Inside Macintosh™
Volume IV

Addison-Wesley Publishing Company, Inc.
Reading, Massachusetts Menlo Park, California Don Mills, Ontario Wokingham, England
Amsterdam Sydney Singapore Tokyo Madrid Bogotá Santiago San Juan

 APPLE COMPUTER, INC.

Simultaneously published in the United States and Canada.

This book was produced using the Apple Macintosh computer and the LaserWriter printer.

ISBN 0-201-05409-4
DEFGHIJ-MU-8987
Fourth Printing, September 1987

Inside Macintosh
Volume IV

Warranty Information

ALL IMPLIED WARRANTIES ON THIS MANUAL, INCLUDING IMPLIED WARRANTIES OF MERCHANTABILITY AND FITNESS FOR A PARTICULAR PURPOSE, ARE LIMITED IN DURATION TO NINETY (90) DAYS FROM THE DATE OF THE ORIGINAL RETAIL PURCHASE OF THIS PRODUCT.

Even though Apple has reviewed this manual, **APPLE MAKES NO WARRANTY OR REPRESENTATION, EITHER EXPRESS OR IMPLIED, WITH RESPECT TO THIS MANUAL, ITS QUALITY, ACCURACY, MERCHANTABILITY, OR FITNESS FOR A PARTICULAR PURPOSE. AS A RESULT, THIS MANUAL IS SOLD "AS IS," AND YOU, THE PURCHASER, ARE ASSUMING THE ENTIRE RISK AS TO ITS QUALITY AND ACCURACY.**

IN NO EVENT WILL APPLE BE LIABLE FOR DIRECT, INDIRECT, SPECIAL, INCIDENTAL, OR CONSEQUENTIAL DAMAGES RESULTING FROM ANY DEFECT OR INACCURACY IN THIS MANUAL, even if advised of the possibility of such damages.

THE WARRANTY AND REMEDIES SET FORTH ABOVE ARE EXCLUSIVE AND IN LIEU OF ALL OTHERS, ORAL OR WRITTEN, EXPRESS OR IMPLIED. No Apple dealer, agent, or employee is authorized to make any modification, extension, or addition to this warranty.

Some states do no allow the exclusion or limitation of implied warranties or liability for incidental or consequential damages, so the above limitation or exclusion may not apply to you. This warranty gives you specific legal rights, and you may also have other rights which vary from state to state.

Contents

PREFACE

ABOUT INSIDE MACINTOSH VOLUME IV

The first three volumes of *Inside Macintosh* provide information you'll need to write software for any of the Apple® Macintosh™ family. This volume, Volume IV, is a companion to the first three volumes that gives specific information on writing software to take advantage of the features of the Macintosh Plus and the Macintosh 512 enhanced. A familiarity with the material presented in the first three volumes is assumed, since most of the information presented in Volume IV consists of changes and additions to that original material.

Practically every chapter in the first three volumes has a corresponding chapter in Volume IV that describes new routines, modified data structures, additional error codes, and so on. Most of these chapters are "delta" documents that present only the new information. In the case of the File Manager chapter, the changes are so extensive that the chapter has been completely rewritten. Finally, four additional chapters—"The System Resource File", "The List Manager", "The SCSI Manager", and "The Time Manager"—introduce entirely new material.

The Language

The routines you'll need to call are written in assembly language, but (with a few exceptions) they're also accessible from high-level languages, such as Pascal on the Lisa Workshop development system. *Inside Macintosh* documents the Lisa Pascal interfaces to the routines and the symbolic names defined for assembly-language programmers using the Lisa Workshop; if you're using a different development system, its documentation should tell you how to apply the information presented here to that system.

Inside Macintosh is intended to serve the needs of both high-level language and assembly-language programmers. Every routine is shown in its Pascal form (if it has one), but assembly-language programmers are told how they can access the routines. Information of interest only to assembly-language programmers is set apart and labeled so that other programmers can conveniently skip it.

Familiarity with Lisa Pascal (or a similar high-level language) is recommended for all readers, since it's used for most examples. Lisa Pascal is described in the documentation for the Lisa Pascal Workshop.

Version Numbers

This edition of *Inside Macintosh Volume IV* describes the following versions of the software:

- version 117 ($75) of the ROM in the Macintosh Plus and Macintosh 512K enhanced
- version 2.0 of the Lisa Pascal interfaces and the assembly-language definitions

Some of the RAM-based software is read from the file named System (usually kept in the System Folder). This manual describes the software in the System file version 3.2 whose creation date is June 4, 1986. In certain cases, a feature can be found in earlier versions of the System file; these cases are noted as they come up.

Compatibility

Version 117 ($75) of the ROM, also known as the 128K ROM, is provided on the Macintosh 512K enhanced and Macintosh Plus.

> **Note:** A partially upgraded Macintosh 512K is identical to the Macintosh 512K enhanced, while a completely upgraded Macintosh 512K includes all the features of the Macintosh Plus.

Version 105 ($69) of the ROM (the version described in the first three volumes of *Inside Macintosh*), also known as the 64K ROM, is provided on the Macintosh 128K and 512K.

Most applications written for the 64K ROM run without modification on machines equipped with the 128K ROM. Applications that use the routines and data structures found in the 128K ROM, however, *may not function* on machines equipped with the 64K ROM.

Programmers may wish to determine which version of the ROM is installed in order to take advantage of the features of the 128K ROM whenever possible. You can do this by checking the ROM version number returned by the Operating System Utility procedure Environs; if the version number is greater than or equal to 117 ($75), it's safe to use the routines and data structures described in this volume.

> **Assembly-language note:** A faster way of determining whether the 128K ROM is present is to examine the global variable Rom85 (a word); it's positive (that is, the high-order bit is 0) if the 128K ROM is installed.

Conventions

The following notations are used in Volume IV to draw your attention to particular items of information:

> **64K ROM note:** A note, found only in chapter 19 of this volume, that points out some difference between the 64K ROM and 128K ROM.

> **Note:** A note that may be interesting or useful.

> **Warning:** A point you need to be cautious about.

> **Assembly-language note:** A note of interest to assembly-language programmers only.

[Not in ROM]

Routines marked with this notation are not part of the Macintosh ROM. Depending on how the interfaces have been set up on the development system you're using, these routines may or may not be available. They're available to users of Lisa Pascal; other users should check the documentation for their development system for more information. (For related information of interest to assembly-language programmers, see chapter 4 of Volume I and chapter 2 of this volume.)

1 THE MACINTOSH USER INTERFACE GUIDELINES

ABOUT THIS CHAPTER

This chapter describes the following new features of the Macintosh user interface:

- the Macintosh Plus arrow keys
- an updated list of reserved Command key combinations
- the new window zooming feature
- a new standard Close dialog box

ARROW KEYS

The Macintosh Plus keyboard includes four arrow keys: Up Arrow, Down Arrow, Left Arrow, and Right Arrow.

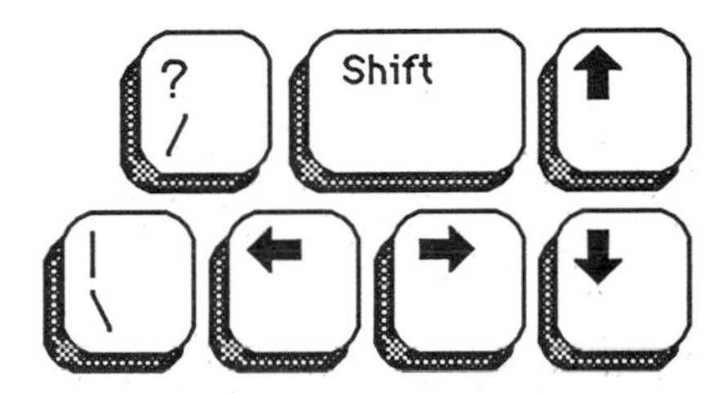

Figure 1. Macintosh Plus Arrow Keys

Appropriate Uses for the Arrow Keys

The arrow keys *do not* replace the mouse. They can be used in addition to the mouse as a shortcut for moving the insertion point and (under some circumstances) for making selections. The following rules are the minimum guidelines for the use of arrow keys, leaving application programmers relatively free to expand on them where things are left undefined. Extensions necessary for a particular application should be done in the spirit of the Macintosh user interface.

It's up to you to decide whether it's worth the effort to create arrow key shortcuts for mouse functions. Many users find that remembering a key combination on the order of Command–Shift–Left Arrow is more trouble than it's worth and would rather use a mouse anyway. In other situations, it's more convenient to use the keyboard. Some people have difficulty using a mouse and appreciate being able to use the keyboard instead.

You should make use of the arrow keys only where it's appropriate to the application. Applications that deal with text or arrays (word processors, spreadsheets, and data bases, for example) have an insertion point. This insertion point can always be moved by the mouse and, with the new keyboard, with the arrow keys as well.

As a general rule, arrow keys are used to move the insertion point and to expand or shrink selections. Arrow keys are *never* used to duplicate the function of the scroll bars or to move the pointer. In a graphics application, the arrow keys should not be used to move a selected object.

Moving the Insertion Point With Arrow Keys

The Left Arrow and Right Arrow keys move the insertion point one character left and right, respectively .

Up Arrow and Down Arrow move the insertion point up and down one line, respectively. The horizontal screen position should be maintained in terms of screen pixels but not necessarily in terms of characters, because the insertion point moves to the nearest character boundary on the new line. (Character boundaries seldom line up vertically when proportional fonts are used.) During successive movements up or down, you should keep track of the original horizontal screen position; otherwise, accumulated round-off errors might cause the insertion point to move a significant distance from the original horizontal position as it moves from line to line.

Moving the Insertion Point in Empty Documents

Various text-editing programs treat empty documents in different ways. Some assume that an empty document contains no characters, in which case clicking at the bottom of a blank screen causes the insertion point to appear at the top. In this situation, Down Arrow cannot move the insertion point into the blank space (because there are no characters there).

Other applications treat an empty document as a page of space characters, in which case clicking at the bottom of a blank screen puts the insertion point where the user clicked and lets the user type characters there, overwriting the spaces. Down Arrow moves the insertion point straight down through the spaces.

Whichever paradigm you choose for your application, be consistent.

Modifier Keys With Arrow Keys

Holding down the Command key while pressing an arrow key should move the insertion point to the appropriate edge of the window. If the insertion point is already at the edge of the window, the document should be scrolled one windowful in the appropriate direction and the insertion point should move to the same edge of the new windowful. Command–Up Arrow moves to the top of the window, Command–Down Arrow to the bottom, Command–Left Arrow to the left edge, and Command–Right Arrow to the right edge.

The Option key is reserved as a "semantic modifier" key. The application determines what the semantic units are. For example, in a word processor, where the basic semantic unit is the character and the next larger unit is the word, Option–Left Arrow and Option–Right Arrow might move the insertion point to the beginning and end, respectively, of a word. (Movement of the insertion point by word boundaries should use the same definition of "word" that the application uses for double clicking.) The next larger semantic unit could be defined as the sentence, in which case Option–Left Arrow and Option–Right Arrow would move the insertion point to the beginning or end of a sentence. In a programming language editor, where the basic semantic unit is the token and the next larger one might be the line, Option–Left Arrow and Option–Right Arrow might move the insertion point left and right to the beginning and end of the line, respectively.

In an application (such as a spreadsheet) that represents itself as an array, the basic semantic unit would be the cell. Option–Left Arrow would designate the cell to the left of the currently active cell as the new active cell, and so on. Using modifier keys with arrow keys doesn't do anything to the data; Option–Left Arrow just moves the selection to the next cell to the left.

Though the use of multiple modifier key combinations (such as Command–Option–Left Arrow) is discouraged, it's fine to use the Shift key with any *one* of the other modifier keys for making a selection (see "Making a Selection With Arrow Keys" below). Keep in mind that if multiple keys must be pressed simultaneously, they should be fairly close together—otherwise many people won't be able to use that combination.

Making a Selection With Arrow Keys

To use arrow keys to make a selection, the user holds down Shift while pressing an arrow key. Application programs that depend (as TextEdit does) on the numeric keypad should not use these Shift–arrow key combinations because the ASCII codes for the four Shift–arrow key combinations are the same as those for the keypad's +, *, /, and = keys. If the use of Shift–arrow for making selections is more important to your application than the numeric keypad, the following paragraphs describe how it should work.

After a Shift–arrow key combination has been pressed, the insertion point moves and the range over which it moves becomes selected. If both the Shift key and another modifier key are held down, the insertion point moves (as defined for the particular modifier key) and the range over which the insertion point moves becomes selected. For example, Shift–Left Arrow selects the character to the left of the insertion point, Command–Shift–Left Arrow selects from the insertion point to the left edge of the window, and Option–Shift–Left Arrow selects the whole word that contains the character to the left of the insertion point (just like double clicking on a word).

A selection made using the mouse is no different from one made using arrow keys. A selection started with the mouse can be extended using Shift and Left Arrow or Right Arrow.

The two ends of a selected range have different characteristics and different names. The place where the insertion point was when selection was started is called the **anchor point**. The place to which the insertion point moves to complete the selection is called the **active end**. Once selection begins, the anchor point cannot be moved except by beginning a new selection. To extend or shrink a selection, the user moves the active end as specified here. As the active end moves, it can cross over the anchor point.

In a text application, pressing Shift and either Left Arrow or Right Arrow selects a single character. Assuming that Left Arrow key was used, the anchor point of the selection is on the right side of the selection, the active end on the left. Each subsequent Shift–Left Arrow adds another character to the left side of the selection. A Shift–Right Arrow at this point shrinks the selection. Figure 2 summarizes these actions.

1. Insertion point is within a word: word
2. Shift-← is pressed: word
3. another Shift-←: word
4. Shift-→: word
5. three more times Shift-→: word

Figure 2. Selecting With Shift–Arrow Keys

In a text application, pressing Option–Shift and either Left Arrow or Right Arrow selects the entire word containing the character to the left of the insertion point. Assuming Left Arrow was used, the anchor point is at the right end of the word, the active end at the left. Each subsequent Option–Shift–Left Arrow adds another word to the left end of the selection, as shown in Figure 3.

1. Insertion point is within a word: another word
2. Option-Shift-← is pressed: another word
3. another Option-Shift-←: another word

Figure 3. Selecting With Option–Shift–Arrow Keys

Pressing Command–Shift–Left Arrow selects the area from the insertion point to the left edge of the window. The anchor point is at the right end of the selection, the active end is at the left. Each subsequent Command–Shift–Left Arrow moves the document one windowful left and extends the selection to the left edge of the new window.

Extending or Shrinking a Selection

To use arrow keys to extend or shrink a selection, the user holds down the Shift key (plus any defined modifiers) while pressing an arrow key. The arrow key moves the insertion point at the active end of the selection.

Collapsing a Selection

When a block of text is selected, pressing either Left Arrow or Right Arrow deselects the range. If Left Arrow is pressed, the insertion point is left at the beginning of the previous selection; if Right Arrow, at the end of the previous selection.

RESERVED COMMAND KEY COMBINATIONS

There are several menu items, particularly in the File and Edit menus, that commonly have keyboard equivalents. For consistency, several of those keyboard equivalents should be used only for the commands listed below and should never be used for any other purpose. Desk accessories, which are accessible from *all* applications, assume that these Command-key combinations have the meanings listed here.

File Menu

Command-N (New)
Command-O (Open)
Command-S (Save)
Command-Q (Quit)

Edit Menu

Command-Z (Undo)
Command-X (Cut)
Command-C (Copy)
Command-V (Paste)

The keyboard equivalents in the Style menu (listed below) are less strictly reserved. Applications that have Style menus shouldn't use these keyboard equivalents for any other purpose, but applications that have no Style menus can use them for other purposes if needed. Remember that you risk confusing users if a given key combination means different things in different applications.

Style Menu

Command-P (Plain)
Command-B (Bold)
Command-I (Italic)
Command-U (Underline)

WINDOW ZOOMING

The more open documents on a desktop, the more difficult it is for the user to locate, select, and resize the one to be worked on. The 128K ROM includes a feature, known as window zooming, that allows users—with a single mouse click—to toggle the active window between its standard size and location and a predefined size and location.

The initial size and placement of a window is known as its standard state. The application program can supply values for the standard state; otherwise the full screen (minus a few border pixels) is assumed (see Figure 4). The standard state should be the most useful size and location for normal operations within the program—usually it's the full screen.

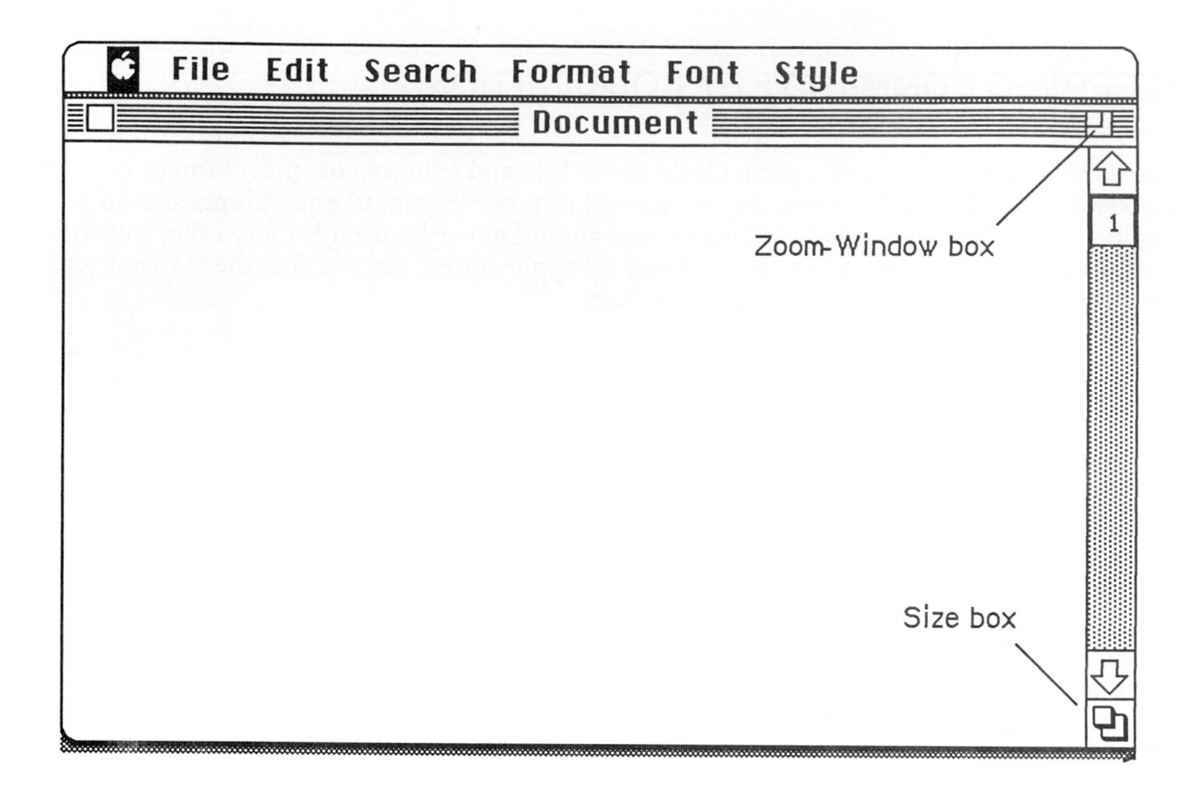

Figure 4. Window in Standard State

The user cannot change the standard state, but the application can change it within context. For example, a word processor might define a size that's wide enough to display a document whose width is as specified in Page Setup. If the user invokes Page Setup to specify a wider or narrower document, the application might then change the standard state to reflect that change.

Your application can also supply initial values for the second window state, known as the user state. If you don't supply initial values, the user state is identical to the standard state until the user moves or resizes the window. When the standard state and user state are different (Figure 5 shows a hypothetical user state), clicking in the zoom-window box acts as a toggle between the two states.

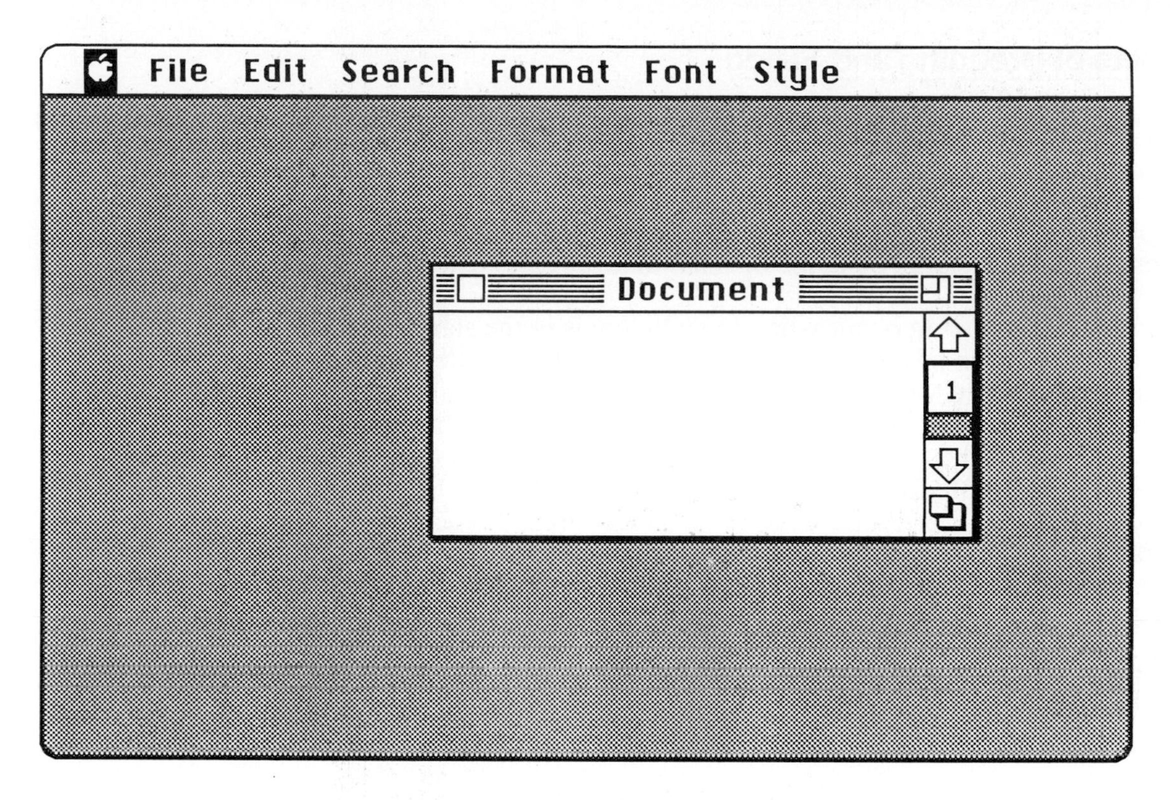

Figure 5. Window in User State

Application developers are encouraged to take advantage of the zoom-window feature; details on using this feature are provided in chapter 6 of this volume. You should not change the shape of the zoom-window box or change the interpretation of clicking on the the zoom-window box (shown in Figure 6). You should add no other elements to the title bar. Except in the zoom-window box and in the close box, clicking within the title bar should have no effect.

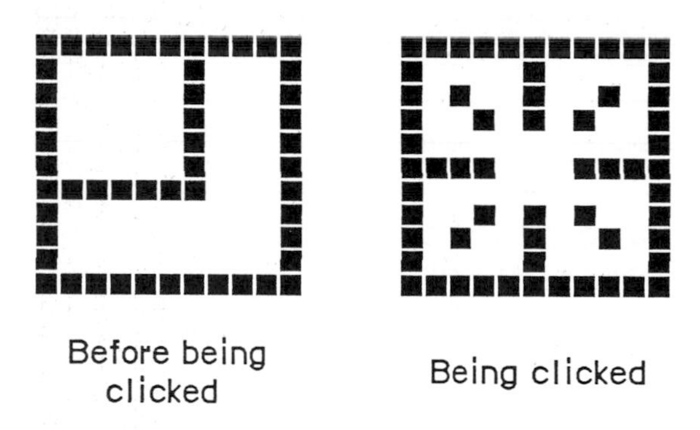

Figure 6. Zoom-Window Box Details

Effects of Dragging and Sizing

Explicit dragging or resizing of the window is handled in the normal way (see "Changing the Size of a Window" in chapter 2 of Volume I), regardless of the presence or absence of the zoom-window feature. The effect of dragging or resizing depends on the state of the window and the degree of movement. A change, either in position or size, of seven pixels or less is insignificant. A change of more than seven pixels is a "significant change".

If dragging or resizing occur when the window is in the standard state, a small change in the size or location of the window does not change the state, nor does it change the application-defined values for the size and location of the standard state. It does, of course, change the size or location of the window. A significant change in the size or location of the window switches the window to the user state and sets the values for the size and location of that state to those of the window.

If dragging or resizing occur when the window is in the user state, a change in size or location that leaves the window within seven pixels of the size and location specified as the standard state changes the state to the standard state, leaving the size and location of the user state unchanged. Any other change in size or location in the user state leaves the window in the user state and sets the values for the size and location of that state to those of the window.

STANDARD CLOSE DIALOG

When a user chooses Close or Quit from the File menu, and the active document has been changed, the Close dialog box appears, asking "Save changes before closing?" A great deal of work can be lost if a user mistakenly clicks the "No" button instead of "Cancel". This is especially important to Switcher users, who often move from one application to another and become less aware of subtle differences between applications. To avoid confusion, all applications should use the same standard Close dialog. As shown in Figure 7, dialogs can have multiple lines of text.

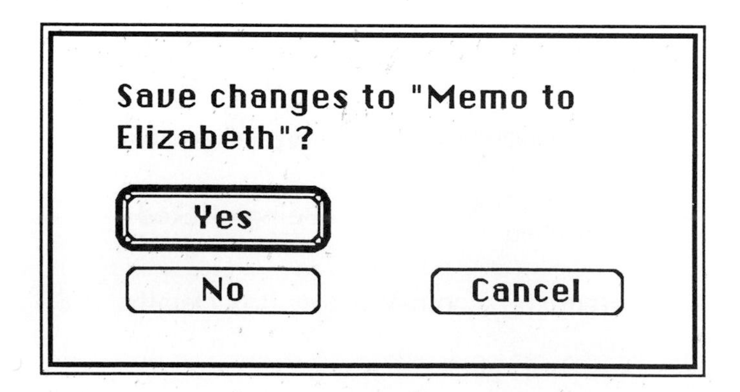

Figure 7. A Standard Close Dialog

Close Box Specifications

"Yes" and "No", the two direct responses to the question "Save changes before closing?" are placed together on the left side of the box. "Yes", the default button, is boldly outlined. "Cancel", which cancels the close command, is to the right, separate from "Yes" and "No".

After the user selects Close from the File menu, the text of the question in the Close box is generally "Save changes before closing?" However, if the user sees this dialog after choosing "Quit", the text would instead be "Save changes before quitting?" If the application supports multiple windows, the text could be "Save changes to [document name] before closing window?" The box should always look the same and appear in the same place on the screen.

The box itself is 120 pixels high by 238 pixels wide. Its standard location is (100,120)(220,358) but other locations may be appropriate.

Here are the other coordinates for the standard close box (assuming standard location):

the text	(12,20)(45,223)
the word "yes"	(58,25)(76,99)
the word "no"	(86,25)(104,99)
the word "cancel"	(86,141)(104,215)

If you must devise a close box different from the one described here, maintain the general arrangement of the buttons and remember that the user's safest choice should be the default button and that the most dangerous choice should be the most difficult to make happen.

2 USING ASSEMBLY LANGUAGE

In the 128K ROM, Toolbox and Operating System traps have separate trap dispatch tables. It's possible for a Toolbox trap and an Operating System trap to have the same trap number.

THE TRAP DISPATCH TABLE

In the 64K ROM, references to both Toolbox and Operating System routines are made through a single trap dispatch table. For compactness, entries in that table are encoded into one word each. The high-order bit of each entry tells whether the routine resides in ROM (0) or RAM (1). The remaining 15 bits give the offset of the routine relative to a base address. For routines in ROM, this base address is the beginning of the ROM; for routines in RAM, it's the beginning of the system heap. The two base addresses are kept in a pair of global variables named ROMBase and RAMBase. Using 15-bit unsigned word offsets, the range of locations that the trap dispatch table can address is limited to 64K bytes. Also, the interleaving of Operating System and Toolbox trap numbers limits the total number of traps to 512 and means that no two traps can be represented by the same number.

In the 128K ROM, the Toolbox and Operating System traps have separate dispatch tables. Instead of a packed format, entries in these dispatch tables are stored as full long-word addresses so the dispatcher makes no distinction between ROM and RAM addresses. The Operating System dispatch table consists of 256 long words, from address $400 through $7FF; this replaces the old dispatch table of 512 words. The Toolbox table consists of 512 long words, from address $C00 through $13FF.

> **Warning:** The format of the trap dispatch tables may be different in future versions of Macintosh system software. If it's absolutely necessary that you manipulate the trap dispatch tables, use the Operating System Utility routines NGetTrapAddress and NSetTrapAddress (or with the 64K ROM, GetTrapAddress and SetTrapAddress); they're described in chapter 25 of this volume.

FORMAT OF TRAP WORDS

As described in chapter 4 of Volume I, a trap word begins with the hexadecimal digit $A (binary 1010); the rest of the word identifies the routine you're calling, along with additional information pertaining to the call.

Figure 1 shows the format of Toolbox and Operating System trap words. Bit 11 of the trap word determines how the remainder of the word will be interpreted; usually it's 0 for Operating System calls and 1 for Toolbox calls, though there are certain exceptions.

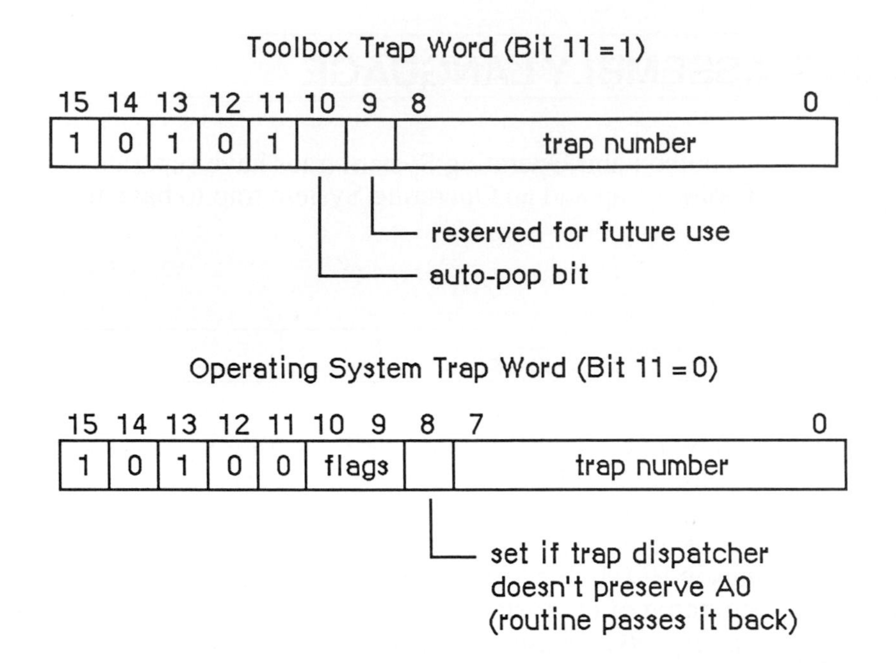

Figure 1. Toolbox and Operating System Trap Words

In the 64K ROM, an Operating System trap and a Toolbox trap cannot have the same trap number; the GetTrapAddress and SetTrapAddress routines do not distinguish between Toolbox and Operating System traps.

Since each group has its own dispatch table in the 128K ROM, there can be a Toolbox trap and an Operating System trap with the same trap number. Two new routines—NGetTrapAddress and NSetTrapAddress—have been added; they use bits 9 and 10 of their trap word for specifying the group to which a routine belongs.

3 THE RESOURCE MANAGER

The speed and efficiency of the Resource Manager have been significantly enhanced in the 128K ROM. Nine routines have been added; seven are functional counterparts of 64K ROM routines but search only the current resource file, and two routines are new. Additional standard resource types have been defined, two new result codes have been added, and the reporting of error conditions has been improved.

RESOURCE MANAGER ROUTINES

```
FUNCTION Count1Types : INTEGER;
```

Count1Types is the same as CountTypes except that it returns the number of resource types in the current resource file only.

```
PROCEDURE Get1IndType (VAR theType: ResType; index: INTEGER);
```

Assembly-language note: The macro you invoke to call Get1IndType from assembly language is named _Get1IxType.

Get1IndType is the same as GetIndType except that it searches the current resource file only. Given an index ranging from 1 to Count1Types (above), Get1IndType returns a resource type in theType. Called repeatedly over the entire range for the index, it returns all the resource types in the current resource file. If the given index isn't in the range from 1 to Count1Types, Get1IndType returns four NUL characters (ASCII code 0).

```
FUNCTION Count1Resources (theType: ResType) : INTEGER;
```

Count1Resources is the same as CountResources except that it returns the total number of resources of the given type in the current resource file only.

```
FUNCTION Get1IndResource (theType: ResType; index: INTEGER) :
           Handle;
```

Assembly-language note: The macro you invoke to call Get1IndResource from assembly language is named _Get1IxResource.

Get1IndResource is the same as GetIndResource except that it searches the current resource file only. Given an index ranging from 1 to Count1Resources(theType), Get1IndResource returns a handle to a resource of the given type (see Count1Resources, above). Called

3 Resource Manager

repeatedly over the entire range for the index, it returns handles to all resources of the given type in the current resource file.

```
FUNCTION Get1Resource (theType: ResType; theID: INTEGER) : Handle;
```

Get1Resource is the same as GetResource except that it searches the current resource file only.

```
FUNCTION Get1NamedResource (theType: ResType; name: Str255) :
         Handle;
```

Get1NamedResource is the same as GetNamedResource except that it searches the current resource file only.

```
FUNCTION Unique1ID (theType: ResType) : INTEGER;
```

Unique1ID is the same as UniqueID except that the ID number it returns is unique only with respect to resources in the current resource file.

```
FUNCTION MaxSizeRsrc (theResource: Handle) : LONGINT;
```

MaxSizeRsrc is similar to SizeResource except that it does *not* cause the disk to be read; instead it determines the size (in bytes) of the resource from the offsets found in the resource map.

Since MaxSizeRsrc does not read from the disk, it returns only the *maximum* size of the resource. In other words, you can count on the resource not being larger than the number of bytes reported by MaxSizeRsrc; it's possible, however, that the resource is actually smaller than the resource map indicates (because the file has not yet been compacted). If called after UpdateResFile, MaxSizeRsrc will return the correct size of the resource.

Advanced Routines

```
FUNCTION RsrcMapEntry (theResource: Handle) : LONGINT;
```

RsrcMapEntry provides a way to access the resource references in the resource map. Given a handle to a resource, RsrcMapEntry returns the offset of the resource's reference from the beginning of the resource map. (For more information on resource references and the structure of a resource map, see the section "Format of a Resource File" in the Resource Manager chapter.) If it doesn't find the resource, RsrcMapEntry returns NIL and the ResError function will return the result code resNotFound. If you pass it a NIL handle, RsrcMapEntry will return garbage but ResError will return the result code noErr.

> **Warning:** Since routines are provided for opening, accessing, and changing resources, there's really no reason to access resources directly. To avoid damaging the resource file, you should be extremely careful if you use RsrcMapEntry.

```
FUNCTION OpenRFPerm (fileName: Str255; vRefNum: INTEGER;
           permission: Byte) : INTEGER;
```

OpenRFPerm is similar to OpenResFile except that it allows you to specify the read/write permission of the resource file the first time it is opened; OpenRFPerm also lets you specify in vRefNum the directory or volume on which the file is located (see chapter 19 of this volume for more details on directories). Permission can have any of the values that you would pass to the File Manager; these values are given in "Low-Level File Manager Routines" in chapter 19 of this volume.

OpenRFPerm, like OpenResFile, will not open the specified file twice; it simply returns the reference number already assigned to the file. In other words, OpenRFPerm cannot be used to open a second access path to a resource file nor can it be used to change the permission of an already open file. Since OpenRFPerm gives no indication of whether the file was already open, there's no way to tell whether the file's open permission is what you specified or what was specified by an earlier call.

Note: The shared read/write permission described in chapter 19 of this volume has no effect with OpenRFPerm since the Resource Manager is unable to deal with a portion of a resource file.

RESOURCE TYPES

The following standard resource types have been defined (System file version 3.0 or later):

Resource type	Meaning
'CACH'	RAM cache code
'FMTR'	3 1/2-inch disk formatting code
'FOND'	Font family record
'NFNT'	128K ROM font
'PRER'	Device type for Chooser
'PRES'	Device type for Chooser
'PTCH'	ROM patch code
'RDEV'	Device type for Chooser
'ROvr'	Code for overriding ROM resources
'ROv#'	List of ROM resources to override
'bmap'	Bit maps used by the Control Panel
'ctab'	Used by the Control Panel
'insc'	Installer script

Uppercase and lowercase letters *are* distinguished in resource types. You can use any four-character sequence, *except* those listed above, those already reserved in chapter 5 of Volume 1, and those sequences consisting entirely of lowercase letters (reserved by Apple), for resource types specific to your application. There's no need to register your resource types with Apple since they'll only be used by your application.

CHECKING FOR ERRORS

In the 64K ROM, some error conditions resulting from certain Resource Manager routines are not reported by the ResError function. Two additional result codes are defined in the 128K ROM version of the Resource Manager:

```
CONST resAttrErr = 198;  {attribute does not permit operation}
      mapReadErr = 199;  {map does not permit operation}
```

In the 128K ROM, the following error conditions are reported by ResError:

- The OpenResFile function checks to see that the information in the resource map is internally consistent; if it isn't, ResError returns mapReadError.
- The CloseResFile procedure calls UpdateResFile. If UpdateResFile returns a nonzero result code, that result code will be returned by CloseResFile.
- If you provide an index to GetIndResource (or Get1IndResource) that's either 0 or negative, the ResError function will return the result code resNotFound.
- If you call DetachResource to detach a resource whose resChanged attribute has been set, ResError will return the result code resAttrErr.
- If you call SetResInfo but the resProtected attribute is set, ResError will return the result code resAttrErr.
- If you call ChangedResource but the resProtected attribute for the modified resource is set, the ResError function will return the result code resAttrErr.
- If you call UpdateResFile but the mapReadOnly attribute for the resource file is set (described in the "Advanced Routines" section of the Resource Manager chapter), ResError will return the result code mapReadErr.

Warning: If you call the GetResource and Get1Resource functions with a resource type that isn't in any open resource file, they return NIL but the ResError function will return the result code noErr. With these calls, you must check that the handle returned is nonzero.

ROM RESOURCES

The information presented in this section is useful only to assembly-language programmers.

With the 64K ROM, many of the system resources are stored in the system resource file. With the 128K ROM, the following system resources are stored in ROM:

Type	ID	Description
'CURS'	1	IBeamCursor
'CURS'	2	CrossCursor
'CURS'	3	PlusCursor
'CURS'	4	WatchCursor
'DRVR'	2	Printer Driver shell (.Print)
'DRVR'	3	Sound Driver (.Sound)
'DRVR'	4	Disk Driver (.Sony)
'DRVR'	9	AppleTalk driver (.MPP)
'DRVR'	A	AppleTalk driver (.ATP)
'FONT'	0	Name of system font
'FONT'	C	System font
'MDEF'	0	Default menu definition procedure
'PACK'	4	Floating-Point Arithmetic Package
'PACK'	5	Transcendental Functions Package
'PACK'	7	Binary-Decimal Conversion Package
'SERD'	0	Serial Driver
'WDEF'	0	Default window definition function

Note: The Sound Driver, Disk Driver, and Serial Driver are in the 64K ROM, but are not stored as resources.

When the Macintosh is turned on, a call is made to the InitResources function. The Resource Manager creates a special heap zone within the system heap, and builds a resource map that points to the ROM resources.

In order to use the ROM resources in your calls to the Resource Manager, the ROM map must be inserted in front of the map for the system resource file prior to making the call. The global variable RomMapInsert is used for this purpose; it tells the Resource Manager to insert the ROM map for the *next call* only. An adjacent global variable, TmpResLoad, is also useful; when RomMapInsert is TRUE, TmpResLoad determines whether the value of the global variable ResLoad is taken to be TRUE or FALSE (overriding the actual value of ResLoad) for the *next call* only. Figure 1 shows these two variables.

RomMapInsert (byte)	TmpResLoad (byte)

Figure 1. RomMapInsert and TmpResLoad

Two global constants, each a word in length, are provided for setting these variables in tandem: mapTrue inserts the ROM map with SetResLoad(TRUE) and mapFalse inserts the ROM map with SetResLoad(FALSE). As noted, both RomMapInsert and TmpResLoad are cleared after each Resource Manager call.

Note: There is no real resource file associated with the ROM resources; the ROM map has a path reference number of 1 (an illegal path reference number). There are two ways to determine if a handle references a ROM resource. First, you can set up TmpResLoad and RomMapInsert and call HomeResFile; if 1 is returned, the handle is to a ROM resource. Second, you can dereference the handle and see if the master pointer points into the ROM space by comparing it to the global variable ROMBase.

Overriding ROM Resources

This section explains how to override ROM resources.

> **Warning**: As with intercepting system traps using the SetTrapAddress procedure, you should override ROM resources *only* if it's absolutely necessary and you understand the situation completely.

You can override some of the ROM resources, such as 'CURS' resources, simply by putting the substitute resource in your application's resource fork. Other ROM resources however, such 'DRVR' and 'PACK' resources, cannot be overridden in this way because they are already referenced and in use when your application is launched.

Whenever InitResource is called, the ROM map is rebuilt. (Do *not* use InitResources to rebuild the ROM map.) Each time the ROM map is rebuilt, the Resource Manager looks in the system resource file for a 'ROvr' resource 0. If it finds such a resource, it loads it into memory and jumps to this resource via a JSR instruction. The code in the 'ROvr' resource looks in the system resource file for all resources of type 'ROv#' whose version word matches the version word of the ROM (see Figure 2). For example, to override a resource in the 128K ROM, the version must be $75.

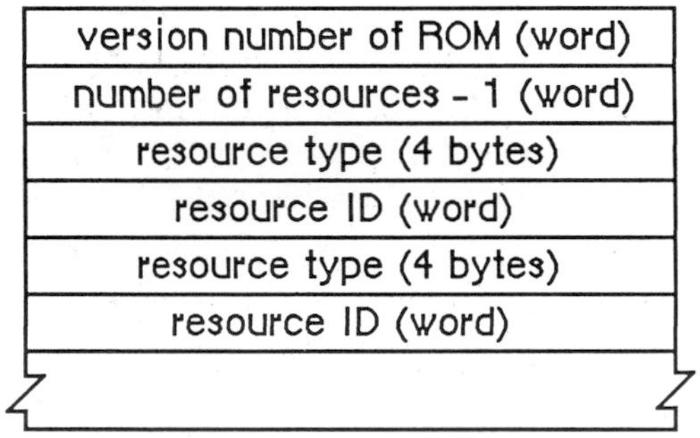

version number of ROM (word)
number of resources - 1 (word)
resource type (4 bytes)
resource ID (word)
resource type (4 bytes)
resource ID (word)

Figure 2. Structure of an 'ROv#' Resource

To override ROM resources in this way, you'll first need a copy of an 'ROvr' resource; you can obtain one by writing to:

Developer Technical Support
Mail Stop 3-T
Apple Computer, Inc.
20525 Mariani Avenue
Cupertino, CA 95014

You'll then need to create an 'ROv#' resource listing the resources you want to override.

SUMMARY OF THE RESOURCE MANAGER

Constants

```
CONST { Resource Manager result codes }

      resAttrErr =  -198;   {attribute inconsistent with operation}
      mapReadErr =  -199;   {map inconsistent with operation}
```

Routines

```
FUNCTION  Count1Types :       INTEGER;
PROCEDURE Get1IndType        (VAR theType: ResType; index: INTEGER);
FUNCTION  Count1Resources    (theType: ResType) : INTEGER;
FUNCTION  Get1IndResource    (theType: ResType; index: INTEGER) :
                             Handle;
FUNCTION  Get1Resource       (theType: ResType; theID: INTEGER) :
                             Handle;
FUNCTION  Get1NamedResource  (theType: ResType; name: Str255) : Handle;
FUNCTION  Unique1ID          (theType: ResType) : INTEGER;
FUNCTION  MaxSizeRsrc        (theResource: Handle) : LONGINT;
FUNCTION  RsrcMapEntry       (theResource: Handle) : LONGINT;
FUNCTION  OpenRFPerm         (fileName: Str255; vRefNum: INTEGER;
                             permission: Byte) : INTEGER;
```

Assembly-Language Information

Constants

```
; Resource Manager result codes

resAttrErr   .EQU   -198  ;attribute inconsistent with operation
mapReadErr   .EQU   -199  ;map inconsistent with operation

; Values for setting RomMapInsert and TmpResLoad

mapTrue     .EQU   $FFFF  ;insert ROM map with TmpResLoad set to TRUE
mapFalse    .EQU   $FF00  ;insert ROM map with TmpResLoad set to FALSE
```

Special Macro Names

Pascal name	**Macro name**
Get1IndType	_Get1IxType
Get1IndResource	_Get1IxResource

Variables

RomMapInsert	Flag for whether to insert map to the ROM resources (byte)
TmpResLoad	Temporary SetResLoad state for calls using RomMapInsert (byte)

4 QUICKDRAW

The performance of QuickDraw in the 128K ROM has been enhanced considerably. New capabilities have been added, and a number of bugs in the 64K ROM version have been fixed. In conjunction with the Font Manager, QuickDraw supports font families, fractional character widths, and the disabling of font scaling; these features are described in chapter 5 of this volume.

The 128K ROM version of QuickDraw supports all eight transfer modes for text drawing, instead of just srcOr, srcBic, and scrXor.

The size of a picture is a long word with a range of over four gigabytes. To get the size of a picture, use GetHandleSize instead of looking at the picSize field, which for compatibility contains the low 16 bits of the real size. Old code will work fine for pictures up to 32767 bytes. To check whether you have run out of memory during picture creation, test EmptyRect(picFrame); it returns TRUE if you have.

The following bugs have been fixed:

- RectInRgn used to return TRUE occasionally when the rectangle intersected the region's enclosing rectangle but not the actual region.
- SectRgn, DiffRgn, UnionRgn, XorRgn, and FrameRgn used to cause a stack overflow for regions with more than 25 rectangles in one scan line. Since this is no longer true, the warning on page I-186 regarding undefined results no longer applies.
- PtToAngle didn't work correctly when the angle was 90 and the aspect ratio was a power of two.
- In some cases where the CopyBits source bitmap overlapped its destination, the transfer would destroy the source bitmap before it was used.
- If you tried to draw a long piece of shadowed text with a tall font, QuickDraw would cause a stack overflow if there wasn't enough stack space for the required off-screen buffer. Now it detects the potential stack overflow and recurses on the left and right halves of the text.
- DrawText did not work correctly in pictures if the character count was greater than 255.

QUICKDRAW ROUTINES

The SeedFill and CalcMask procedures operate on a portion of a bitmap. In both routines, srcPtr and dstPtr point to the beginning of the data to be filled or calculated, *not* to the beginning of the bitmap; both parameters must point to word boundaries in memory. SrcRow and dstRow specify the row width in bytes (in other words, the rowBytes field of the BitMap record) of the source and destination bitmaps respectively. Height and words determine the number of bits to be filled or calculated; words is the width of the rectangle in words and height is the height of the rectangle in pixels. Figure 1 illustrates the use of these parameters.

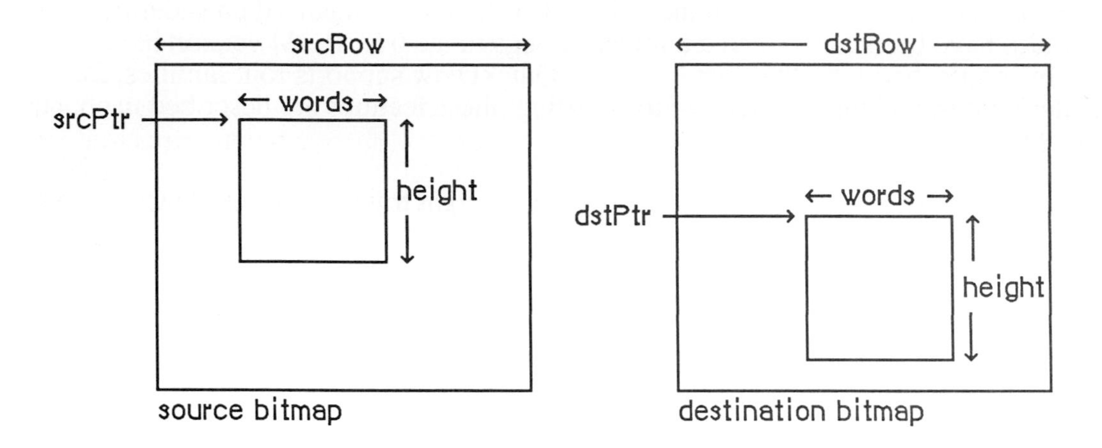

Figure 1. Parameters Used by SeedFill and CalcMask

```
PROCEDURE SeedFill (srcPtr,dstPtr: Ptr;  srcRow,dstRow,height,
          words,seedH,seedV: INTEGER);
```

Given a source bit image, SeedFill computes a destination bit image with 1's only in the pixels where paint can leak from the starting seed point, like the MacPaint paint-bucket tool. SeedH and seedV specify horizontal and vertical offsets, in pixels, from the beginning of the data pointed to by dstPtr, determining how far into the destination bit image filling should begin. Calls to SeedFill are not clipped to the current port and are not stored into QuickDraw pictures.

```
PROCEDURE CalcMask (srcPtr,dstPtr: Ptr;  srcRow,dstRow,height,
          words: INTEGER);
```

Given a source bit image, CalcMask computes a destination bit image with 1's only in the pixels where paint could not leak from any of the outer edges, like the MacPaint lasso tool. Calls to CalcMask are not clipped to the current port and are not stored into QuickDraw pictures.

```
PROCEDURE CopyMask (srcBits,maskBits,dstBits: BitMap;  srcRect,
          maskRect,dstRect: Rect);
```

CopyMask is a new version of the CopyBits procedure; it transfers a bit image from the source bitmap to the destination bitmap only where the corresponding bit of the mask rectangle is a 1. (Note that the mask is specified as a rectangle instead of as a handle to a region.) It can be used along with CalcMask to implement the lasso copy as in MacPaint; it's also useful for drawing icons. CopyMask doesn't check for overlap between the source and destination bitmaps, doesn't stretch the bit image, and doesn't store into QuickDraw pictures. CopyMask does, however, respect the current port's visRgn and clipRgn if dstBits is the portBits of the current grafPort.

```
PROCEDURE MeasureText (count: INTEGER; textAddr,charLocs: Ptr);
```

This procedure is designed to improve performance in specialized applications such as word processors by providing an array version of the TextWidth function; it's like calling TextWidth repeatedly for a given set of characters. TextAddr points to an arbitrary piece of text in memory, and count specifies how many characters are to be measured.

MeasureText moves along the string and, for each character, computes the distance from TextAddr to the right edge of the character. CharLocs should point to an array of count + 1 integers. Upon return, the first element in the array will always contain 0; the other elements will contain pixel positions on the screen for all of the specified characters.

> **Note:** MeasureText only works with text displayed on the screen; since it doesn't go through the QuickDraw procedure StdText, it can't be used to measure text to be printed.

Advanced Routine

The function GetMaskTable, accessible only from assembly language, returns in register A0 a pointer to a ROM table containing the following useful masks:

```
.WORD $0000,$8000,$C000,$E000     ;Table of 16 right masks
.WORD $F000,$F800,$FC00,$FE00
.WORD $FF00,$FF80,$FFC0,$FFE0
.WORD $FFF0,$FFF8,$FFFC,$FFFE

.WORD $FFFF,$7FFF,$3FFF,$1FFF     ;Table of 16 left masks
.WORD $0FFF,$07FF,$03FF,$01FF
.WORD $00FF,$007F,$003F,$001F
.WORD $000F,$0007,$0003,$0001

.WORD $8000,$4000,$2000,$1000     ;Table of 16 bit masks
.WORD $0800,$0400,$0200,$0100
.WORD $0080,$0040,$0020,$0010
.WORD $0008,$0004,$0002,$0001
```

SUMMARY OF QUICKDRAW

Routines

```
PROCEDURE SeedFill    (srcPtr,dstPtr: Ptr; srcRow,dstRow,height,words,
                       seedH,seedV: INTEGER);

PROCEDURE CalcMask    (srcPtr,dstPtr: Ptr; srcRow,dstRow,height,words:
                       INTEGER);

PROCEDURE CopyMask    (srcBits,maskBits,dstBits: BitMap; srcRect,
                       maskRect,dstRect: Rect);

PROCEDURE MeasureText (count: INTEGER; textAddr,charLocs: Ptr);
```

Assembly-Language Information

Routine

Trap macro	On entry	On exit
_GetMaskTable		A0: ptr to mask table in ROM

5 THE FONT MANAGER

ABOUT THE FONT MANAGER

The Font Manager has been significantly improved by the addition of new data structures, most notably the family record. Containing additional typographic information about a font, the family record allows more fonts, fractional character widths (that is, character widths expressed as fixed-point numbers rather than simple integers) for greater precision on high-resolution devices such as the LaserWriter, and the option of disabling font scaling for improved speed and legibility.

The addition of the family record and its related data structures is transparent to most existing applications and is of interest only to advanced programmers designing specialized fonts for the LaserWriter or writing their own font editors.

Most programmers will simply want to take advantage of the new features. Two routines, SetFractEnable and SetFScaleDisable, are provided for this purpose; they're described in "Font Manager Routines" below.

FONTS AND THEIR FAMILIES

In the 64K ROM version of the Font Manager, **font** is defined as the complete set of characters of one typeface; it doesn't include the size of the characters, and usually doesn't include any stylistic variations. In other words, fonts are defined in the plain style and stylistic variations, such as bold and italic, are applied to them. For example, Times plain (or roman) defines the font, while Times italic is a stylistic variation applied to that font.

In the 128K ROM version, the definition of a font is broadened to include stylistic variations. That is, a separate font can be defined for certain stylistic variations of a typeface. The set of available fonts for a given typeface is known as a **font family**.

This allows QuickDraw to use an actual font instead of modifying a plain font, thereby improving speed and readability. For example, suppose the user of a word processor selects a phrase in 12-point Times Roman and chooses the italic style from a menu. QuickDraw asks for an italic Times and, assuming that the proper resources are available, the Font Manager returns a 12-point Times Italic font. QuickDraw could then draw the phrase from an actual italic font rather than having to slant the plain font.

> **Note:** The standard stylistic variations will still be performed by QuickDraw when they're not available as actual fonts.

Information about fonts and their families is stored as resources in resource files; the Font Manager calls the Resource Manager to read them into memory. Fonts are stored as resources of type 'FONT' or 'NFNT'. Fonts known to the system are stored in the system resource file; you may also define your own fonts and include them in your application's resource file or even in the resource file for a document. The information about a font family is stored as a resource of type 'FOND'; this includes the resource IDs of all the fonts in the family, as shown in Figure 1.

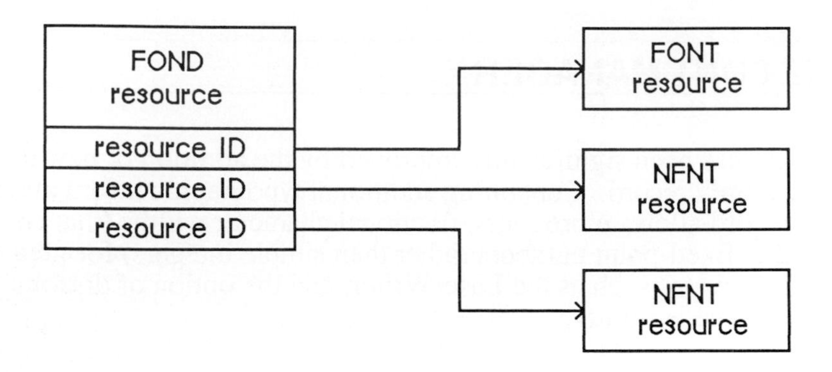

Figure 1. Font Manager Resources

The 'NFNT' resource is new to the 128K ROM version of the Font Manager; it has the same format as the 'FONT' resource and allows for many more fonts. An 'NFNT' resource type can also be used to mask all but plain fonts from appearing in a font menu. In this way, the system resource file can contain Times, Times Italic, Times Bold, and Times Bold Italic, yet only Times will appear on the Font Menu. (The user would need to choose Italic from the Style menu.)

The 64K ROM can only handle 'FONT' resources; it ignores resources of type 'NFNT' and 'FOND'.

> **Warning:** If you're creating a font, be sure to read the section "Restrictions on the 'FONT' type" below for information on maintaining compatibility with the 64K ROMs.

It's crucial that all new fonts have a corresponding 'FOND' resource. A minimal 'FOND' resource can be made for a font by using the Font/DA Mover (version 3.0 or later) to copy the font into a different file that has no font with the same name.

> **Note:** A 'FOND' resource created this way does not contain any optional tables, but it does contain the font association table (described below) that maps family numbers and font sizes into resource IDs.

> **Warning:** Be aware that when a 'FOND' is present, the Font Manager uses it exclusively to determine which fonts are available. Fonts should be added to or deleted from the System file with a tool like the Font/DA Mover, which correctly updates the 'FOND' as well as the 'FONT'.

The Font Manager uses these resources to build two data structures in the application heap. The **font record** contains information about a font and the **family record** contains information about a font family.

About Names and Numbers

In the 64K ROM version of the Font Manager, a font is identified by its font number, which is always between 0 and 255. Each font also has a name that's used to identify it in menus. Font families are identified by a family number and a family name. Since existing routines rely on passing and returning the font number in Font Manager routines, the family number must be the same as the font number, and the family name must be the same as the font name. Family numbers 0 through 127 are reserved for use by Apple; numbers 128 through 255 are assigned by Apple for fonts created by software developers.

Assembly-language note: You can determine the system family number and size by reading the global variables SysFontFam and SysFontSiz, respectively. This is highly recommended, especially if your application is intended to run on Macintoshes that are localized for non-English-speaking countries, as the localization process may change the system font.

You can get the family number of the application font from the global variable ApFontID. You can substitute a different family number in this variable but the application font is reset to its default value (it's stored in parameter RAM) whenever a new application is launched.

Since font numbers only range from 0 to 255, only font families with family numbers in this range are recognized by the 64K ROM version of the Font Manager. All fonts with family numbers from 0 through 255 are stored as resources of type 'FONT', so that the 64K ROM's version of the Font Manager can recognize them.

It's very important that all new fonts and font families be registered with Apple to avoid conflict. To register the name of a font family, write to:

Developer Technical Support
Mail Stop 3-T
Apple Computer, Inc.
20525 Mariani Avenue
Cupertino, CA 95014

When there's a conflict, font families may be renumbered by the Font/DA Mover. For instance, when the Font/DA Mover moves a font or font family into a file in which there's already a font (or font family) with that number (but with a different name), the new font (or font family) is renumbered. For this reason, you should always call GetFNum to verify the number of a font you want to access.

FONT MANAGER ROUTINES

To improve the speed and readability of text display in your application, use the SetFractEnable and SetFScaleDisable procedures to enable fractional character widths and disable font scaling. Certain applications do not work properly when fractional character widths are used and font scaling is disabled, so these features are turned off by default.

The FontMetrics function is much like QuickDraw's GetFontInfo function except that it returns fixed-point values, letting you draw characters in more precise locations on the screen.

If there's a 'FOND' resource associated with the most recently drawn font, making the font resource purgeable or unpurgeable with the SetFontLock procedure will make the 'FOND' resource resource purgeable or unpurgeable as well.

```
PROCEDURE FontMetrics (VAR theMetrics: FMetricRec);
```

FontMetrics is similar to the QuickDraw procedure GetFontInfo except that it returns fixed-point values for greater accuracy in high-resolution printing.

The FMetricRec data structure is defined as follows:

```
TYPE FMetricRec =
        RECORD
          ascent:      Fixed;    {ascent}
          descent:     Fixed;    {descent}
          leading:     Fixed;    {leading}
          widMax:      Fixed;    {maximum character width}
          wTabHandle:  Handle;   {handle to global width table}
        END;
```

Ascent, descent, leading, and widMax are identical in function to their counterparts in GetFontInfo. WTabHandle is a handle to the global width table (described below).

`PROCEDURE SetFractEnable (fractEnable: BOOLEAN)` [Not in ROM]

SetFractEnable lets you enable or disable fractional character widths. If fractEnable is TRUE, fractional character widths are enabled; if it's FALSE, the Font Manager uses integer widths. To ensure compatibility with existing applications, fractional character widths are disabled by default.

Assembly-language note: From assembly language, you can change the value of the global variable FractEnable.

```
PROCEDURE SetFScaleDisable (fontScaleDisable: BOOLEAN);
```

SetFScaleDisable lets you disable or enable font scaling. If fontScaleDisable is TRUE, font scaling is disabled and the Font Manager returns an unscaled font with more space around the characters; if it's FALSE, the Font Manager scales fonts. To ensure compatibility with existing applications, the Font Manager defaults to scaling fonts.

Assembly-language note: All programmers should use the SetFScaleDisable procedure to disable and enable font scaling. In particular, setting the global variable FScaleDisable is insufficient.

COMMUNICATION BETWEEN QUICKDRAW AND THE FONT MANAGER

The basic structure of the font input and output records passed between QuickDraw and the Font Manager is unchanged.

> **Note:** Advanced programmers who use the FMSwapFont function should be aware that the Font Manager may attach optional tables to the font output record it returns.

The information QuickDraw passes to the Font Manager includes the font or family number, the font size, and the scaling factors QuickDraw wants to use; the search for an appropriate font is as follows.

The Font Manager first looks for a 'FOND' resource matching the ID of the requested font or font family. If it finds one, it searches the family record's font association table (detailed below) for a an 'NFNT' or 'FONT' resource matching the requested style and size. If it can match the size but not the style, it returns a font that matches as many properties as possible, giving priority first to italic, then to bold. Quickdraw must then add any needed stylistic variations (using the information passed in the bold, italic, ulOffset, ulShadow, ulThick, and shadow fields of the font output record).

If the Font Manager can't find a 'FOND' resource, it looks for a 'FONT' resource with the requested font number and size. (It doesn't look for a 'NFNT' resource since these occur only in conjunction with 'FOND' resources.)

If the Font Manager cannot find a font for a particular style, the Font Manager and QuickDraw derive a font (as in the 64K ROM version).

Font Scaling

If the Font Manager can't find a font of the requested size and font scaling is enabled, it follows the standard scaling algorithm (described in chapter 7 of Volume I) with one exception: If it can't find a font that's double or half the requested size, it looks for the font that's closest to the request size, either larger or smaller.

If it can't find a font of the requested size and font scaling is disabled, the Font Manager looks for a smaller font closest to the requested size and returns with it with the widths for the *requested* size. Thus, QuickDraw draws the smaller font with the spacing of the larger, requested font. This is generally preferable to font scaling since it's faster and more readable. Also, it accurately mirrors the word spacing and line breaks that the document will have when printed, especially if fractional character widths are used.

Fractional Character Widths

The use of fractional character widths allows more accurate character placement on high-resolution output devices such as the LaserWriter. It also enables character placement on the screen to match more closely that on the LaserWriter (although QuickDraw cannot actually draw a letter 3.5 pixels wide, for instance). The Font Manager will, however, store the locations of characters more accurately than any particular screen can display. Given exact widths for characters, words, and lines, the LaserWriter can print faster and give better spacing. A price must be paid, however; since screen characters are made up of whole pixels, spacing between characters and words will be uneven as the fractional parts are rounded off. The extent of the distortion depends on the font size relative to the screen resolution.

The Font Manager communicates fractional character widths QuickDraw via the **global width table**, a data structure allocated in the system heap. The Font Manager gathers the width data for this table from one of three data structures.

> **Warning:** You should always obtain character widths from the global width table since you can't really know where the Font Manager obtained the width information from. A handle to the global width table is returned by the FontMetrics procedure.

First, it looks for a font character-width table in the font record. In this table, the actual widths of each character in the font are stored in a 16-bit fixed-point format with an integer part in the high-order byte and a fractional part in the low-order byte.

If it doesn't find this table, it looks in the family record for a family character-width table. For each font in the family, this table contains the fractional widths for every character as if a hypothetical one-point font; the actual values for the characters are calculated by multiplying these widths by the font size. The widths in this table are stored in a 16-bit fixed-point format with an integer part in the high-order 4 bits and a fractional part in the low-order 12 bits.

If no family character-width table is found, the global character widths are derived from the integer widths contained in the offset/width table in the font record (described in chapter 7 of Volume I).

To use fractional character widths effectively, an application must get accurate widths for the characters, either by using the QuickDraw function TextWidth or by looking in the global width table.

> **Warning:** Applications that derive their own character widths may not function properly when fractional widths are enabled.

FONT MANAGER DATA STRUCTURES

This section describes the data structures that define fonts and font families; you need to read it only if you're going to define your own fonts or write your own font editor. Most of the information in this section is useful only to assembly-language programmers.

Figure 2 shows some of the relationships between the various data structures used by the Font Manager. Handles are shown as dotted lines; the one pointer is shown by a solid line.

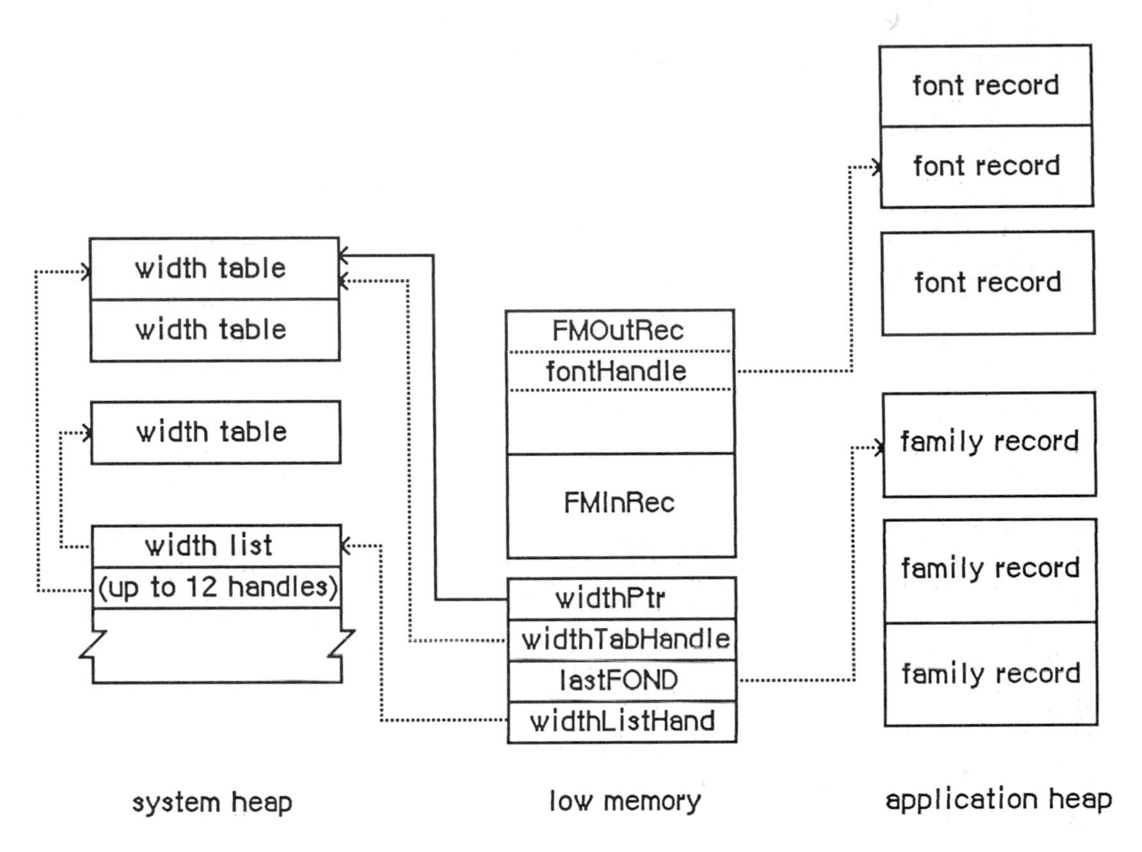

Figure 2. Font Manager Data Structures

Font records and family records, the structures from which global width tables are derived, are kept in the application heap. Global width tables, which are used constantly, are kept in the system heap.

Font Records

To maintain compatibility with existing applications, the order of the fields in the font record remains unchanged; two variable-length arrays are added at the end of the record, however, to implement fractional character widths.

Additional constants have been defined for use in the fontType field; it can now contain any of the following values:

```
CONST propFont    = $9000;    {proportional font}
      prpFntH     = $9001;    { with height table}
      prpFntW     = $9002;    { with width table}
      prpFntHW    = $9003;    { with height & width tables}

      fixedFont   = $B000;    {fixed-width font}
      fxdFntH     = $B001;    { with height table}
      fxdFntW     = $B002;    { with width table}
      fxdFntHW    = $B003;    { with height & width tables}

      fontWid     = $ACB0;    {font width data: 64K ROM only}
```

The low-order two bits of the fontType field tell whether the two optional tables are present. If bit 0 is set, there's an image-height table; if bit 1 is set, there's a character width table.

The optional character-width table immediately follows the offset/width table; it's a variable-length array specifying the fixed-point character widths for each character in the font. Each entry is a word in length. For compactness, a special 16-bit fixed-point format is used with an unsigned integer part in the high-order byte and a fractional part in the low-order byte.

The optional image-height table, which speeds the drawing of characters, may also be appended after the character-width table; it's a variable-length array specifying the image height of each character in the font. Each entry is a word in length; the high-order byte is the offset of the first non-white row in the character; the low-order byte is the number of rows that must be drawn. The image height is the height of the character image and is less than or equal to the font height; it's used in conjunction with QuickDraw for improved character plotting. Most font resources don't contain this table; it's typically generated by the Font Manager when the font is swapped in.

Note: The 64K ROM version of the Resource Manager limits the total space occupied by the bit image, location table, offset/width table, and character-width and image-height tables to 32K bytes. For this reason, the practical limit on the font size of a full font is about 40 points.

Family Records

A family record defines a font family; the information is loaded from the 'FOND' resource.

Assembly-language note: The global variable LastFOND is a handle to the last family record used. You can read the contents of the family record by using this handle. You should not alter the contents of this record.

The data type for a family record is as follows:

```
TYPE FamRec =
    RECORD
      ffFlags:       INTEGER;      {flags for family}
      ffFamID:       INTEGER;      {family ID number}
      ffFirstChar:   INTEGER;      {ASCII code of the first character}
      ffLastChar:    INTEGER;      {ASCII code of the last character}
      ffAscent:      INTEGER;      {maximum ascent for 1-pt.font}
      ffDescent:     INTEGER;      {maximum descent for 1-pt.font}
      ffLeading:     INTEGER;      {maximum leading for 1-pt.font}
      ffWidMax:      INTEGER;      {maximum width for 1-pt.font}
      ffWTabOff:     LONGINT;      {offset to width table}
      ffKernOff:     LONGINT;      {offset to kerning table}
```

```
      ffStylOff:     LONGINT;        {offset to style-mapping table}
      ffProperty:    ARRAY[1..9] OF INTEGER; {style property info}
      ffIntl:        ARRAY[1..2] OF INTEGER; {reserved}
      ffVersion:     INTEGER;        {version number}
    { ffAssoc:       FontAssoc;}     {font association table}
    { ffWidthTab:    WidTable;}      {width table}
    { ffStyTab:      StyleTable;}    {style-mapping table}
    { ffKernTab:     KernTable;}     {kerning table}
    END;
```

Note: The variable-length arrays appear as comments because they're not valid Pascal syntax; they're used only as conceptual aids.

The ffFlags field defines general characteristics of the font family, as follows:

Bit	Meaning
0	Set if there's an image-height table
1	Set if there's a character-width table
2–11	Reserved (should be zero)
12	Set to ignore FractEnable when deciding whether to use fixed-point values for stylistic variations (see bit 13), clear to treat FractEnable as usual
13	Set to use integer extra width for stylistic variations, clear to compute fixed-point extra width from the family style-mapping table when FractEnable is TRUE
14	Set if family fractional-width table is not used, clear if table is used
15	Set for fixed-width font, clear for proportional font

The values in the ffAscent, ffDescent, ffLeading, and ffWidMax describe the maximum dimensions of the family as they would be for a hypothetical one-point font to be scaled up. They use a special 16-bit fixed-point format with an integer part in the high-order 4 bits and a fractional part in the low-order 12 bits. The FontMetrics procedure calculates the true values by multiplying this number by the actual point size.

The ffWTabOff, ffKernOff, and ffStylOff fields are offsets from the top of the record to the start of the width table, kerning table, and style-mapping table, respectively; if any of these fields is zero, the corresponding table does not exist.

The ffProperty field is the family style-property table, shown in Figure 3.

extra width for Plain text -set to 0 (word)
extra width for Bold text (word)
extra width for Italic text (word)
extra width for Underline text (word)
extra width for Outline text (word)
extra width for Shadow text (word)
extra width for Condensed text (word)
extra width for Extended text (word)
not used - set to 0 (word)

Figure 3. Family Style-Property Table

Each entry is a 16-bit fixed-point number with a signed integer part in the high-order 4 bits and a fractional part in the low-order 12 bits. These numbers are used to calculate the amount of extra width for special stylistic variations; each of these values is multiplied by the point size of the font actually being used. If the font already exists for a given style, the value in its field is ignored.

The ffAssoc field contains the font association table. This table, shown in Figure 4, is used to match a given font size and style combination with the resource ID of an actual font.

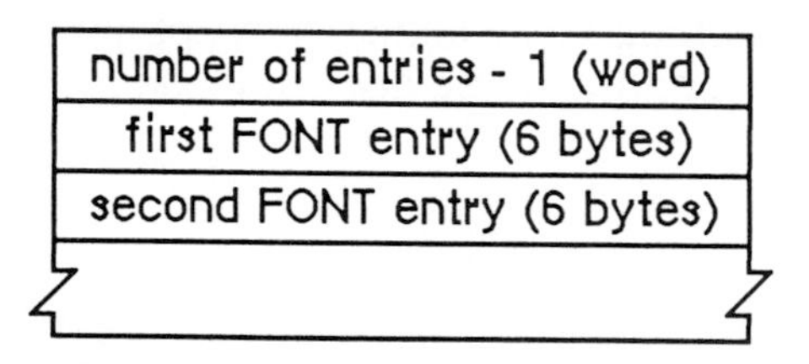

Figure 4. Font Association Table

> **Note:** In order to reduce search time, the Font Manager requires that the entries be sorted according to the fontSize field, with the smallest sizes first. If multiple fonts from the same family, the plain (roman) fonts come first. The Font Manager is optimized to look first for 'NFNT' resources, then 'FONT' resources.

Each entry in the font association table has the format shown in Figure 5.

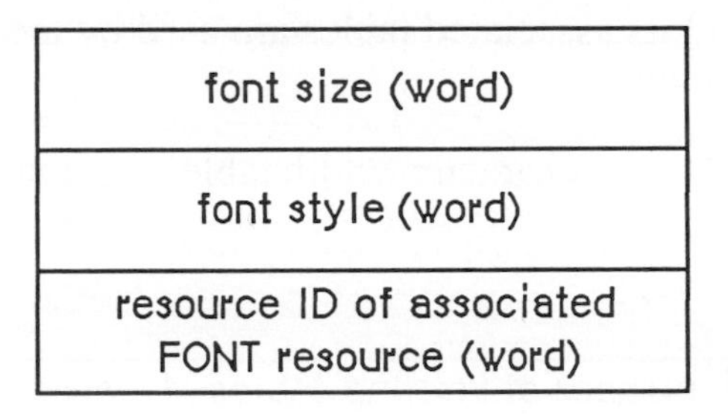

Figure 5. Font Association Table Entry

The font association table is followed by the family character-width table. As shown in Figure 6, this table is actually a number of width tables (since a font family may include numerous styles).

number of width tables - 1 (word)
style code (word)
first width table
style code (word)
second width table

Figure 6. Family Character-Width Table

Each character-width table is preceded by a style code; the low-order byte of this word specifies stylistic variations (see Figure 7). The widths in each table are for a hypothetical one-point font; the actual values for the characters are calculated by multiplying these widths by the font size. The widths in this table are stored in a 16-bit fixed-point format with an unsigned integer part in the high-order 4 bits and a fractional part in the low-order 12 bits.

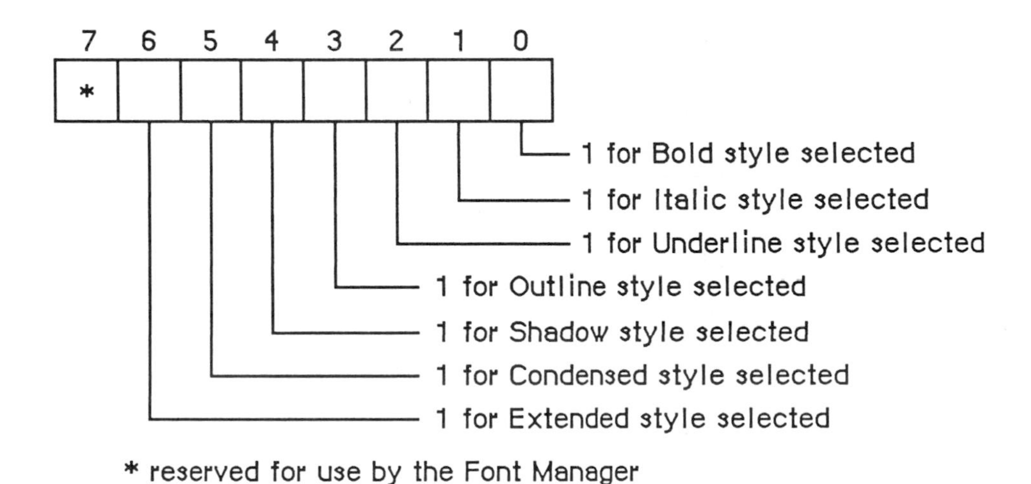

Figure 7. Style Codes

The style-mapping table and its associated tables are used by the LaserWriter driver and are described in *Inside LaserWriter*.

The kerning table, like the family character-width table, is actually a number of kerning tables (see Figure 8).

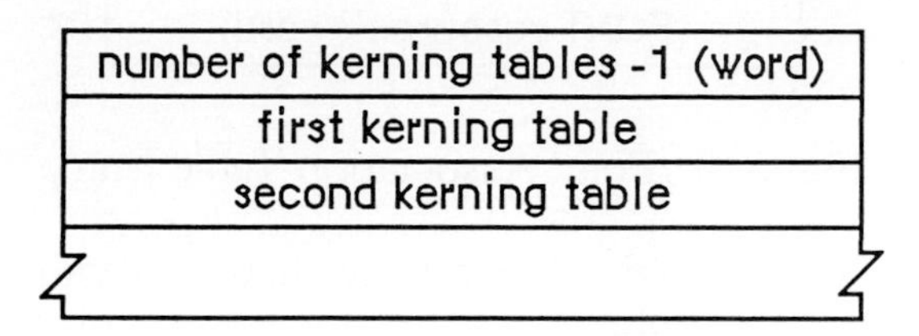

Figure 8. Kerning Table

Each kerning table is preceded by a style code; stored in the low-order byte of the word, this style information has the same format shown in Figure 7 above. The number of entries in the table follows the style word (see Figure 9).

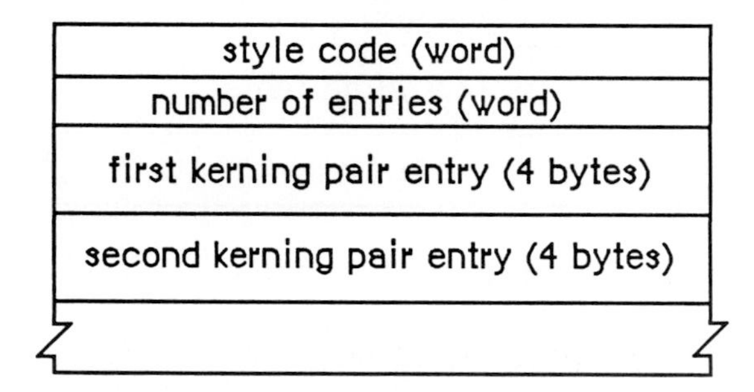

Figure 9. Structure of a Kerning Table

The entries in each kerning table (shown in Figure 10) consist of a pair of characters followed by a kerning offset for a hypothetical one-point font. This value, represented by an integer part in the high-order 4 bits and a fractional part in the low-order 12 bits, is multiplied by the size of the font to obtain the actual offset.

first character of kerning pair (byte)
second character of kerning pair (byte)
kerning offset (word)

Figure 10. Kerning Table Entry

Global Width Tables

The Font Manager communicates fractional character widths to QuickDraw via a **global width table**, a data structure allocated in the system heap. A handle to the global width table is returned by the FontMetrics procedure. The format of the global width table is follows:

```
TYPE  WidthTable =
        RECORD
          tabData:     ARRAY[1..256] OF Fixed; { character widths}
          tabFont:     Handle;     {font record used to build table}
          sExtra:      LONGINT;    {space extra used for table}
          style:       LONGINT;    {extra due to style}
          fID:         INTEGER;    {font family ID}
          fSize:       INTEGER;    {font size request}
          face:        INTEGER;    {style (face) request}
          device:      INTEGER;    {device requested}
          inNumer:     Point;      {numerators of scaling factors}
          inDenom:     Point;      {denominators of scaling factors}
          aFID:        INTEGER;    {actual font family ID for table}
          fHand:       handle;     {family record used to build table}
          usedFam:     BOOLEAN;    {used fixed-point family widths}
          aFace:       Byte;       {actual face produced}
          vOutput:     INTEGER;    {vertical factor for expanding }
                                   { characters}
          hOutput:     INTEGER;    {horizontal factor for expanding }
                                   { characters}
          vFactor:     INTEGER;    {not used}
          hFactor:     INTEGER;    {horizontal factor for increasing }
                                   { character widths}
          aSize:       INTEGER;    {actual size of actual font used}
          tabSize:     INTEGER     {total size of table}
        END;
```

TabData is an array containing a character width for each of the 255 possible characters in a font, plus one long word for the font's missing symbol. The widths are stored in the standard 32-bit fixed-point format. If a character is missing, its entry contains the width of the missing symbol. (For efficiency, the Font Manager will store up to 12 recently used global width tables.) InNumer and inDenom contain the vertical and horizontal scaling factors copied from the font input record.

Scaling is effected in two ways: by expanding characters of the chosen font and by artificially increasing the widths of the chosen font in the width table. HOutput and vOutput give the factors by which characters are to be expanded horizontally and vertically. HFactor is the factor by which the widths of the chosen font, after stylistic variations, have been increased. (VFactor is not used.) Thus, multiplying hOutput and vOutput by hFactor and vFactor gives the true font scaling; the product of hOutput and an entry in the width table is that character's true scaled width. HOutput,vOutput, hFactor, and vFactor are all 16-bit fixed-point numbers, with an integer part in the high-order byte and a fractional part in the low-order byte.

If font scaling has been enabled, hFactor and vFactor both have a value of 1. In any case, hOutput, vOutput, hFactor, and vFactor are adjusted so that the values of hFactor and vFactor lie between 1 and 2, including 1.

Assembly-language note: A handle to the global width table is contained in the global variable WidthTabHandle. A pointer to the table is contained in the global variable WidthPtr; it's reliable immediately after a call to FMSwapFont but, like all pointers, may become invalid after a call to the Memory Manager.

The global variable WidthListHand is a handle to a list of handles to up to 12 recently-used width tables. You can scan this list, looking for width tables that match the family number, size, and style of the font you wish to measure. If you reach a width handle that's equal to –1, that width table is invalid, and you must make an FMSwapFont call to get a valid one. When you reach a handle that's zero, you've reached the end of the list.

You should not use the global width table when special international interface software is being used to accommodate non-Roman alphabets. You can recognize such software by looking at the global variable IntlSpec; if it's greater than 0, special international software is installed. If your application uses non-Roman alphabets, write to

Developer Technical Support
Mail Stop 3-T
Apple Computer, Inc.
20525 Mariani Avenue
Cupertino, CA 95014

for the latest version of the International Utilities Package, which will be extended to handle non-Roman alphabets.

FONT AND FONT FAMILY RESOURCES

The various sizes of a font are each stored as separate resources. The resource type for a font is either 'FONT' or 'NFNT'; the two have identical formats:

Number of bytes	Contents
2 bytes	FontType field of font record
2 bytes	FirstChar field of font record
2 bytes	LastChar field of font record
2 bytes	WidMax field of font record
2 bytes	KernMax field of font record
2 bytes	NDescent field of font record
2 bytes	FRectWidth field of font record
2 bytes	FRectHeight field of font record
2 bytes	OWTLoc field of font record
2 bytes	Ascent field of font record
2 bytes	Descent field of font record

Number of bytes	Contents
2 bytes	Leading field of font record
2 bytes	RowWords field of font record
n bytes	Bit image of font n = 2 * rowWords * fRectHeight
m bytes	Location table of font m = 2 * (lastChar–firstChar+3)
m bytes	Offset/width table of font m = 2 * (lastChar–firstChar+3)
m bytes	Optional character-width table of font m = 2 * (lastChar–firstChar+3)
m bytes	Optional image-height table of font m = 2 * (lastChar–firstChar+3)

The resource type 'FRSV' is reserved by the Font Manager; it identifies fonts used by the system. Fonts whose resource IDs are contained in a 'FRSV' resource 1 will not be removed from the system resource file by the Font/DA Mover. The format of a 'FRSV' resource is as follows:

Number of bytes	Contents
2 bytes	Number of font resource IDs
n * 2 bytes	n font resource IDs

Family Record Format

A font family is stored as a resource of type 'FOND'; it consists of the following:

Number of bytes	Contents
2 bytes	FONDFlags field of family record
2 bytes	FONDFamID field of family record
2 bytes	FONDFirst field of family record
2 bytes	FONDLast field of family record
2 bytes	FONDAscent field of family record
2 bytes	FONDDescent field of family record
2 bytes	FONDLeading field of family record
2 bytes	FONDWidMax field of family record
4 bytes	FONDWTabOff of family record
4 bytes	FONDKernOff of family record
4 bytes	FONDStylOff of family record
24 bytes	FONDProperty field of family record
6 bytes	FONDIntl field of family record
m bytes	FONDAssoc field of family record (variable length)
n bytes	FONDWidTable field of family record (variable length)
p bytes	FONDStylTab field of family record (variable length)
q bytes	FONDKerntab field of family record (variable length)

Restrictions on the 'FONT' Type

For backward compatibility, all 'FONT' resources that are part of a 'FOND' have certain restrictions:

1. The font name and family name must be identical.

2. The font number and family number must be identical since the Font Manager interprets a family number as a font number.

3. The resource ID of the font must be the same number that would be produced by concatenating the font number and the font size (as described in chapter 7 of Volume I).

These restrictions ensure that both the 64K ROM and 128K ROM versions of the Font Manager will associate the family number and point size with the proper corresponding font resource ID, whether or not there's a family resource. 'NFNT' resources are not bound by these restrictions (but neither will they be found by the 64K ROM version of the Font Manager).

SUMMARY OF THE FONT MANAGER

Constants

```
CONST { Font types }

      propFont     = $9000;     {proportional font}
      prpFntH      = $9001;     { with height table}
      prpFntW      = $9002;     { with width table}
      prpFntHW     = $9003;     { with height & width tables}

      fixedFont    = $B000;     {fixed-width font}
      fxdFntH      = $B001;     { with height table}
      fxdFntW      = $B002;     { with width table}
      fxdFntHW     = $B003;     { with height & width tables}

      fontWid      = $ACB0;     {font width data: 64K ROM only}
```

Data Types

```
  FMetricRec =
  RECORD
     ascent:     Fixed;          {ascent}
     descent:    Fixed;          {descent}
     leading:    Fixed;          {leading}
     widMax:     Fixed;          {maximum character width}
     wTabHandle: Handle          {handle to font width table}
  END;

FamRec =
  RECORD
     ffFlags:     INTEGER;       {flags for family}
     ffFamID:     INTEGER;       {family ID number}
     ffFirstChar: INTEGER;       {ASCII code of the first character}
     ffLastChar:  INTEGER;       {ASCII code of the last character}
     ffAscent:    INTEGER;       {maximum ascent for 1-pt.font}
     ffDescent:   INTEGER;       {maximum descent for 1-pt.font}
     ffLeading:   INTEGER;       {maximum leading for 1-pt.font}
     ffWidMax:    INTEGER;       {maximum width for 1-pt.font}
     ffWTabOff:   LONGINT;       {offset to width table}
     ffKernOff:   LONGINT;       {offset to kerning table}
     ffStylOff:   LONGINT;       {offset to style-mapping table}
     ffProperty:  ARRAY[1..9] OF INTEGER; {style property info}
     ffIntl:      ARRAY[1..2] OF INTEGER; {reserved}
     ffVersion:   INTEGER;       {version number}
  {  ffAssoc:     FontAssoc;}    {font association table}
  {  ffWidthTab:  WidTable;}     {width table}
  {  ffStyTab:    StyleTable;}   {style-mapping table}
  {  ffKernTab:   KernTable;}    {kerning table}
  END;
```

5 Font Manager

```
WidthTable =
RECORD
   tabData:     ARRAY[1..256] OF Fixed; { character widths}
   tabFont:     Handle;       {font record used to build table}
   sExtra:      LONGINT;      {space extra used for table}
   style:       LONGINT;      {extra due to style}
   fID:         INTEGER;      {font family ID}
   fSize:       INTEGER;      {font size request}
   face:        INTEGER;      {style (face) request}
   device:      INTEGER;      {device requested}
   inNumer:     Point;        {numerators of scaling factors}
   inDenom:     Point;        {denominators of scaling factors}
   aFID:        INTEGER;      {actual font family ID for table}
   fHand:       handle;       {family record used to build table}
   usedFam:     BOOLEAN;      {used fixed-point family widths}
   aFace:       Byte;         {actual face produced}
   vOutput:     INTEGER;      {vertical factor for expanding }
                              { characters}
   hOutput:     INTEGER;      {horizontal factor for expanding }
                              { characters}
   vFactor:     INTEGER;      {not used}
   hFactor:     INTEGER;      {horizontal factor for increasing }
                              { character widths}
   aSize:       INTEGER;      {size of actual font used}
   tabSize:     INTEGER       {total size of table}
END;
```

Routines

```
PROCEDURE FontMetrics (VAR theMetrics: FMetricRec);
PROCEDURE SetFScaleDisable(fontScaleDisable: BOOLEAN);
PROCEDURE SetFractEnable (fractEnable: BOOLEAN);    [Not in ROM]
```

Assembly-Language Information

Constants

```
; Font types

propFont      .EQU     $9000 ;proportional font
prpFntH       .EQU     $9001 ; with height table
prpFntW       .EQU     $9002 ; with width table
prpFntHW      .EQU     $9003 ; with height & width tables


fixedFont     .EQU     $B000 ;fixed-width font
fxdFntH       .EQU     $B001 ; with height table
fxdFntW       .EQU     $B002 ; with width table
fxdFntHW      .EQU     $B003 ; with height & width tables


fontWid       .EQU     $ACB0 ;font width data
```

Font Metric Record Data Structure

ascent	Ascent (word)
descent	Descent (word)
leading	Leading (word)
widMax	Maximum character width (word)
wTabHandle	Handle to global width table (long)

Font Record ('FONT' or 'NFNT') Data Structure

fFontType	Font type (word)
fFirstChar	ASCII code of first character (word)
fLastChar	ASCII code of last character (word)
fWidMax	Maximum character width (word)
fKernMax	Negative of maximum character kern (word)
fNDescent	Negative of descent (word)
fFRectWidth	Width of font rectangle (word)
fFRectHeight	Height of font rectangle (word)
fOWTLoc	Offset to offset/width table (word)
fAscent	Ascent (word)
fDescent	Descent (word)
fLeading	Leading (word)
fRowWords	Row width of bit image / 2 (word)

Family Record ('FOND') Data Structure

fondFlags	Flags for family (word)
fondFamID	Family ID number (word)
fondFirst	ASCII code of first character (word)
fondLast	ASCII code of last character (word)
fondAscent	Maximum ascent expressed for 1 pt. font (word)
fondDescent	Maximum descent expressed for 1 pt. font (word)
fondLeading	Maximum leading expressed for 1 pt. font (word)
fondWidMax	Maximum widMax expressed for 1 pt. font (word)
fondWTabOff	Offset to width table (long)
fondKernOff	Offset to kerning table (long)
fondStylOff	Offset to style-mapping table (long)
fondProperty	Style property info (12 words)
fondIntl	Reserved (3 words)
fondAssoc	Font association Table (variable length)
fondWidTab	Optional character-width table (variable length)
fondStylTab	Style-mapping table (variable length)
fondKerntab	Kerning table (variable length)

Global Width Table Data Structure

widTabData	Character widths (1024 bytes)
widTabFont	Font handle used to build table (long)
widthSExtra	Space extra used for table (long)
widthStyle	Extra due to style (long)
widthFID	Font family ID (word)
widthFSize	Font size request (word)
widthFace	Style (face) request (word)
widthDevice	Device requested (word)
inNumer	Numerators of scaling factors (long)
inDenom	Denominators of scaling factors (long)
widthAFID	Actual font family ID for table (word)
widthFHand	Font family handle for table (long)
widthUsedFam	Used fixed point family widths? (boolean)
widthAFace	Actual face produced (byte)
widthVOutput	Not used (word)
widthHOutput	Horizontal factor for increasing character widths (word)
widthVFactor	Vertical scale output value (word)
widthHFactor	Horizontal scale output value (word)
widthASize	Actual size of actual font used (word)
widTabSize	Total size of table (word)

Global Variables

ApFont ID	Font number of application font (word)
FractEnable	Nonzero to enable fractional widths (byte)
IntlSpec	International software installed if greater than 0 (long)
WidthListHand	Handle to a list of handles to recently-used width tables
WidthPtr	Pointer to global width table
WidthTabHandle	Handle to global width table
SysFontFam	If nonzero, the font number to use for system font (byte)
SysFontSiz	If nonzero, the size of the system font (byte)
LastFOND	Handle to last family record used

6 THE WINDOW MANAGER

A new variation of the window definition function implements a feature known as window zooming; a description of window zooming is found in chapter 1 of this volume.

If you're using the standard document window, you can implement a zoom-window box by specifying a window definition function with a resource ID of 0 and a variation code of 8 when you call either the NewWindow or GetNewWindow functions. Two fields in the window record, dataHandle and spareFlag, are used only when variation code 8 is specified (otherwise they're not used).

DataHandle contains a handle to two rectangles that specify the standard and user states of the window:

```
TYPE WStateData =  RECORD;
                     userState:  Rect;
                     stdState: Rect
                   END;
```

If you wish, your application can access both states. You might want to provide initial values for the user state. Or you might want to save and restore all windows to the same state the next time your application is launched. To do this, you would save the two states and determine which of the two is current. The next time the application is launched, you would then create the window using the saved current state, and set the user and standard states to their previous values, after the GetNewWindow or NewWindow call.

SpareFlag is TRUE if zooming has been requested (that is, if a variation code of 8 has been specified).

If you create a custom window, you can give your window definition function any variation code you wish. If you want to implement zooming in the custom window, you must supply values for WStateData.

When there's a mouse-down event in the zoom-window box and your application calls the FindWindow function, the integer returned will be one of the following predefined constants:

```
CONST inZoomIn   = 7;   {in zoom box for zooming in}
      inZoomOut  = 8;   {in zoom box for zooming out}
```

InZoomIn and inZoomOut both indicate that the mouse button was pressed in the zoom-window box of the window. FindWindow returns inZoomIn when the window is in the standard state (and will be zoomed in), and inZoomOut when it's in the user state (and will be zoomed out).

If either of these constants are returned by FindWindow, call the TrackBox function (described below) to handle the highlighting of the zoom-window box and to determine whether the mouse is inside the box when the button is released. If TrackBox returns TRUE, call the ZoomWindow procedure (described below) to resize the window appropriately.

Advanced programmers: Two additional constants have been defined for your window definition function to return in response to a wHit message:

```
CONST wInZoomIn  = 5;   {in zoom box for zooming in}
      wInZoomOut = 6;   {in zoom box for zooming out}
```

WINDOW MANAGER ROUTINES

```
FUNCTION TrackBox (theWindow: WindowPtr; thePt: Point; partCode:
           INTEGER) : BOOLEAN;
```

When there's a mouse-down event in the zoom-window box of theWindow, the application should call TrackBox with thePt equal to the point where the mouse button was pressed (in global coordinates, as stored in the where field of the event record). The partCode parameter contains the constant (either inZoomIn or inZoomOut) returned by FindWindow. TrackBox keeps control until the mouse button is released; it highlights the zoom-window box in the same way as a window's close box is highlighted. When the mouse button is released, TrackBox unhighlights the zoom-window box and returns TRUE if the mouse is inside the zoom-window box or FALSE if it's outside the box (in which case the application should do nothing).

```
PROCEDURE ZoomWindow (theWindow: WindowPtr; partCode: INTEGER;
           front: BOOLEAN);
```

Call ZoomWindow after a call to TrackBox that returns TRUE. The partCode parameter contains the constant (either inZoomIn or inZoomOut) returned by FindWindow. The window will be zoomed either out or in, depending on the state of the window specified by partCode. If the window is already in the state specified by partCode, ZoomWindow does nothing. If the front parameter is TRUE, the window will be brought to the front; otherwise, the window is left where it is. (This means a window can be zoomed without necessarily becoming the active window.)

For best results, call the QuickDraw procedure EraseRect with the portRect field of theWindow's grafPort before calling ZoomWindow.

> **Warning:** Using the QuickDraw procedure SetPort, set thePort to the window's port before calling ZoomWindow.

> **Note:** ZoomWindow is in no way tied to the TrackBox function and could just as easily be called in response to a selection from a menu.

SUMMARY OF THE WINDOW MANAGER

Constants

```
CONST { Additional values returned by FindWindow }

      inZoomIn   =  7;   {in zoom box for zooming in}
      inZoomOut  =  8;   {in zoom box for zooming out}

      { Values returned by window definition function's hit routine }

      wInZoomIn  =  5;   {in zoom box for zooming in}
      wInZoomOut =  6;   {in zoom box for zooming out}
```

Data Types

```
TYPE WStateData =  RECORD;
                     userState: Rect;  {user state}
                     stdState:  Rect   {standard state}
                   END;
```

Routines

```
FUNCTION   TrackBox     (theWindow: WindowPtr; thePt: Point; partCode:
                         INTEGER) : BOOLEAN;
PROCEDURE ZoomWindow    (theWindow: WindowPtr; partCode: INTEGER; front:
                         BOOLEAN);
```

Assembly-Language Information

Constants

```
; Additional values returned by FindWindow

inZoomIn        .EQU    7      ;in zoom box for zooming in
inZoomOut       .EQU    8      ;in zoom box for zooming out

; Values returned by window definition function's hit routine

wInZoomIn       .EQU    5      ;in zoom box for zooming in
wInZoomOut      .EQU    6      ;in zoom box for zooming out
```

Window Record Data Structure

windowPort	Window's grafPort (portRec bytes)
windowKind	Window class (word)
wVisible	Nonzero if window is visible (byte)
wHilited	Nonzero if window is highlighted (byte)
wGoAway	Nonzero if window has go-away region (byte)
wZoom	Nonzero if window has a zoom-window box (byte)
structRgn	Handle to structure region of window
contRgn	Handle to content region of window
updateRgn	Handle to update region of window
windowDef	Handle to window definition function
wDataHandle	Handle to standard and user window states
wTitleHandle	Handle to window's title (preceded by length)
wTitleWidth	Width of title in pixels (word)
wControlList	Handle to window's control list
nextWindow	Pointer to next window in window list
windowPic	Picture handle for drawing window
wRefCon	Window's reference value (long)
windowSize	Size in bytes of window record

Window State Data Structure

userState	Window's user state (rectangle; 8 bytes)
stdState	Window's standard state (rectangle; 8 bytes)

7 THE CONTROL MANAGER

Two new routines, UpdtControl and Draw1Control, have been added to the Control Manager. In addition, there's a new control definition function that supports multiple lines of text in controls.

CONTROL MANAGER ROUTINES

```
PROCEDURE UpdtControl (theWindow: WindowPtr; updateRgn: RgnHandle);
```

UpdtControl is a faster version of the DrawControls procedure. Instead of drawing all of the controls in theWindow, UpdtControl draws only the controls that are in the specified update region. UpdtControl is called in response to an update event, and is usually bracketed by calls to the Window Manager procedures BeginUpdate and EndUpdate. UpdateRgn should be set to the visRgn of theWindow's port (for more details, see the BeginUpdate procedure in the Window Manager chapter).

> **Note:** In general, controls are in a dialog box and are automatically drawn by the DrawDialog procedure.

```
PROCEDURE Draw1Control (theControl: ControlHandle);
```

Draw1Control draws the specified control if it's visible within the window.

THE CONTROL DEFINITION FUNCTION

A new version of the control definition function (version 4 or greater) in the 128K ROM allows buttons, check boxes, and radio buttons to have multiple lines of text in their titles. When specifying the title with either NewControl or SetCTitle, simply separate the lines with the ASCII character code $0D (carriage return). You can also use a version of the Resource Editor that supports the 128K ROM to specify multiline titles.

> **Note:** This feature will work with the 64K ROM if the new version of the control definition function is in the system resource file.

If the control is a button, each line is horizontally centered and separated from the neighboring lines by the font's leading. (Since the height of each line is equal to the ascent plus descent plus leading of the font used, be sure to make the total height of the enclosing rectangle greater than the number of lines times this height.)

If the control is a check box or a radio button, the text is left-justified and the check box or button is vertically centered within the enclosing rectangle, cntrlRect.

SUMMARY OF THE CONTROL MANAGER

Routine

```
PROCEDURE UpdtControl  (theWindow: WindowPtr; updateRgn: RgnHandle);
PROCEDURE Draw1Control (theControl: ControlHandle);
```

8 THE MENU MANAGER

The AddResMenu and InsertResMenu procedures have been modified to work with the font family resource type ('FOND'). If you call either routine for a resource of type 'FONT', they first add all instances of type 'FOND' and then all instances of type 'FONT'. The Menu Manager ignores resources of type 'NFNT'. Both routines, before adding a new item to the menu, first check to see that an item with the same name is not already in the menu. If an item with the same name is already there, the new item is not added. This prevents duplication and gives items of type 'FOND' precedence over items of type 'FONT'.

AddResMenu and InsertResMenu *both* sort the items alphabetically as they're placed in the menu; the order of items already in the menu, however, is unaffected. Neither routine enables the items.

> **Note:** If the name of your desk accessory appears not to have been sorted and is inserted at the end of the Apple menu, the name is missing the leading null character.

Two new routines, InsMenuItem and DelMenuItem, let you insert and delete individual items from an existing menu. Use of these routines is discouraged except in certain situations where the user expects a menu to change (such as list of open windows).

> **Warning:** Menu resources should *never* be marked as purgeable. If a Menu Manager routine tries to access a menu that's been purged, a system error (ID 84) will occur.

> **Note:** In the 64K ROM version of the Menu Manager, if the user attempted to pull down an empty menu (one with no items), an unsightly empty menu of arbitrary size was displayed. In the 128K ROM version, the menu title is highlighted but the menu is not pulled down at all.

MENU MANAGER ROUTINES

```
PROCEDURE InsMenuItem (theMenu: MenuHandle; itemString: Str255;
           afterItem: INTEGER);
```

InsMenuItem inserts an item or items into the given menu where specified by the afterItem parameter. If afterItem is 0, the items are inserted before the first menu item; if it's the item number of an item in the menu, they're inserted after that item; if it's equal to or greater than the last item number, they're appended to the menu.

The contents of itemString are parsed as in the AppendMenu procedure. Multiple items are inserted in the *reverse* of their order in itemString.

```
PROCEDURE DelMenuItem (theMenu: MenuHandle; item: INTEGER);
```

DelMenuItem deletes the specified item from the given menu.

> **Note:** DelMenuItem is intended for maintaining dynamic menus (such as a list of open windows). It should not be used for disabling items; you should use DisableItem instead.

THE MENU DEFINITION PROCEDURE

This section describes changes to the default menu definition procedure ('MDEF' resource 0); some of the information presented in this section is accessible only through assembly language.

> **Note:** These features will work with the 64K ROM if the new menu definition procedure is in the system resource file.

Variable Size Fonts

Menus are displayed in the system font. Since the system font and font size can now be changed, the menu definition procedure calls the QuickDraw procedure GetFontInfo for the system font to determine the height of menu items

Scrolling Menus

The default menu definition procedure allows longer menus by implementing automatic scrolling. If the entire menu cannot be drawn on screen, dragging the cursor below the last displayed item will cause the items in the menu to scroll up. Similarly, if items have been scrolled past the top of the menu, dragging the cursor into the highlighted portion of the menu bar will cause the menu to scroll back down. The maximum number of items that can be drawn on the standard Macintosh screen with this new menu definition function is 19 (instead of 20).

> **Warning:** You should not disable any menu items in a menu containing more than 31 items because the enableFlags field of the MenuInfoRec can only handle 31 items.

SUMMARY OF THE MENU MANAGER

Routines

```
PROCEDURE InsMenuItem  (theMenu: MenuHandle; itemString: Str255;
                        afterItem: INTEGER);
PROCEDURE DelMenuItem  (theMenu: MenuHandle; item: INTEGER);
```

9 TEXTEDIT

Automatic scrolling of text (when the user is making a selection and drags the cursor out of the view rectangle) is now supported by TextEdit.

To enable and disable automatic scrolling, call the procedure TEAutoView. TESelView will, if automatic scrolling is enabled, automatically scroll the selection range into view. TEPinScroll scrolls text within the view rectangle but stops when the last line comes into view.

> **Note**: When enabled, automatic scrolling can occur in response to TESelView, TEKey, TEPaste, TEDelete, and TESetSelect.

When used with the System file version 3.0 or later, TextEdit also automatically supports the movement of the insertion point with the Macintosh Plus arrow keys; this is described in chapter 1 of this volume.

> **Warning**: Command–arrow key combinations are not supported by TextEdit and must be handled by your application. Selection expansion must also be handled by your application.

TEXTEDIT ROUTINES

```
PROCEDURE TESelView (hTE: TEHandle);
```

If automatic scrolling has been enabled (by a call to TEAutoView, described below), TESelView makes sure that the selection range is visible, scrolling it into the view rectangle if necessary. If automatic scrolling is disabled, TESelView does nothing.

> **Note**: The top left of the insertion is scrolled into view; if text is being displayed in a rectangle that's not tall enough, automatic scrolling could cause the text to jump up and down at times.

```
PROCEDURE TEPinScroll (dh,dv: INTEGER; hTE: TEHandle);
```

TEPinScroll is similar to TEScroll except that it stops scrolling when the last line scrolls into the view rectangle.

```
PROCEDURE TEAutoView (auto: BOOLEAN; hTE: TEHandle);
```

TEAutoView enables and disables automatic scrolling of text in the edit record specified by hTe. If the auto parameter is FALSE, automatic scrolling is disabled and calling TESelView has no effect.

DEFAULT CLICK LOOP ROUTINE

TextEdit now installs a default click loop routine in the edit record that supports automatic scrolling; you still need, however, to update the scroll bars. If automatic scrolling is enabled, this routine checks to see if the mouse has been dragged out of the view rectangle; if it has, the routine scrolls the text using TEPinScroll. The amount by which the text is scrolled, whether horizontally or vertically, is determined by the lineHeight field of the edit record.

SUMMARY OF TEXTEDIT

Routines

```
PROCEDURE TESelView    (hTE: TEHandle);
PROCEDURE TEPinScroll  (dh,dv: INTEGER; hTE: TEHandle);
PROCEDURE TEAutoView   (auto: BOOLEAN; hTE: TEHandle);
```

10 THE DIALOG MANAGER

Four routines—HideDItem, ShowDItem, FindDItem, and UpdtDialog—have been added to the Dialog Manager.

Advanced programmers: The standard filterProc function called by ModalDialog now returns 1 in itemHit and a function result of TRUE only if the first item is *enabled.*

Automatic scrolling is supported in editText items.

DIALOG MANAGER ROUTINES

```
PROCEDURE HideDItem (theDialog: DialogPtr; itemNo: INTEGER);
```

HideDItem hides the item numbered itemNo in the given dialog's item list by giving the item a display rectangle that's off the screen. (Specifically, if the left coordinate of the item's display rectangle is less than 8192, ShowDItem adds 16384 to both the left and right coordinates the rectangle.) If the item is already hidden (that is, if the left coordinate is greater than 8192), HideDItem does nothing.

HideDItem calls the EraseRect procedure on the item's enclosing rectangle and adds the rectangle that contained the item (not necessarily the item's display rectangle) to the update region. If the specified item is an active editText item, the item is first deactivated (by calling TEDeactivate).

> **Note:** If you have items that are close to each other, be aware that the Dialog Manager draws outside of the enclosing rectangle by 3 pixels for editText items and by 4 pixels for a default button.

An item that's been hidden by HideDItem can be redisplayed by the ShowDItem procedure.

> **Note:** To create a hidden item in a dialog item list, simply add 16384 to the left and right coordinates of the display rectangle.

```
PROCEDURE ShowDItem (theDialog: DialogPtr; itemNo: INTEGER);
```

ShowDItem redisplays the item numbered itemNo, previously hidden by HideDItem, by giving the item the display rectangle it had prior to the HideDItem call. (Specifically, if the left coordinate of the item's display rectangle is greater than 8192, ShowDItem subtracts 16384 from both the left and right coordinates the rectangle.) If the item is already visible (that is, if the left coordinate is less than 8192), ShowDItem does nothing.

ShowDItem adds the rectangle that contained the item (not necessarily the item's display rectangle) to the update region so that it will be drawn. If the item becomes the only editText item, ShowDItem activates it (by calling TEActivate).

```
FUNCTION FindDItem (theDialog: DialogPtr; thePt: Point) : INTEGER;
```

FindDItem returns the item number of the item containing the point specified, in local coordinates, by thePt. If the point doesn't lie within the item's rectangle, FindDItem returns –1. If there are overlapping items, it returns the item number of the first item in the list containing the point. FindDItem is useful for changing the cursor when it's over a particular item.

Note: FindDItem will return the item number of disabled items as well.

```
PROCEDURE UpdtDialog (theDialog: DialogPtr; updateRgn:
          RgnHandle);
```

UpdtDialog is a faster version of the DrawDialog procedure. Instead of drawing the entire contents of the given dialog box, UpdtDialog draws only the items that are in a specified update region. UpdtDialog is called in response to an update event, and is usually bracketed by calls to the Window Manager procedures BeginUpdate and EndUpdate. UpdateRgn should be set to the visRgn of theWindow's port. (For more details, see the BeginUpdate procedure in chapter 9 of Volume I.)

SUMMARY OF THE DIALOG MANAGER

Routines

```
PROCEDURE HideDItem  (theDialog: DialogPtr; itemNo: INTEGER);
PROCEDURE ShowDItem  (theDialog: DialogPtr; itemNo: INTEGER);
FUNCTION  FindDItem  (theDialog: DialogPtr; thePt: Point) : INTEGER;
PROCEDURE UpdtDialog (theDialog: DialogPtr; updateRgn: RgnHandle);
```

11 THE SCRAP MANAGER

The desk scrap is now written on the system startup volume (that is, the volume that contains the currently open System file) rather than the default volume. With hierarchical volumes, the scrap file is placed in the folder containing the currently open System file and Finder.

In addition, the GetScrap and PutScrap functions will never return the result code noScrapErr; if the scrap has not been initialized, the ZeroScrap function will be called. The InfoScrap function also calls ZeroScrap if the scrap is uninitialized.

12 TOOLBOX UTILITIES

A new fixed-point type, Fract, has been defined. Useful in graphics software, the Fract type allows accurate representation of small numbers (between –2 and 2). Like the type Fixed, a Fract number is a 32-bit quantity, but its implicit binary point is to the right of bit 30 of the number; that is, a Fract number has 2 integer bits and 30 fraction bits. As with the type Fixed, a number is negated by taking its two's complement. Thus Fract values range between –2 and $2-(2^{-30})$, inclusive. Figure 1 shows the weight of each binary place of a Fract number.

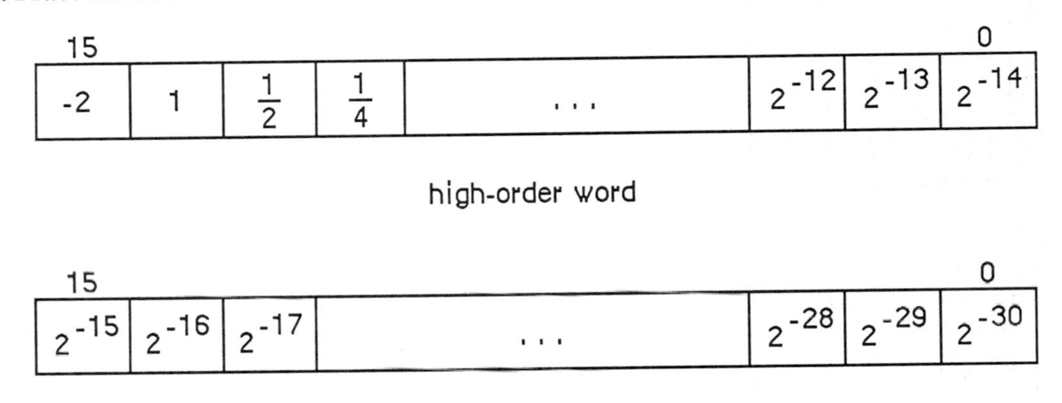

Figure 1. A Fract Number

In the 128K ROM, *all* fixed-point functions (that is, functions with Fixed or Fract arguments or results) handle boundary cases uniformly. Results are rounded by adding half a unit in magnitude in the last place of the stored precision and then chopping toward zero. Overflows are set to the maximum representable value with the correct sign (typically $80000000 for negative results and $7FFFFFFF for positive results). Division by zero in any of the four divide routines results in $80000000 if the numerator is negative and $7FFFFFFF otherwise; thus the special case 0/0 yields $7FFFFFFF.

Warning: Some applications may depend on spurious values returned by the 64K ROM: FixRatio and FixMul overflowed unpredictably, FixRatio returned $80000001 when a negative number was divided by 0, and FixRound malfunctioned with negative arguments.

TOOLBOX UTILITY ROUTINES

The 128K ROM version of the Toolbox Utilities supports fifteen new fixed-point functions. Pascal typing will allow any of the operand combinations suggested here without redefinition of the function.

Arithmetic Operations

```
FUNCTION FracMul (x,y: Fract) : Fract;
```

FracMul returns x * y. Note that FracMul effects "type * Fract —> type":

Fract	*	Fract	—>	Fract
LONGINT	*	Fract	—>	LONGINT
Fract	*	LONGINT	—>	LONGINT
Fixed	*	Fract	—>	Fixed
Fract	*	Fixed	—>	Fixed

```
FUNCTION FixDiv (x,y: Fixed) : Fixed;
```

FixDiv returns x / y. Note that FixDiv effects "type / type —> Fixed" and "type / Fixed —> type":

Fixed	/	Fixed	—>	Fixed
LONGINT	/	LONGINT	—>	Fixed
Fract	/	Fract	—>	Fixed
LONGINT	/	Fixed	—>	LONGINT
Fract	/	Fixed	—>	Fract

```
FUNCTION FracDiv (x,y: Fract) : Fract;
```

FracDiv returns x / y. Note that FracDiv effects "type / type —> Fract" and "type / Fract —> type":

Fract	/	Fract	—>	Fract
LONGINT	/	LONGINT	—>	Fract
Fixed	/	Fixed	—>	Fract
LONGINT	/	Fract	—>	LONGINT
Fixed	/	Fract	—>	Fixed

```
FUNCTION FracSqrt (x: Fract) : Fract;
```

FracSqrt returns the square root of x, with x interpreted as unsigned in the range 0 through $4-(2^{-30})$, inclusive: That is, bit 15 in Figure 1 has weight 2 rather than –2. The result, too, is unsigned in the range 0 through 2, inclusive.

```
FUNCTION FracCos (x: Fixed) : Fract;
FUNCTION FracSin (x: Fixed) : Fract;
```

FracCos and FracSin return the cosine and sine of their radian arguments, respectively. The hexadecimal value 0.C910 (which is FixATan2(1,1)) is the approximation to $\pi/4$ used for argument reduction. Thus, FracCos and FracSin are nearly periodic, but with period 2*P instead of $2*\pi$, where P=3.1416015625 and π, of course, is 3.14159265....

```
FUNCTION FixATan2 (x,y: LONGINT) : Fixed;
```

FixATan2 returns the arctangent of y / x in radians. Note that FixATan2 effects "arctan(type / type) —> Fixed":

arctan(LONGINT / LONGINT)	—>	Fixed
arctan(Fixed / Fixed)	—>	Fixed
arctan(Fract / Fract)	—>	Fixed

Conversion Functions

```
FUNCTION Long2Fix (x: LONGINT) : Fixed;
FUNCTION Fix2Long (x: Fixed) : LONGINT;
FUNCTION Fix2Frac (x: Fixed) : Fract;
FUNCTION Frac2Fix (x: Fract) : Fixed;
```

Long2Fix, Fix2Long, Fix2Frac, and Frac2Fix convert between fixed-point types.

```
FUNCTION Fix2X    (x: Fixed) : Extended;
FUNCTION X2Fix    (x: Extended) : Fixed;
FUNCTION Frac2X   (x: Fract) : Extended;
FUNCTION X2Frac   (x: Extended) : Fract;
```

Fix2X, X2Fix, Frac2X, and X2Frac convert between Fixed and Fract and the Extended floating-point type. These functions do not set floating-point exception flags.

Examples

Examples of the use of these fixed-point functions are provided below; all numbers are decimal unless otherwise noted.

Function		Result	Comment
FixDiv	(X2Fix(1.95), X2Fix(1.30))	$00018000	1.5 = 01.10 bin
FracDiv	(X2Frac(1.95), X2Frac(1.30))	$60000000	1.5 = 01.10 bin
FracMul	(X2Frac(1.50), X2Frac(1.30))	$7CCCCCCD	1.95 rounded
FracSqrt	(X2Frac(1.96))	$5999999A	1.4 rounded
FracSin	(X2Fix(3.1416015625))	$00000000	0
FracCos	(X2Fix(3.1416015625))	$C0000000	-1
Fix2Long	(X2Fix(1.75))	$00000002	2
Fix2Frac	(X2Fix(1.75))	$70000000	1.75 = 01.11 bin
Frac2Fix	(X2Frac(1.75))	$0001C000	1.75 = 01.11 bin
FixATan2	(X2Fix(1.00), X2Fix(1.00))	$0000C910	0.C910 hex = X2Fix (π/4)
FixDiv	(X2Fix(-1.95), X2Fix(1.30))	$FFFE8000	-1.5
FracDiv	(X2Frac(-1.95), X2Frac(1.30))	$A0000000	-1.5
FracMul	(X2Frac(-1.50), X2Frac(1.30))	$83333333	-1.95 rounded
FracSin	(X2Fix(-3.1416015625))	$00000000	0
FracCos	(X2Fix(-3.1416015625))	$C0000000	-1
Fix2Long	(X2Fix(-1.75))	$FFFFFFFE	-2
Fix2Frac	(X2Fix(-1.75))	$90000000	-1.75
Frac2Fix	(X2Frac(-1.75))	$FFFE4000	-1.75
FixATan2	(X2Fix(-1.00), X2Fix(-1.00))	$FFFDA4D0	-3*X2Fix(π/4) = 3*0.C910 hex

SUMMARY OF THE TOOLBOX UTILITIES

Routines

Arithmetic Operations

```
FUNCTION FracMul   (x,y : Fract) : Fract;
FUNCTION FixDiv    (x,y: Fixed) : Fixed;
FUNCTION FracDiv   (x,y: Fract) : Fract;
FUNCTION FracSqrt  (x: Fract) : Fract;
FUNCTION FracCos   (x: Fixed) : Fract;
FUNCTION FracSin   (x: Fixed) : Fract;
FUNCTION FixATan2  (x,y: LONGINT) : Fixed;
```

Conversion Functions

```
FUNCTION Long2Fix  (x: LONGINT) : Fixed;
FUNCTION Fix2Long  (x: Fixed) : LONGINT;
FUNCTION Fix2Frac  (x: Fixed) : Fract;
FUNCTION Frac2Fix  (x: Fract) : Fixed;
FUNCTION Fix2X     (x: Fixed) : Extended;
FUNCTION X2Fix     (x: Extended) : Fixed;
FUNCTION Frac2X    (x: Fract) : Extended;
FUNCTION X2Frac    (x: Extended) : Fract;
```

13 THE PACKAGE MANAGER

The following Macintosh packages, previously stored only in the system resource file, are now also found in the 128K ROM:

- The Binary-Decimal Conversion Package, for converting integers to decimal strings and vice versa.
- The Floating-Point Arithmetic Package, which supports extended-precision arithmetic according to IEEE Standard 754.
- The Transcendental Functions Package, which contains trigonometric, logarithmic, exponential, and financial functions, as well as a random number generator.

For compatibility with the 64K ROM, the above resources are still stored in the system resource file. The system resource file contains the following additional packages as well:

- The List Manager Package, for creating, displaying, and manipulating lists.
- The Standard File Package, for presenting the standard user interface when a file is to be saved or opened.
- The Disk Initialization Package, for initializing and naming new disks.
- The International Utilities Package, for accessing country-dependent information such as the formats for numbers, currency, dates, and times.

Packages have the resource type 'PACK' and the following resource IDs:

```
CONST listMgr = 0;     {List Manager}
      dskInit = 2;     {Disk Initialization}
      stdFile = 3;     {Standard File}
      flPoint = 4;     {Floating-Point Arithmetic}
      trFunct = 5;     {Transcendental Functions}
      intUtil = 6;     {International Utilities}
      bdConv  = 7;     {Binary-Decimal Conversion}
```

The Package Manager has been extended to allow for eight additional packages. All packages are reserved for use by Apple.

SUMMARY OF THE PACKAGE MANAGER

Constants

```
CONST { Resource IDs for packages }

      listMgr    =  0;    {List Manager}
      dskInit    =  2;    {Disk Initialization}
      stdFile    =  3;    {Standard File}
      flPoint    =  4;    {Floating-Point Arithmetic}
      trFunct    =  5;    {Transcendental Functions}
      intUtil    =  6;    {International Utilities}
      bdConv     =  7;    {Binary-Decimal Conversion}
```

Assembly-Language Information

Constants

```
; Resource IDs for packages

listMgr      .EQU   0     ;List Manager
dskInit      .EQU   2     ;Disk Initialization
stdFile      .EQU   3     ;Standard File
flPoint      .EQU   4     ;Floating-Point Arithmetic
trFunct      .EQU   5     ;Transcendental Functions
intUtil      .EQU   6     ;International Utilities
bdConv       .EQU   7     ;Binary-Decimal Conversion
```

Trap Macros for Packages

List Manager	_Pack0	
Disk Initialization	_Pack2	
Standard File	_Pack3	
Floating-Point Arithmetic	_Pack4	(synonym: _FP68K)
Transcendental Functions	_Pack5	(synonym: _Elems68K)
International Utilities	_Pack6	
Binary-Decimal Conversion	_Pack7	

14 THE BINARY-DECIMAL CONVERSION PACKAGE

Three new routines have been added to the Binary-Decimal Conversion Package. These routines supplement the Floating-Point Arithmetic and Transcendental Functions Packages in providing the the Standard Apple Numeric Environment (SANE) for the Macintosh.

Detailed documentation for these new routines is included with the rest of the SANE documentation in the *Apple Numerics Manual*—in particular, see the chapter "Conversions" in Part I and the three chapters "Conversions", "Numeric Scanner and Formatter", and "Examples" in Part III.

The new routines, two numeric scanners and a numeric formatter, are intended for programmers with special needs beyond what their development language provides. For example, developers of programming languages can use these routines to implement the floating-point I/O routines—such as read and write for Pascal or scanf and printf for C—that are appropriate for their particular languages. The scanners can be used for scanning numbers embedded in text and for numbers received character by character. The scanners differ only in that one accepts a pointer to a Pascal strings (with an initial length byte) as input, while the other accepts a pointer to the first character of a character stream.

The scanners convert ASCII string representations of numbers into SANE decimal records. The formatter converts SANE decimal records into ASCII string representations. The Floating-Point Arithmetic Package converts between this decimal record format and the SANE binary data formats.

The three routines handle the usual number representations, like –1.234 and 5e–7, throughout the range and precision of the extended data format. They also handle the special NaN, infinity, and signed-zero representations specified by the IEEE Floating-Point Standard.

15 THE STANDARD FILE PACKAGE

The Standard File Package has been modified to work with the hierarchical file system. (This chapter assumes some familiarity with the new material presented in chapter 19 of this volume.) Since a volume's files are no longer necessarily contained in a single flat directory, the Standard File Package must provide some way for the user to select a file that's contained in a folder (or subdirectory). It must also provide the user with a way of indicating the directory into which a particular file should be saved.

The dialog box displayed in response to the SFGetFile procedure shows the names of folders (if any) as well as files. Files and folders are distinguished by miniature icons preceding their names. Notice that there are two types of mini-icons for files—one for applications and another for documents. Figure 1 shows the files and folders contained on a sample desktop.

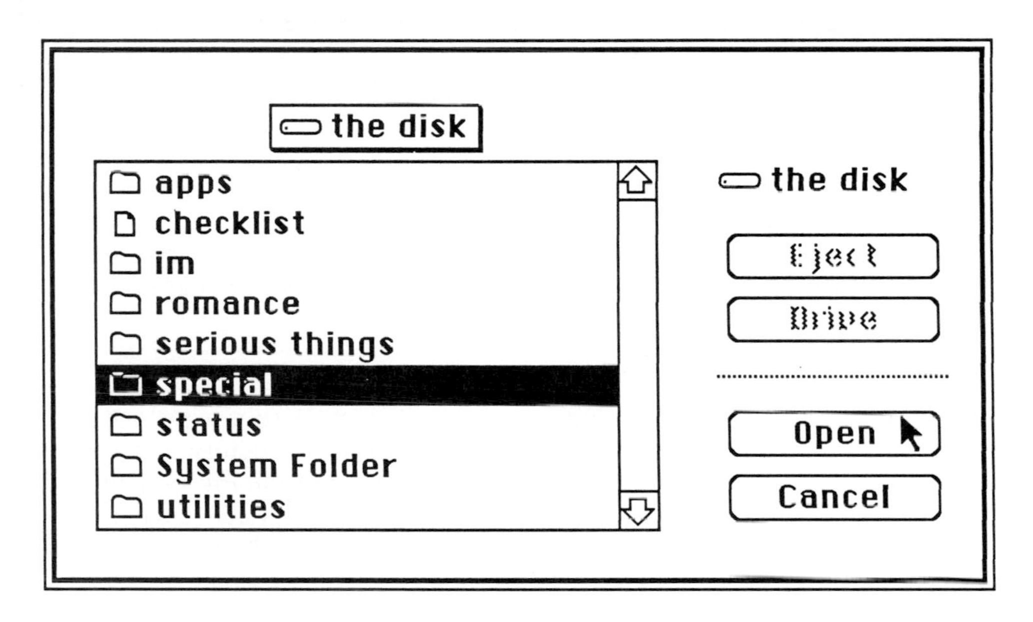

Figure 1. Open Dialog (at the Desktop Level)

To view the files and folders contained in a particular folder, the user must open the folder by clicking it and then clicking the Open button, or by double-clicking on the folder name; this causes the contents of the folder to be displayed. Figure 2 shows the contents of the sample folder special.

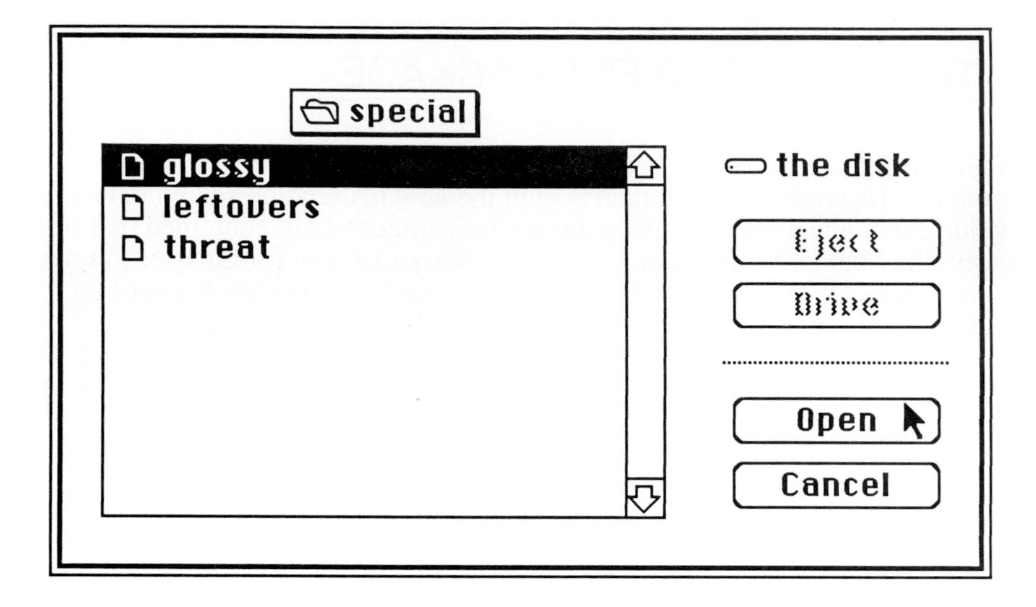

Figure 2. Open Dialog (at a Folder Level)

A current directory button above the list shows the name of the directory whose files and folders are displayed in the list below. If the contents of the desktop (or root directory) are being displayed, the button will show the name of the volume next to either a 3 1/2-inch disk mini-icon or a hard disk mini-icon (as in Figure 1). If the contents of a particular folder (or subdirectory) are being displayed, the button will show the name of that folder next to an open folder mini-icon (as in Figure 2 for instance).

Assembly-language note: The global variable SFSaveDisk always contains the negative of the volume reference number (never a working directory reference number) of the volume to use. If the hierarchical version of the File Manager is running, the global variable CurDirStore contains the directory ID of whatever directory (including the root) was last opened (regardless of whether a document was actually opened or saved). With the 64K ROM version of the File Manager, CurDirStore is not needed and is set to 0.

The current directory button provides a way of moving back up through the hierarchical directory structure of a volume. If the user is at the level of a particular folder (or subdirectory), clicking on the button causes a list to pop down. This list gives the path from the current directory back up to the root directory. The rules for displaying and selecting items from this "pop down" list are identical to those for items in a menu. To change levels, select the desired folder and the files and folders at that level will be displayed.

When the user chooses Save As, or Save when the document is untitled, the SFPutFile dialog box contains a list of files and folders similar to the list displayed in response to the Open command. This allows the user to specify the directory into which the file should be placed. A current directory button above the list lets the user move about in the hierarchical structure. File names in the list are dimmed (but displayed, so that the user can see what other files are in the directory). Figure 3 shows an example.

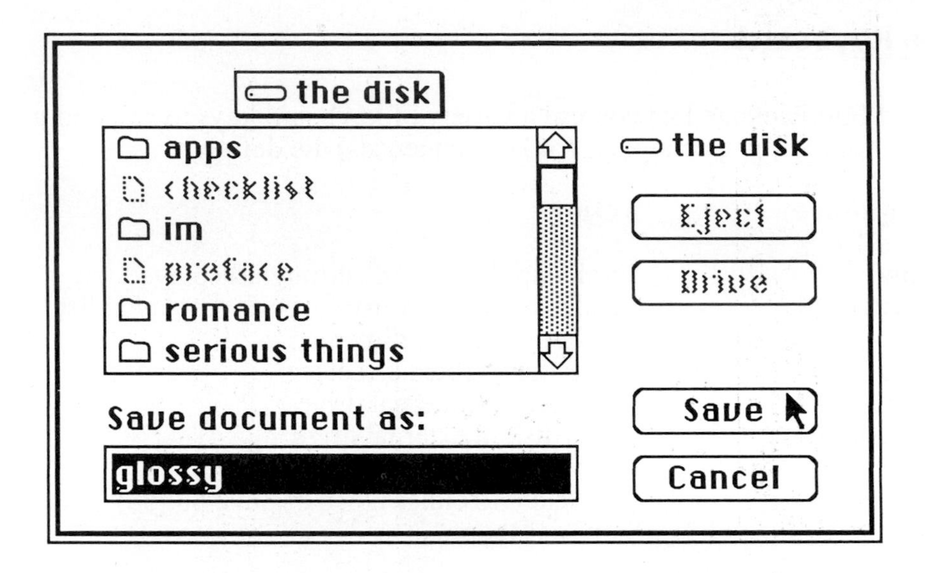

Figure 3. Save Dialog Box (at the Desktop Level)

In both dialog boxes, the Drive, Eject, and Open/Save buttons function as they always have, although their positions have changed. The Save button is always dimmed if the current volume is locked.

> **Note**: No new buttons have been added, so programmers need not worry about interference with controls they've added. The new dialog boxes, however, are larger than the old boxes; the Standard File Package does its best to position nonstandard dialogs in a visible and pleasing position. (Additional details are provided below in the section "Creating Your Own Dialog Box".)

When the user dismisses the dialog, whether by Cancel or Save or Open, the directory currently displayed is set to be the working directory (in other words, a call is made to the File Manager function OpenWD).

USING THE STANDARD FILE PACKAGE

No new routines have been added to the Standard File Package. Applications that use the Standard File Package properly need no modification to operate on machines equipped with the 128K ROM. The specification of a directory in the SFGetFile and SFPutFile procedures is transparent, due to the fact that working directory reference numbers can always be used in place of volume reference numbers. (The relationship between volume reference numbers and working directory reference numbers is described in detail in the File Manager chapter.) If the user specifies that a given file be opened from or saved to a particular subdirectory, the vRefNum field of the reply record you pass with these routines will be filled with a working directory reference number instead of a volume reference number.

> **Warning**: Programmers who have written their own "standard file" routines or who rely on SFReply.vRefNum being a volume reference number may find that their applications are not compatible with the 128K ROM version of the File Manager.

Using the Keyboard

The Standard File Package lets you use a variety of keyboard keys to respond to its dialogs. The following special keys (or key sequences) are defined:

Key Sequence	Action
Up Arrow	Scrolls up (backward) through displayed list
Down Arrow	Scrolls down (forward) through displayed list
Command–Up Arrow	Closes the current directory
Command–Down Arrow	Opens the selected directory
Command–Shift–1	Ejects disk in internal drive
Command–Shift–2	Ejects disk in external drive
Tab	Equivalent to Drive button
Return	Equivalent to either Open or Save button
Enter	Same as Return

Note: The Up Arrow and Down Arrow keys are available on the standard Macintosh Plus keyboard, and on the optional numeric keypad for the Macintosh 128K and 512K, as well as on the Macintosh XL keypad. (See chapter 1 of this volume for details on using the arrow keys.) In addition, with the SFGetFile dialog the user can type characters to locate files in the list; each time a character is typed, the list selects and displays the first file whose initial character matches the typed character.

CREATING YOUR OWN DIALOG BOX

This section is for advanced programmers who want to create their own dialog boxes rather than use the standard SFPutFile and SFGetFile dialogs.

Warning: Future compatibility is *not* guaranteed if you don't use the standard dialogs.

The addition of the file name list to the SFPutFile dialog, as well as the addition of current directory buttons to both SFPutFile and SFGetFile, requires that the dialog boxes for each call be made larger and the items in the box moved down. Although new dialog templates and item lists are provided, the Standard File Package also needs an algorithm for transforming old or nonstandard dialog templates and item lists.

To maintain compatibility with existing applications, the Standard File Package uses only the existing dialog items. In SFPutFile, a userItem for the new file name list replaces the dotted line in item number 8. In SFGetFile, the scroll bar userItem in item number 8 is no longer used. For both SFPutFile and SFGetFile, the information for the current directory button and the scroll bars is maintained internally.

The Standard File Package determines if a dialog needs to be transformed by looking at the width of item number 8 (the dotted line or scroll bar) as specified in the item's rectangle. If the width of item number 8 specifies either a dotted line (a width of 1) or a scroll bar (a width of 16), the dialog will be transformed.

Note: If a dialog needs to be transformed, the box is enlarged to make room for both the scrolling list and the current directory button. All of the items are moved down to their original position relative to the bottom of the box, and the scrolling list and current directory button are added. The dialog is then centered on the screen. If it overlaps the menu bar, it's moved down. If it extends below or to the right of the screen, it's repositioned to make the entire dialog visible. In the case of certain unusual dialogs, the bottom of the dialog may not be visible.

To create nonstandard dialogs that will not be transformed (in other words, ones in which you leave room for the list and current directory button), simply set item number 8 to the desired size and location of your file name list, including scroll bars (for SFPutFile), and set item number 8 to have a width other than 16 (for SFGetFile). The scroll bar is placed within the specified file name list's rectangle.

The DlgHook Function

In the old Standard File Package, a dlgHook routine could not accurately monitor what file was being opened, since it could not detect a double-click. In the new Standard File Package, double-clicks on files are interpreted as clicks on the Open button (item number 1), allowing the dlgHook to intercept files to be opened. With folders, however, both clicks on the Open button and double-clicks are passed to the hook as "fake" item number 103.

A new fake item number 102 is generated by a click in the current directory button; it causes the file list to be pulled down and tracked.

To redisplay the file list in GetFile (which you might do if your dialog box contains radio buttons that let you choose different file types to be displayed), change item number 100 (a null event) into item number 101 (which means redisplay the list) from within the dialog hook.

Note: Disk-inserted events are handled internally; they are not (and never have been) returned as "fake" item number 100. Item number 100 is returned only when no event has taken place.

Before the dlgHook routine is called, information for the selected file or folder is stuffed in the reply record (which can be examined on null events). If no file or folder is selected, fName and fType are both NIL. If a file is selected, fName will not be NIL and will contain the file name. If a folder is selected, fType will not be NIL and will contain the dirID. This is done before the dialog hook is called, regardless of which event is being returned.

Three of the new Standard File Package alerts display an OK button instead of a Cancel button:

Alert	Resource ID
Disk not found	–3994
System error	–3995
Locked disk	–3997

Also, the text of the alert number –3994 (previously "Can't find that disk.") has been changed to "Bad character in name, or can't find that disk." This reflects the fact that this alert is generated if there's a colon in the name.

With nonhierarchical volumes, SFGetFile passes the fileFilter function the file information it gets by calling the File Manager function GetFileInfo. With hierarchical volumes, it gets this information from the GetCatInfo function. SFPutFile does *not* support a fileFilter function.

SUMMARY OF THE STANDARD FILE PACKAGE

Variables

CurDirStore	Directory ID of directory last opened (long)
SFSaveDisk	Negative of volume reference number (word)

16 THE MEMORY MANAGER

Many existing Memory Manager routines have been improved; most of these improvements are transparent to the programmer.

SetHandleSize is smarter about finding free space below, as well as above, the relocatable block.

Routines have been provided for the setting and clearing of handle flags.

MEMORY MANAGER ROUTINES

Two Memory Manager routines—MaxApplZone and MoveHHi—that were not in the 64K ROM (but were available in the Lisa Pascal interfaces) have been added to the 128K ROM.

Assembly-language note: The calling information for MaxApplZone and MoveHHi is as follows:

Trap macro	_MaxApplZone
On exit	D0: result code (word)
Trap macro	_MoveHHi
On entry	A0: h (handle)
On exit	D0: result code (word)

```
FUNCTION MaxBlock : LONGINT;
```

Trap macro	_MaxBlock _MaxBlock ,SYS (applies to system heap)
On exit	D0: function result (word)

MaxBlock returns the maximum contiguous space in bytes that could be obtained by compacting the current zone (without actually doing the compaction).

```
PROCEDURE PurgeSpace (VAR total,contig: LONGINT);
```

Trap macro	_PurgeSpace _PurgeSpace ,SYS (applies to system heap)
On exit	A0: contig (long word) D0: total (long word)

PurgeSpace returns in total the total amount of space in bytes that could be obtained by a general purge (without actually doing the purge); this amount includes space that is already free. The maximum contiguous space in bytes (including already free space) that could be obtained by a purge is returned in contig.

```
FUNCTION StackSpace : LONGINT;
```

Trap macro	_StackSpace
On exit	D0: function result (word)

StackSpace returns the current amount of stack space between the current stack pointer and the application heap (at the instant of return from the trap).

Advanced Routine

```
FUNCTION NewEmptyHandle : Handle;
```

Trap macro	_NewEmptyHandle _NewEmptyHandle ,SYS (applies to system heap)
On exit	A0: function result (handle) D0: result code (word)

NewEmptyHandle is similar in function to NewHandle except that it does not allocate any space; the handle returned is empty (in other words, it points to a NIL master pointer). NewEmptyHandle is used extensively by the Resource Manager; you may not need to use it.

Properties of Relocatable Blocks

The master pointer associated with each handle contains flags for use by the Memory Manager. Routines are provided for setting and clearing each of these flags, as well as for saving and restoring the entire byte.

Warning: Failure to use these routines virtually guarantees incompatibility with future versions of the Macintosh. You should *not* set and clear these flags directly.

The HLock and HUnlock procedures lock and unlock a given relocatable block by setting and clearing the lock flag. The HPurge and HNoPurge mark a given relocatable block as purgeable or unpurgeable by setting and clearing the purge flag.

A third flag, the resource flag, is used internally by the Resource Manager. The HSetRBit and HClrRBit procedures set and clear this flag.

The HSetState and HGetState routines let you save and restore the state of the flags byte.

```
PROCEDURE HSetRBit (h: Handle);
```

Trap macro	_HSetRBit
On entry	A0: h (handle)
On exit	D0: result code (word)

HSetRBit sets the resource flag of a relocatable block's master pointer.

```
PROCEDURE HClrRBit (h: Handle);
```

Trap macro	_HClrRBit
On entry	A0: h (handle)
On exit	D0: result code (word)

HClrRBit clears the resource flag of a relocatable block's master pointer.

```
FUNCTION HGetState (h: Handle) : SignedByte;
```

Trap macro	_HGetState
On entry	A0: h (handle)
On exit	D0: flags (byte)

HGetState returns the byte that contains the flags of the master pointer for the given handle; it's used in conjunction with HSetState to save and restore the state of the flags contained in this byte. You can save this byte, change the state of any of the flags (using the routines described above), and then restore their original state by passing the byte back to the HSetState procedure (described below).

```
PROCEDURE HSetState (h: Handle; flags: SignedByte);
```

Trap macro	_HSetState
On entry	A0: h (handle) D0: flags (byte)
On exit	D0: result code (word)

HSetState is used in conjunction with HGetState; it sets the byte that contains the flags of the master pointer for the given handle to the byte specified by flags.

ERROR REPORTING

All Memory Manager routines (including the RecoverHandle function) return a result code that you can examine by calling the MemError function.

Assembly-language note: The trap _RecoverHandle doesn't return a result code in register D0. The result code of the most recent call, however, is always stored in the global variable MemErr.

SUMMARY OF THE MEMORY MANAGER

Constants

```
CONST { Result codes }

      memROZErr  =  -99;    {operation on a read-only zone}
```

Routines

```
FUNCTION  MaxBlock :          LONGINT;
PROCEDURE PurgeSpace          (VAR total,contig: LONGINT);
FUNCTION  StackSpace :        LONGINT;
FUNCTION  NewEmptyHandle : Handle;
PROCEDURE HSetRBit            (h: Handle);
PROCEDURE HClrRBit            (h: Handle);
FUNCTION  HGetState           (h: Handle) : SignedByte;
PROCEDURE HSetState           (h: Handle; flags: SignedByte);
```

Assembly-Language Information

Constants

```
; Result codes

memROZErr      .EQU    -99    ;operation on a read-only zone
```

Routines

Trap macro	On entry	On exit
_MaxApplZone		D0: result code (word)
_MoveHHi	A0: h (handle)	D0: result code (word)
_MaxBlock		D0: function result (word)
_PurgeSpace		A0: contig (long) D0: total (long)
_StackSpace		D0: function result (word)
_NewEmptyHandle		A0: function result (word)

Trap macro	On entry	On exit
_HSetRBit	A0: h (handle)	D0: result code (word)
_HClrRBit	A0: h (handle)	D0: result code (word)
_HGetState	A0: h (handle)	D0: function result (byte)
_HSetState	A0: h (handle) D0: flags (byte)	D0: result code (word)

Variables

MemErr   Current value of MemError (word)

17 THE SEGMENT LOADER

Advanced programmers: The LoadSeg procedure has been modified to help reduce heap fragmentation. If the code segment to be loaded is unlocked (that is, if it's not in memory and its resLocked attribute is clear, or if it is in memory and is unlocked), LoadSeg calls the Memory Manager procedure MoveHHi to move the segment toward the top of the current heap zone.

To maintain compatibility with the 64K ROM, your code segments should be locked in the resource file. They will, however, be unlocked when they're unloaded and may float up in the heap; subsequent loading may then cause heap fragmentation.

If your application will never run on a 64K ROM machine, all segments except the main segment ('CODE' resource 1) can be unlocked in the resource file. Your application's initialization routine must call the Memory Manager procedure MaxApplZone, however; otherwise the heap zone will grow incrementally and calls to MoveHHi may leave your segments scattered throughout the heap.

18 THE OPERATING SYSTEM EVENT MANAGER

A new routine, PPostEvent, posts application-defined events into the event queue and returns a pointer to the created queue element.

```
FUNCTION PPostEvent (eventCode: INTEGER; eventMsg: LONGINT; VAR qEl:
          EvQEl) : OSErr);
```

Trap macro	_PPostEvent
On entry	A0: eventCode (word) D0: eventMsg (long word)
On exit	A0: pointer to event queue entry

PPostEvent is identical to PostEvent except that it returns a pointer to the created queue entry.

SUMMARY OF THE OPERATING SYSTEM EVENT MANAGER

Routines

```
FUNCTION PPostEvent (eventCode: INTEGER; eventMsg: LONGINT; VAR qEl:
                     EvQEl) : OSErr);
```

Assembly-Language Information

Routines

Trap macro	On entry	On exit
_PPostEvent	A0: eventCode (word) D0: eventMsg (long)	A0: ptr to event queue entry

19 THE FILE MANAGER

ABOUT THIS CHAPTER

This chapter describes the File Manager, the part of the Operating System that controls the exchange of information between a Macintosh application and files. The File Manager allows you to create and access any number of files containing whatever information you choose.

The changes to the File Manager are so extensive that the chapter has been completely rewritten. For most programmers, the changes are transparent and require no modification of code. All operations on the 64K ROM version of the File Manager are supported.

ABOUT THE FILE MANAGER

The File Manager is the part of the Operating System that handles communication between an application and files on block devices such as disk drives. (Block devices are discussed in the Device Manager chapter.) Files are a principal means by which data is stored and transmitted on the Macintosh. A **file** is a named, ordered sequence of bytes. The File Manager contains routines used to read from and write to files.

Volumes and the File Directory

A **volume** is a piece of storage medium, such as a disk, formatted to contain files. A volume can be an entire disk or only part of a disk. A 3 1/2-inch Macintosh disk is one volume. Specialized memory devices, such as hard disks and file servers, can contain many volumes. The size of a volume also varies from one type of device to another. Macintosh volumes are formatted into chunks known as **logical blocks**, each able to contain up to 512 bytes. Files are stored in **allocation blocks**, which are multiples of logical blocks.

Each volume has a **file directory** containing information about the files on the volume. With small volumes (containing only a few dozen files), a “flat” file directory organized as a simple, unsorted list of file names is sufficient. Volumes initialized by the 64K ROM have such a flat file directory.

> **64K ROM note:** The 128K ROM version of the File Manager supports all operations on flat file directories.

With the introduction of larger storage devices (several megabytes per volume) containing a large number of files (thousands per volume), the flat file directory proves inadequate, since an exhaustive, linear search of all the files is so time-consuming. A major feature of the 128K ROM version of the File Manager is the implementation of a hierarchical file directory (sometimes referred to as the **file catalog**), that significantly speeds up access to large volumes.

The hierarchical file directory allows a volume to be divided into smaller units known as **directories**. Directories can contain files as well as other directories. Directories contained within directories are also known as **subdirectories**.

The hierarchical directory structure is equivalent to the user's perceived desktop hierarchy, where folders contain files or additional folders. In the 64K ROM version of the File Manager, however, this desktop hierarchy was essentially an illusion maintained completely by the Finder (at considerable expense). The introduction of an actual hierarchical directory containing subdirectories greatly enhances the performance of the Finder by relieving it of this task.

Figure 1 illustrates these two ways of organizing the files on a volume.

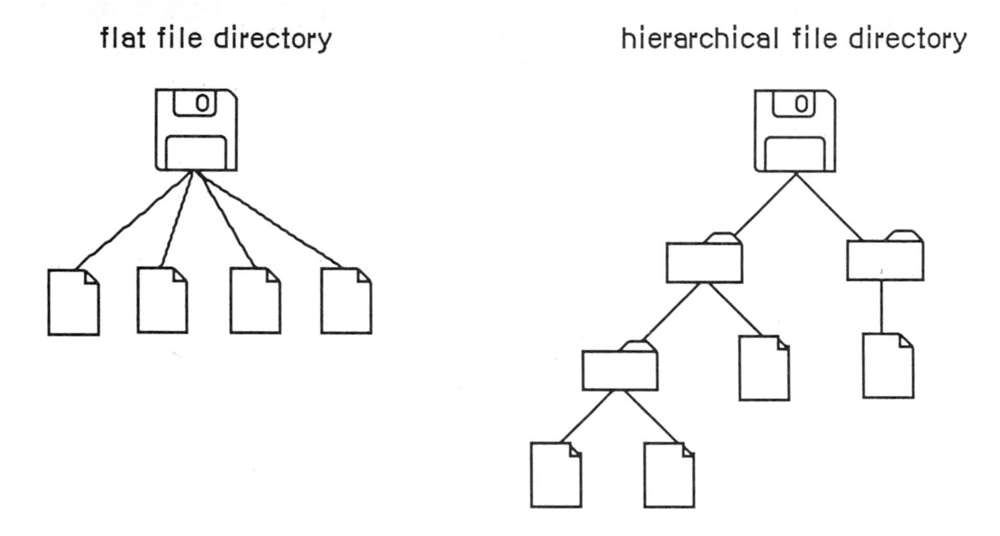

Figure 1. Flat and Hierarchical Directories

About Names

Volumes, directories, and files all have names. A volume name consists of any sequence of 1 to 27 printing characters, excluding colons (:). File names and directory names consist of any sequence of 1 to 31 printing characters, excluding colons. You can use uppercase and lowercase letters when naming things, but the File Manager ignores case when comparing names (it doesn't ignore diacritical marks).

> **64K ROM note:** The 64K ROM version of the File Manager allows file names of up to 255 characters. File names should be constrained to 31 characters, however, to maintain compatibility with the 128K ROM version of the File Manager. The 64K ROM version of the File Manager also allows the specification of a version number to distinguish between different files with the same name. Version numbers are generally set to 0, though, because the Resource Manager, Segment Loader, and Standard File Package won't operate on files with nonzero version numbers, and the Finder ignores version numbers.

About Directories

A few terms are needed to describe the relationships between directories on a hierarchical volume. Figure 2 shows what looks to be an upside-down tree; it's a sample hierarchical volume.

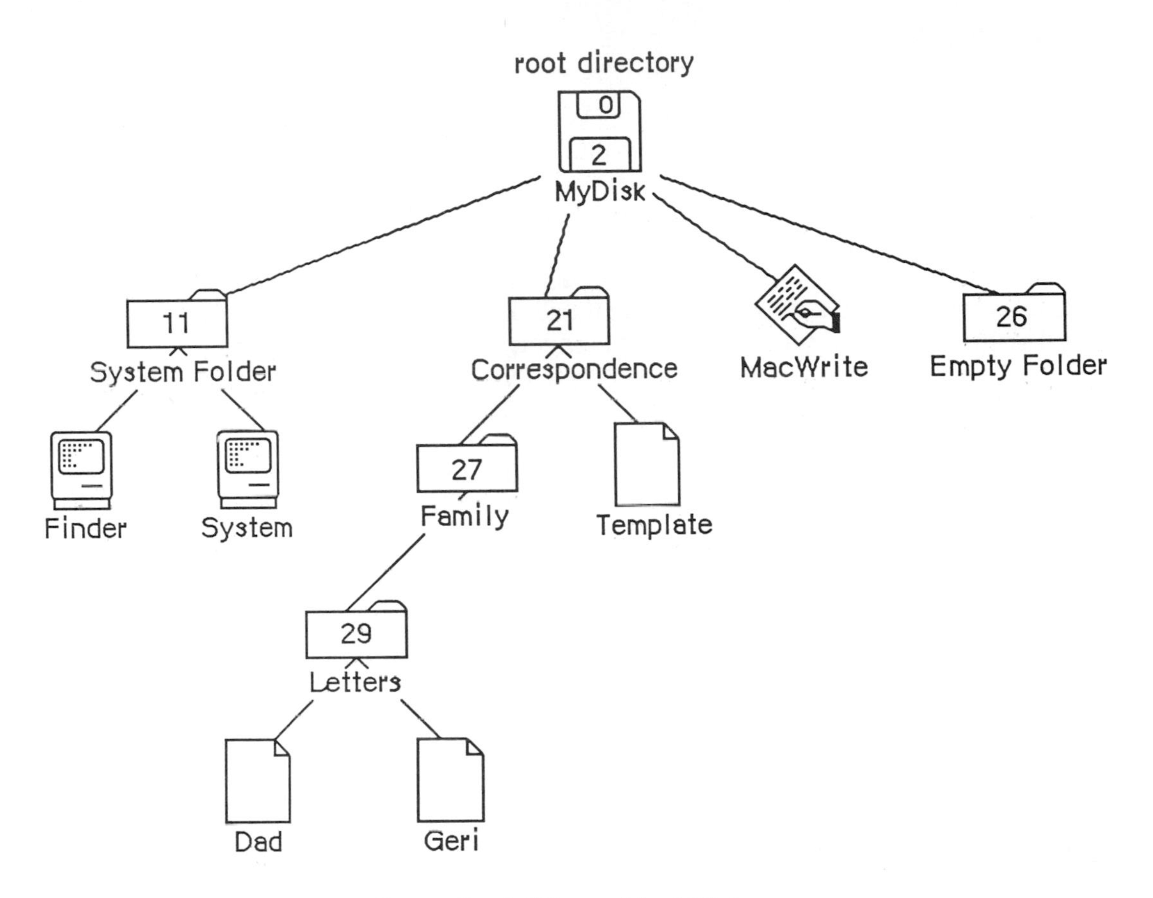

Figure 2. A Hierarchical Volume

All of the volume's files stem from the directory labeled MyDisk; this is the **root directory** and is none other than the volume itself. The name of the root directory of a volume is the same as the volume name.

> **Note**: The volume name, constrained to 27 characters, is the sole exception to the rule that directory names can be up to 31 characters long.

Each directory, including the root directory, is a distinct, addressable entity. Each directory has its own set of **offspring** (possibly an empty set), which is those files or directories contained in it. For instance, the directory Letters has the files Dad and Geri as offspring, while the root directory contains the file MacWrite and the directories System Folder and Empty Folder. Borrowing a term from physics, the number of offspring is known as the directory's **valence;** for instance, the valence of the directory Correspondence is 2. Similarly, for a given file or directory, the directory immediately above it is known as its **parent**. The root directory is the only directory that doesn't have a parent.

When created, every directory is given a **directory ID** that's unique (and assigned sequentially) for any given volume. The root directory always has a directory ID of 2. In Figure 2, for instance, the directory Empty Folder has a directory ID of 26. The directory ID of a given offspring's parent is known as its **parent ID**; for example, the parent ID of the file Template is 21.

About Volumes

A volume can be mounted or unmounted. When a volume is **mounted**, the File Manager reads descriptive information about the volume into memory. For each mounted volume, part of this information is placed in a data structure known as a **volume control block** (described in detail in the section "Data Structures in Memory").

Ejectable volumes (such as the 3 1/2-inch disks) are mounted when they're inserted into a disk drive; nonejectable volumes (such as those on hard disks) are always mounted. Only mounted volumes are known to the File Manager, and an application can access information on mounted volumes only. When a volume is **unmounted**, the File Manager releases the information stored in the volume control block.

A mounted volume can be on-line or off-line. A mounted volume is **on-line** as long as the volume buffer and all the descriptive information read from the volume when it was mounted remain in memory (about 1K to 1.5K bytes); it becomes **off-line** when all but the volume control block is released. You can access information on on-line volumes immediately, but off-line volumes must be placed on-line before their information can be accessed. When an application ejects a 3 1/2-inch disk from a drive, the File Manager automatically places the volume off-line. Whenever the File Manager needs to access a mounted volume that's been placed off-line and ejected, the dialog box shown in Figure 3 is displayed, and the File Manager waits until the user inserts the disk named volName into a drive.

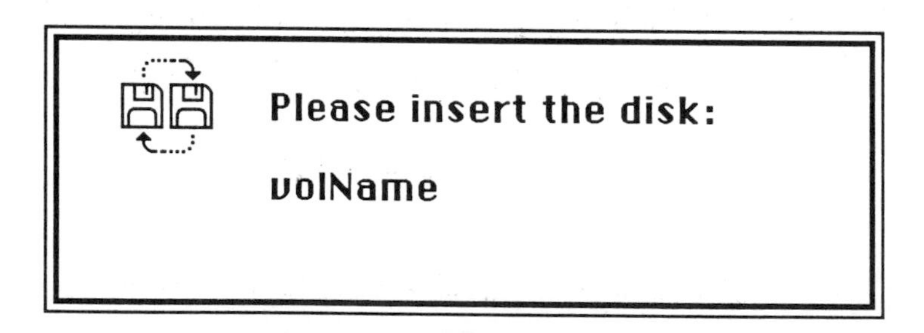

Figure 3. Disk-Switch Dialog

Note: This dialog is actually a system error alert, as described in the System Error Handler chapter.

Mounted volumes share a common set of **volume buffers**, which is temporary storage space in the heap used when reading or writing information on the volume. The number of volumes that may be mounted at any time is limited only by the number of drives attached and available memory.

64K ROM note: In the 64K ROM version of the File Manager, each mounted volume was assigned its own volume buffer.

To prevent unauthorized writing to a volume, volumes can be **locked**. Locking a volume involves either setting a software flag on the volume or changing some part of the volume physically (for example, sliding a tab from one position to another on a 3 1/2-inch disk). Locking a volume ensures that none of the data on the volume can be changed.

Each volume has a name that you can use to identify it. On-line volumes in disk drives can also be accessed via the **drive number** of the drive on which the volume is mounted; the internal drive is number 1, the external drive is number 2, and any additional drives connected to the Macintosh will have larger numbers. In most routines, however, you'll identify a volume by its **volume reference number**, which is assigned to a volume when it's mounted. When accessing an on-line volume, you should always use the volume reference number or the volume name rather than a drive number, because the volume may have been ejected or placed off-line. Whenever possible, use the volume reference number (to avoid confusion between volumes with the same name).

Note: In the case of specialized storage devices (such as hard disks) containing several volumes, only the first on-line volume can be accessed using the drive number of the device.

About Files

A file is a finite sequence of numbered bytes. Any byte or group of bytes in the sequence can be accessed individually. A byte within a file is identified by its position within the ordered sequence.

There are two parts, or **forks**, to a file: the **data fork** and the **resource fork**. Normally the resource fork of an application file contains the resources used by the application, such as menus, fonts, and icons, and also the application code itself. The data fork can contain anything an application wants to store there. Information stored in resource forks should always be accessed via the Resource Manager. Information in data forks can only be accessed via the File Manager. For simplicity, "file" will be used instead of "data fork" in this chapter.

The size of a file is limited only by the size of the volume it's on. Space is allocated to a file in allocation blocks (multiples of 512 bytes). Two numbers are used to describe the size of a file. The **physical end-of-file** is the number of bytes currently allocated to the file; it's 1 greater than the number of the last byte in its last allocation block (since the first byte is byte number 0). The **logical end-of-file** is the number of those allocated bytes that currently contain data; it's 1 greater than the number of the last byte in the file that contains data. For example, given an allocation block size of two logical blocks (that is, 1024 bytes), a file with 50 bytes of data has a logical end-of-file of 50 and a physical end-of-file of 1024 (see Figure 4).

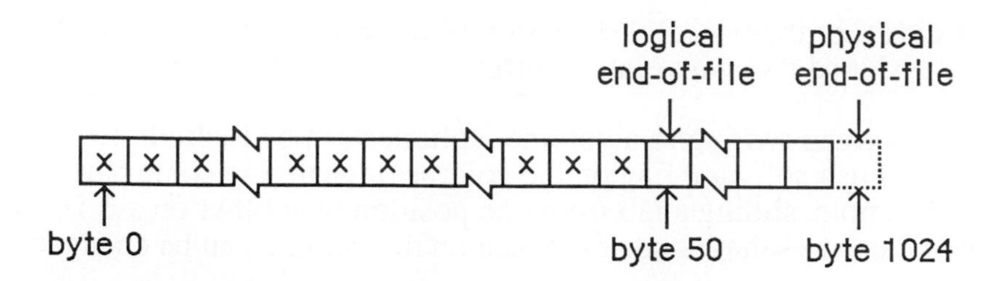

Figure 4. Logical and Physical End-of-File

The File Manager maintains a current position marker, called the **mark**, to keep track of where it is in the file during a read or write operation. The mark is the number of the next byte that will be read or written; each time a byte is read or written, the mark is moved.

When, during a write operation, the mark reaches the number of the last byte currently allocated to the file, another allocation block is added to the file.

You can read bytes from and write bytes to a file either singly or in sequences of unlimited length. You can specify where each read or write operation should begin by setting the mark; if you don't, the operation begins at the byte where the mark currently points. You can find the current position of the mark by calling GetFPos. You can set the mark before the read or write operation with SetFPos; you can also set it in the Read or Write call itself.

You can move the logical end-of-file to adjust the size of the file (such as after a resource file has been compacted); when the logical end-of-file is moved to a position more than one allocation block short of the current physical end-of-file, the unneeded allocation block will be deleted from the file. You can also increase the size of a file by moving the logical-end-file past the physical end-of-file.

A file can be **open** or **closed**. An application can perform only certain operations, such as reading and writing, on open files; other operations, such as deleting, can be performed only on closed files.

Your application can **lock** a file to prevent unauthorized writing to it. Locking a file ensures that none of the data in it can be changed; this is the same as the user-accessible lock maintained by the Finder.

When a file is opened, the File Manager reads useful information about the file from its volume and stores it in a data structure known as a **file control block**. The contents of the file control block (described in detail in the section "Data Structures in Memory") are used frequently and can be obtained with the function GetFileInfo.

When a file is opened, the File Manager creates an **access path**, a description of the route to be followed when accessing the file. The access path specifies the volume on which the file is located and the location of the file on the volume. Every access path is assigned a unique **path reference number** (a number greater than 0) that's used to refer to it. A file can have multiple access paths open; each access path is separate from all other access paths to the file.

Each file has **open permission** information, which indicates whether data can be written to it or not. When you open a file, you request permission to read or write via an access path. You can request permission to read only, write only (rarely done), or both read and write. There are two types of read/write permission—exclusive and shared. Applications will generally want to request exclusive read/write permission. If an access path requests and is granted exclusive read/write permission, no other access path will be granted permission to write (whether write only, exclusive read/write, or shared read/write).

A second type of read/write permission allows multiple access paths to be open for writing. If you'll be using only a portion, or range, of a file, you can request shared read/write permission. With shared read/write permission, the application must see to it that the file's data integrity is preserved. Before writing to a particular range of bytes, you need to "lock" it so that other access paths cannot write to that range at the same time. In the meantime, other access paths opened with shared read/write access can lock and write to other parts of the file.

The shared read/write permission has no utility on a single Macintosh; this permission is intended for, and will be passed by, external file systems, where multiple read/write operations are performed.

> **Note:** If an access path is open with shared read/write permission, no access path can be granted exclusive read/write access.

> **64K ROM note:** Shared read/write permission is not implemented in the 64K ROM version of the File Manager.

If the file's open permission doesn't allow I/O as requested, a result code indicating the error is returned.

Each access path can move its own mark and read at the position it indicates. All access paths to the same file share common logical and physical end-of-file markers.

When an application requests that data be read from a file, the File Manager reads the data from the file and transfers it to the application's **data buffer**. Any part of the data that can be transferred in entire 512-byte blocks is transferred directly. Any part of the data composed of fewer than 512 bytes is also read from the file in one 512-byte block, but placed in temporary storage space in memory. Then, only the bytes containing the requested data are transferred to the application.

When an application writes data to a file, the File Manager transfers the data from the application's data buffer and writes it to the file. Any part of the data that can be transferred in entire 512-byte blocks is written directly. Any part of the data composed of fewer than 512 bytes is placed in temporary storage space in memory until 512 bytes have accumulated; then the entire block is written all at once.

> **Note:** Advanced programmers: The File Manager can also read a continuous stream of characters or a line of characters. In the first case, you ask the File Manager to read a specific number of bytes: When that many have been read or when the mark has reached the logical end-of-file, the read operation terminates. In the second case, called **newline mode**, the read will terminate when either of the above conditions is met or when a specified character, the **newline character**, is read. The newline character is usually Return (ASCII code $0D), but it can be any character. Information about newline mode is associated with each access path to a file, and can differ from one access path to another.

Normally the temporary space in memory used for all reading and writing is the volume buffer, but an application can specify that an **access path buffer** be used instead for a particular access path (see Figure 5).

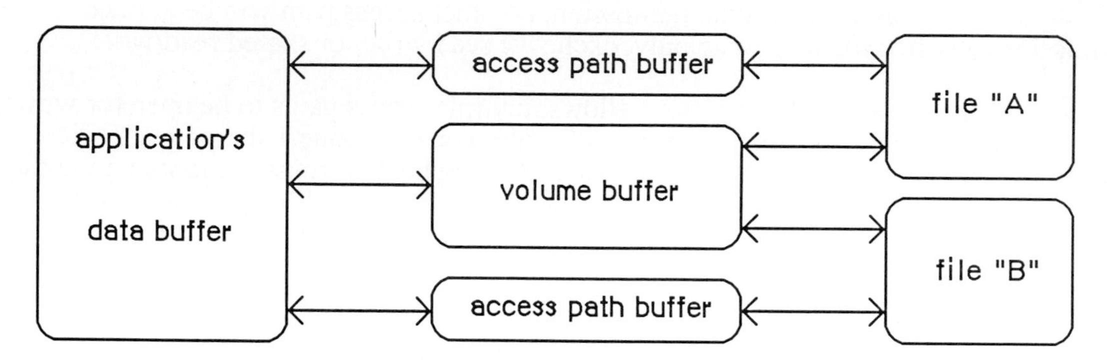

Figure 5. Buffers for Transferring Data

Warning: You must lock any access path buffers of files in relocatable blocks, so their location doesn't change while the file is open.

USING THE FILE MANAGER

This section outlines the routines provided by the File Manager and explains some basic concepts needed to use them. The actual routines are presented later in the chapter.

The File Manager is automatically initialized each time the system starts up.

You can call most File Manager routines via three different methods: high-level Pascal calls, low-level Pascal calls, and assembly language. The high-level Pascal calls are designed for Pascal programmers interested in using the File Manager in a simple manner; they provide adequate file I/O and don't require much special knowledge to use. The low-level Pascal and assembly-language calls are designed for advanced Pascal programmers and assembly-language programmers interested in using the File Manager to its fullest capacity; they require some special knowledge to be used most effectively.

Note: The names used to refer to File Manager routines in text (as opposed to in particular routine descriptions) are actually the assembly-language macro names for the low-level routines, but the Pascal routine names are very similar.

Hierarchical Routines

Many new routines are introduced in the hierarchical version of the File Manager; they can be divided into two groups. These routines are used primarily by the File Manager itself.

Routines in the first group are slight extensions of certain basic File Manager routines that allow the specification of a directory ID in addition to the other parameters; in certain cases they set or obtain additional information. These specialized routines have the same names as their general-purpose counterparts, but preceded by the letter "H". For instance, the routine HOpen is identical to the Open call except that it allows the specification of a directory ID. The routines in this first group are: HOpen, HOpenRF, HRename, HCreate, HDelete, HGetFileInfo, HSetFileInfo, and HGetVInfo. The calls in this group will work with the 64K ROM version of the File Manager, but most applications will never need to use them.

The second group of hierarchical routines consists of calls that perform operations unique to the hierarchical file directory. The routines in this group are: SetVolInfo, LockRng, UnlockRng, DirCreate, GetCatInfo, SetCatInfo, CatMove, OpenWD, CloseWD, GetWDInfo, and GetFCBInfo.

> **Warning:** Using any of the routines in this second group on a Macintosh equipped only with the 64K ROM version of the File Manager will result in a system error. Using them on a flat volume will have no effect on "folders" and will result in File Manager errors.

In general, you will want your application to be independent of any particular version of the File Manager. The benefits of the hierarchical file system are transparent to your application and do not require use of the hierarchical routines. You may, however, want to use the hierarchical routines under certain circumstances. One way of determining whether the hierarchical version of the File Manager is present is to check which version of the ROM is running by calling the Operating System Utilities procedure Environs.

RAM-based hierarchical versions of the File Manager may also be encountered, however; a better way of determining which version of the File Manager is running is to examine the contents of the global variable FSFCBLen. Located at address $3F6, this variable is a word (two bytes) in length; it contains a positive value if the hierarchical version of the File Manager is active or –1 if the 64K ROM version of the File Manager is running. You could test the value of this global variable in the following way:

```
CONST FSFCBLen = $3F6; {address of global variable}

VAR HFS:   ^INTEGER;
...
HFS := POINTER(FSFCBLen);
IF HFS^ > 0
  THEN
    BEGIN
      {we're running under the hierarchical version}
    END;
  ELSE
    BEGIN
      {we're running under the 64K ROM version}
    END;
```

Even after determining that the hierarchical version is running, you'll still need to check that a mounted volume is hierarchical by calling the HGetVInfo function.

Assembly-language note: You can tell whether a Macintosh is equipped with the 64K ROM version or the hierarchical version of the File Manager by examining the contents of the global variable FSFCBLen; if the 64K ROM version is running, FSFCBLen will contain –1. You can determine if a mounted volume is flat or hierarchical by calling the HGetVInfo function.

Working Directories

It's useful to look at the relationship between the 64K ROM and 128K ROM versions of the File Manager. In the 64K ROM version, the entire volume is a single directory (you could consider it a barren root directory). It would seem that existing applications, when introduced on a machine equipped with the 128K ROM version of the File Manager, would be unable to handle the specification of which directory a file is in, since they only exchange volume reference numbers and file names with the Finder and the File Manager. The 128K ROM version, however, introduces the notion of a **working directory** to allow existing applications to operate with the hierarchical file system.

When the File Manager makes a particular directory a working directory (using the function OpenWD), it stores the directory ID, as well as the volume reference number of the volume on which the directory is located, in a **working directory control block**. The File Manager then returns a unique **working directory reference number** which you can use in subsequent calls to refer to that directory.

Directories can be seen as mini-volumes. (The root directory is, in fact, just another mini-volume; it contains only the files and directories immediately below it in the tree structure.) A working directory reference number is just like a volume reference number for a directory. It's a temporary reference number that specifies where a file is located on a hierarchical volume.

This relationship allows the hierarchical file system to be compatible with existing applications. A working directory reference number can be used in place of a volume reference number in any File Manager call. When you provide a working directory reference number, the File Manager uses it to determine which directory a file is in, as well as which volume the directory and file are on.

An example of the use of working directories is a situation where the Finder opens a document. With the 64K ROM version of the File Manager, when the Finder launches the application that handles the document, it has only to pass the volume reference number and file name of the document. With the 128K ROM version, the Finder makes the directory containing the file a working directory, and passes the application a working directory reference number instead of the volume reference number. Upon being launched, the application opens the file, passing the File Manager the working directory reference number received from the Finder.

Warning: The possibility of incompatibility arises for programmers who (despite numerous warnings) have written code that accesses and manipulates low-level data structures directly (such as volume control blocks and file control blocks). Programmers in this category will want to study the sections "Data Organization on Volumes" and "Data Structures in Memory".

Pathnames

The 128K ROM version of the File Manager also permits the specification of files (and directories) using concatenations of volume names, directory names, and file names. Separated by colons, these concatenations of names are known as **pathnames**.

A **full pathname** always begins with the name of the root directory; it names the path from the root to a given file or directory, and includes each of the directories visited on that path (see Figure 2). For instance, a full pathname to the file Geri is:

```
MyDisk:Correspondence:Letters:Family:Geri
```

A full pathname is a complete and unambiguous identification of a file or directory. You should avoid using full pathnames; they are cumbersome to enter and it takes longer to process them.

Another type of identification is a **partial pathname**, which describes the path to a file or directory starting from a given directory. When using a partial pathname, you must also specify the directory from which the partial pathname begins; this is discussed below.

> **64K ROM note:** In the 64K ROM version of the File Manager, the combination of volume name followed by the file name constitutes a full pathname. A file name alone constitutes a partial pathname; the directory from which this partial pathname begins (the root directory) is specified by the volume reference number.

To distinguish them from full pathnames, partial pathnames must begin with a colon, except in the case where the partial pathname contains only one name. (This exception is needed to maintain compatibility with 64K ROM version of the File Manager, where the only partial pathnames—file names—do not begin with a colon.) For the file Geri in Figure 2, a valid partial pathname, starting from the directory Letters, would be:

```
:Family:Geri
```

The above pathname begins at the directory Letters and moves down the tree to the file Status. It's also possible to move up the tree by using consecutive colons (::). This notation indicates, for instance, that the name following a double colon is an offspring of the current location's *parent*, rather than an offspring of the directory preceding the double colon. In Figure 2, for example, the file Letter Form can be specified by the full pathname

```
MyDisk:Correspondence:Letters:Family:::Template
```

where the consecutive colons signify a move up the tree from Family to Letters and finally to Correspondence.

If a full pathname consists of only one name (the volume name), the pathname must end in a colon. For pathnames to other directories, if the last name is followed by a colon, the colon is ignored. Multiname pathnames describing a file should not end in a colon.

To summarize, if the first character of a pathname is a colon, or if the pathname contains no colons, it must be a partial pathname; otherwise, it's a full pathname.

> **Warning:** While there's no limit to the number of levels of subdirectories allowed, it may not always be possible in the case of a large volume to specify every file and

directory with a full pathname, since character strings are limited to 255 characters. In such cases, you can obtain the directory ID of a subdirectory somewhere along the path and use it with a partial pathname to specify the desired file or directory.

Specifying Volumes, Directories, and Files

A volume can be specified explicitly by its name, its volume reference number, or its drive number, and implicitly by a working directory reference number or a full pathname. The File Manager searches for volume specifications in the following order:

1. It looks for a volume name. (Remember, it must be followed by a colon.)

2. If the name specified is NIL or an improper name, the File Manager looks for either a volume reference number, a drive number, or a working directory reference number.

With routines that operate on a volume, such as mounting or ejecting, if you don't provide any of these specifications, the File Manager assumes you want to perform the operation on the **default volume**. Initially, the volume used to start up the application is set as the default volume, but an application can designate any mounted volume as the default volume.

With routines that access files (or directories), if no directory is specified *and* the volume reference number passed is zero, the File Manager assumes that the file or directory is located in the **default directory**. Initially, the default directory is set to the root directory of the volume used to start up the application, but an application can designate any directory as the default directory.

To access a file or directory, you need to specify its name, the directory it's in, and which volume it's on. There are a number of ways of doing this:

- Full pathname. A full pathname completely specifies a file or directory. Since the first name in a full pathname (the name of the root directory) is always the name of the volume, no separate volume specification is needed. In fact, a full pathname will override an explicit volume specification. (This specification runs the risk of ambiguity since there could be two mounted volumes with the same name.)

- Volume reference number and partial pathname. This is the most common type of specification, since it's the *only* form of specification in the 64K ROM version of the File Manager. The volume reference number specifies the volume as well as the directory (the root) to be used with the partial pathname (the file name).

- Directory ID and partial pathname. Another way to specify a file or directory is to use the directory ID of any directory in the catalog along with a partial pathname from that directory. Since neither the directory ID nor the partial pathname indicates the name of the volume, a separate volume specification is also needed.

- Working directory reference number and partial pathname. This is the most common type of specification in the 128K ROM version of the File Manager. It's similar to the previous one; it does not, however, require a separate volume specification. The working directory reference number is used to obtain both the directory ID (to be used with the partial pathname) and the volume reference number.

If both a directory ID and a working directory reference number are specified, the directory ID is used to identify the directory on the volume indicated by the working directory reference number. In other words, a directory ID specified by the caller will override the directory referred to by the working directory reference number.

Advanced programmers: If the File Manager doesn't find a given file in the directory specified, it looks in the directory containing the currently open System file (obtained from the global variable BootDrive), provided it's on the volume specified by the call. If the file isn't found there, the File Manager looks in the folder, on the volume specified by the call, whose directory ID is returned in the vcbFndrInfo field by the HGetVInfo function.

> **Warning:** It's important to be aware of this search path. You can't assume that a given file is located in the directory that you specified when accessing it.

Indexing

In most of the File Manager routines, you'll be referring to a particular file, directory, or volume by its name or some sort of reference number. With a routine such as GetFileInfo, however, you may want to make the same call repeatedly for all files in a given directory without specifying each file individually. Such routines provide a parameter where you can simply specify an index number. In the first iteration of the GetFileInfo function, for example, you would pass an index of 1 and get information about the first file in a given directory. In the second iteration you would pass an index of 2, and so on.

It's possible to determine how many files are contained in a given directory and thereby specify the number of iterations for a GetFileInfo indexing loop. The presence of subdirectories, however, complicates the situation. A faster and more reliable technique is to begin with an index of 1 and continue until the result code fnfErr (file not found) is returned.

The routines that allow you to provide an index are: GetVolInfo, GetFileInfo, GetCatInfo, GetWDInfo, and GetFCBInfo. Respectively, they provide information about mounted volumes, files in a given directory, files and directories in a given directory, working directories, and file control blocks.

On flat volumes, programmers can use the function GetFileInfo to index through all the files on a volume. On hierarchical volumes, files can be in subdirectories, which may themselves contain other subdirectories and files. With such volumes, you should instead use GetCatInfo since it returns information about both files and directories.

Advanced programmers: While it's questionable whether an application would want to index through all the files on a hierarchical volume (since such a volume may contain a large number of files), you may want to index through a particular directory or portion of the tree structure. You can use GetCatInfo in a recursive way to do this. While indexing through the initial directory, if a subdirectory is found, you need to interrupt the indexing of the initial directory and index through the subdirectory.

Accessing Files

To create a new, empty file, call Create. Create allows you to set some of the information stored on the volume about the file. DirCreate allows you to create directories.

To open a file, call Open. The File Manager creates an access path and returns a path reference number that you'll use every time you want to refer to it. Before you open a file, you may want to call the Standard File Package, which presents the standard interface through which the user can specify the file to be opened. The Standard File Package will return the name of the file, the volume reference number or working directory reference number, and additional information. (If the user inserts an unmounted volume into a drive, the Standard File Package will automatically call the Disk Initialization Package to attempt to mount it.)

After opening a file, you can transfer data from it to an application's data buffer with Read, and send data from an application's data buffer to the file with Write. If you've opened a file with shared read/write permission, you need to call LockRng before writing to it in order to prevent another access path from writing to the same portion of the file. When you're done writing, call UnlockRng to release that portion of the file.

You can't use Write on a file whose open permission only allows reading, or on a file on a locked volume. In addition, you can't write to a range that's been locked by another access path with the LockRng call.

You can specify the byte position of the mark before calling Read or Write by calling SetFPos. GetFPos returns the byte position of the mark.

Once you've completed whatever reading and writing you want to do, call Close to close the file. Close writes the contents of the file's access path buffer to the volume and deletes the access path. You can remove a closed file (both forks) from a volume by calling Delete.

Applications will normally use the Resource Manager to open resource forks and change the information contained within, but programmers writing unusual applications (such as a disk-copying utility) might want to use the File Manager to open resource forks. This is done by calling OpenRF. As with Open, the File Manager creates an access path and returns a path reference number that you'll use every time you want to refer to this resource fork.

Accessing Volumes

When the Toolbox Event Manager function GetNextEvent receives a disk-inserted event, it calls the Desk Manager function SystemEvent. SystemEvent calls the File Manager function MountVol, which attempts to mount the volume on the disk. GetNextEvent then returns the disk-inserted event: The low-order word of the event message contains the number of the drive, and the high-order word contains the result code of the attempted mounting. If the result code indicates that an error occurred, you'll need to call the Disk Initialization Package to allow the user to initialize or eject the volume.

> **Note:** Applications that rely on the Operating System Event Manager function GetOSEvent to learn about events (and don't call GetNextEvent) must explicitly call MountVol to mount volumes.

After a volume has been mounted, your application can call GetVolInfo, which will return the name of the volume, the amount of unused space on the volume, and a volume reference number that you can use to refer to that volume. The volume reference number is also returned by MountVol.

To minimize the amount of memory used by mounted volumes, an application can unmount or place off-line any volumes that aren't currently being used. To unmount a volume, call UnmountVol, which flushes a volume (by calling FlushVol) and releases all of the memory used for it. To place a volume off-line, call OffLine, which flushes a volume and releases all of the memory used for it except for the volume control block. Off-line volumes are placed on-line by the File Manager as needed, but your application must remount any unmounted volumes it wants to access. The File Manager itself may place volumes off-line during its normal operation.

To protect against power loss or unexpected disk ejection, you should periodically call FlushVol (probably after each time you close a file), which writes the contents of the volume buffer and all access path buffers (if any) to the volume and updates the descriptive information contained on the volume.

Whenever your application is finished with a disk, or when the user chooses Eject from a menu, call Eject. Eject calls FlushVol, places the volume off-line, and then physically ejects the volume from its drive.

If you would like all File Manager calls to apply to one volume, you can specify that volume as the default. You can use SetVol to set the default volume to any mounted volume, and GetVol to learn the name and volume reference number of the default volume.

The preceding paragraphs covered the basic File Manager routines. The remainder of this section describes some less commonly used routines.

Advanced Routines

Normally, volume initialization and naming is handled by the Standard File Package, which calls the Disk Initialization Package. If you want to initialize a volume explicitly or erase all files from a volume, you can call the Disk Initialization Package directly. When you want to change the name of a volume, call the File Manager function Rename.

Whenever a disk has been reconstructed in an attempt to salvage lost files (because its directory or other file-access information has been destroyed), the logical end-of-file of each file will probably be equal to its physical end-of-file, regardless of where the actual logical end-of-file is. The first time an application attempts to read from a file on a reconstructed volume, it will blindly pass the correct logical end-of-file and read misinformation until it reaches the new, incorrect logical end-of-file. To prevent this from happening, an application should always maintain an independent record of the logical end-of-file of each file it uses. To determine the File Manager's conception of the size of a file, or to find out how many bytes have yet to be read from it, call GetEOF, which returns the logical end-of-file. You can change the length of a file by calling SetEOF.

Allocation blocks are automatically added to and deleted from a file as necessary. If this happens to a number of files alternately, each of the files will be contained in allocation blocks scattered throughout the volume, which increases the time required to access those files. To prevent such fragmentation of files, you can allocate a number of contiguous allocation blocks to an open file by calling Allocate or AllocContig.

Instead of calling FlushVol, an unusual application might call FlushFile. FlushFile forces the contents of a file's volume buffer and access path buffer (if any) to be written to its volume. FlushFile doesn't update the descriptive information contained on the volume, so the volume information won't be correct until you call FlushVol.

To get information about a file in a given directory (such as its name and creation date), call GetFileInfo; you can change this information by calling SetFileInfo. On hierarchical volumes, you can get information about both files and directories by calling GetCatInfo; you can change this information with SetCatInfo. Changing the name of a file is accomplished by calling Rename. You can lock a file by calling SetFilLock; to unlock a file, call RstFilLock. Given a path reference number, you can get the volume reference number of the volume containing that file by calling either GetVRefNum or GetFCBInfo (described in the section "Data Structures in Memory").

> **64K ROM note**: You can change the version number of a file by calling SetFilType.

To make a particular directory a working directory, call OpenWD; you can remove a working directory with CloseWD. To get information about a working directory (from its working directory control block), call GetWDInfo.

INFORMATION USED BY THE FINDER

The file directory (whether hierarchical or flat) lists information about all the files and directories on a volume. This information is returned by the GetFileInfo and GetCatInfo functions.

Flat Volumes

On flat volumes, all of the information used by the Finder is contained in a data structure of type FInfo. (This data structure is also used with hierarchical volumes, along with additional structures described below.) The FInfo data type is defined as follows:

```
TYPE FInfo = RECORD
               fdType:      OSType;   {file type}
               fdCreator:   OSType;   {file's creator}
               fdFlags:     INTEGER;  {flags}
               fdLocation:  Point;    {file's location}
               fdFldr:      INTEGER   {file's window}
             END;
```

Normally an application need only set the file type and creator when a file is created, and the Finder will manipulate the other fields. (File type and creator are discussed in the Finder Interface chapter.)

FdFlags indicates whether the file's icon is invisible, whether the file has a bundle, and other characteristics used internally by the Finder:

Bit	**Meaning**
0	Set if file is on desktop (hierarchical volumes only)
13	Set if file has a bundle
14	Set if file's icon is invisible

Masks for these three bits are available as predefined constants:

```
CONST fOnDesk    = 1;       {set if file is on desktop (hierarchical }
                            { volumes only)}
      fHasBundle = 8192;    {set if file has a bundle}
      fInvisible = 16384;   {set if file's icon is invisible}
```

For more information about bundles, see the Finder Interface chapter.

FdLocation contains the location of the file's icon in its window, given in the local coordinate system of the window; it's used by the Finder to position the icon. FdFldr indicates the window in which the file's icon will appear, and may contain one of the following values:

```
CONST fTrash   = -3; {file is in Trash window}
      fDesktop = -2; {file is on desktop}
      fDisk    =  0; {file is in disk window}
```

64K ROM note: The fdFldr field of FInfo is not used with hierarchical volumes.

Hierarchical Volumes

On hierarchical volumes, in addition to the FInfo record, the following information about files is maintained for the Finder:

```
TYPE FXInfo = RECORD
                fdIconID:   INTEGER;  {icon ID}
                fdUnused:   ARRAY[1..4] OF INTEGER; {reserved}
                fdComment:  INTEGER;  {comment ID}
                fdPutAway:  LONGINT;  {home directory ID}
              END;
```

On hierarchical volumes, the following information about directories is maintained for the Finder:

```
     DInfo = RECORD
               frRect:     Rect;      {folder's rectangle}
               frFlags:    INTEGER;   {flags}
               frLocation: Point;     {folder's location}
               frView:     INTEGER;   {folder's view}
             END;
```

```
DXInfo = RECORD
           frScroll:     Point;     {scroll position}
           frOpenChain:  LONGINT;   {directory ID chain of }
                                    { open folders}
           frUnused:     INTEGER;   {reserved}
           frComment:    INTEGER;   {comment ID}
           frPutAway:    LONGINT;   {directory ID}
         END;
```

When a file (or folder) is moved to the desktop on a hierarchical volume, it's actually moved to the root level of the file directory. (This permits all the desktop icons to be enumerated by one simple scan of the root.) The fOnDesk bit of fdFlags is set. FDPutAway (or frPutAway for directories) contains the directory ID of the folder that originally contained the file (or folder); this allows the file (or folder) to be returned there from the desktop.

HIGH-LEVEL FILE MANAGER ROUTINES

This section describes all the high-level Pascal routines of the File Manager. For information on calling the low-level Pascal and assembly-language routines, see the next section.

When accessing a volume other than the default volume, you must identify it by its volume name, its volume reference number, the drive number of its drive, or a working directory reference number. The parameter volName is a pointer, of type StringPtr, to the volume name. DrvNum is an integer that contains the drive number, and vRefNum is an integer that can contain either the volume reference number or a working directory reference number.

> **Note:** VolName is declared as type StringPtr instead of type STRING to allow you to pass NIL in routines where the parameter is optional.

> **Warning:** Before you pass a parameter of type StringPtr to a File Manager routine, be sure that memory has been allocated for the variable. For example, the following statements will ensure that memory is allocated for the variable myStr:

```
VAR myStr: Str255;
     . . .

result := GetVol(@myStr,myRefNum)
```

FileName can contain either the file name alone or both the volume name and file name.

> **Note:** The high-level File Manager routines will work only with files having a version number of 0.

You can't specify an access path buffer when calling high-level Pascal routines.

All high-level File Manager routines return an integer result code of type OSErr as their function result. Each routine description lists all of the applicable result codes, along with a short description of what the result code means. Lengthier explanations of all the result codes can be found in the summary at the end of this chapter.

Accessing Volumes

```
FUNCTION GetVInfo (drvNum: INTEGER; volName: StringPtr; VAR
            vRefNum: INTEGER; VAR freeBytes: LONGINT) : OSErr;   [Not
            in ROM]
```

GetVInfo returns the name, reference number, and available space (in bytes), in volName, vRefNum, and freeBytes, for the volume in the drive specified by drvNum.

Result codes	noErr	No error
	nsvErr	No default volume
	paramErr	Bad drive number


```
FUNCTION GetVRefNum (pathRefNum: INTEGER; VAR vRefNum: INTEGER) :
            OSErr;   [Not in ROM]
```

Given a path reference number in pathRefNum, GetVRefNum returns the volume reference number in vRefNum.

Result codes	noErr	No error
	rfNumErr	Bad reference number

```
FUNCTION GetVol (volName: StringPtr; VAR vRefNum: INTEGER) : OSErr;
            [Not in ROM]
```

GetVol returns the name of the default volume in volName and its volume reference number in vRefNum.

Result codes	noErr	No error
	nsvErr	No such volume

```
FUNCTION SetVol (volName: StringPtr; vRefNum: INTEGER) : OSErr;
            [Not in ROM]
```

SetVol sets the default volume to the mounted volume specified by volName or vRefNum.

Result codes	noErr	No error
	bdNamErr	Bad volume name
	nsvErr	No such volume
	paramErr	No default volume

```
FUNCTION FlushVol (volName: StringPtr; vRefNum: INTEGER) : OSErr;
```
[Not in ROM]

On the volume specified by volName or vRefNum, FlushVol writes the contents of the associated volume buffer and descriptive information about the volume (if they've changed since the last time FlushVol was called).

Result codes	noErr	No error
	bdNamErr	Bad volume name
	extFSErr	External file system
	ioErr	I/O error
	nsDrvErr	No such drive
	nsvErr	No such volume
	paramErr	No default volume

```
FUNCTION UnmountVol (volName: StringPtr; vRefNum: INTEGER) : OSErr;
```
[Not in ROM]

UnmountVol unmounts the volume specified by volName or vRefNum, by calling FlushVol to flush the volume buffer, closing all open files on the volume, and releasing the memory used for the volume.

Warning: Don't unmount the startup volume.

Result codes	noErr	No error
	bdNamErr	Bad volume name
	extFSErr	External file system
	ioErr	I/O error
	nsDrvErr	No such drive
	nsvErr	No such volume
	paramErr	No default volume

```
FUNCTION Eject (volName: StringPtr; vRefNum: INTEGER) : OSErr;
```
[Not in ROM]

Eject flushes the volume specified by volName or vRefNum, places it off-line, and then ejects the volume.

Result codes	noErr	No error
	bdNamErr	Bad volume name
	extFSErr	External file system
	ioErr	I/O error
	nsDrvErr	No such drive
	nsvErr	No such volume
	paramErr	No default volume

Accessing Files

```
FUNCTION FSOpen (fileName: Str255; vRefNum: INTEGER; VAR refNum:
            INTEGER) : OSErr;    [Not in ROM]
```

FSOpen creates an access path to the file having the name fileName on the volume specified by vRefNum. A path reference number is returned in refNum. The access path's read/write permission is set to whatever the file's open permission allows.

Note: There's no guarantee that any bytes have been written until FlushVol is called.

Result codes	noErr	No error
	bdNamErr	Bad file name
	extFSErr	External file system
	fnfErr	File not found
	ioErr	I/O error
	nsvErr	No such volume
	opWrErr	File already open for writing
	tmfoErr	Too many files open

```
FUNCTION OpenRF (fileName: Str255; vRefNum: INTEGER; VAR refNum:
            INTEGER) : OSErr;    [Not in ROM]
```

OpenRF is similar to FSOpen; the only difference is that OpenRF opens the resource fork of the specified file rather than the data fork. A path reference number is returned in refNum. The access path's read/write permission is set to whatever the file's open permission allows.

Note: Normally you should access a file's resource fork through the routines of the Resource Manager rather than the File Manager. OpenRF doesn't read the resource map into memory; it's really only useful for block-level operations such as copying files.

Result codes	noErr	No error
	bdNamErr	Bad file name
	extFSErr	External file system
	fnfErr	File not found
	ioErr	I/O error
	nsvErr	No such volume
	opWrErr	File already open for writing
	tmfoErr	Too many files open

```
FUNCTION FSRead (refNum: INTEGER; VAR count: LONGINT; buffPtr: Ptr)
            : OSErr;    [Not in ROM]
```

FSRead attempts to read the number of bytes specified by the count parameter from the open file whose access path is specified by refNum, and transfer them to the data buffer pointed to by buffPtr. The read operation begins at the current mark, so you might want to precede this with a call to SetFPos. If you try to read past the logical end-of-file, FSRead moves the mark to the end-of-file and returns eofErr as its function result. After the read is completed, the number of bytes actually read is returned in the count parameter.

Result codes	noErr	No error
	eofErr	End-of-file
	extFSErr	External file system
	fnOpnErr	File not open
	ioErr	I/O error
	paramErr	Negative count
	rfNumErr	Bad reference number

```
FUNCTION FSWrite (refNum: INTEGER; VAR count: LONGINT; buffPtr:
            Ptr) : OSErr;    [Not in ROM]
```

FSWrite takes the number of bytes specified by the count parameter from the buffer pointed to by buffPtr and attempts to write them to the open file whose access path is specified by refNum. The write operation begins at the current mark, so you might want to precede this with a call to SetFPos. After the write is completed, the number of bytes actually written is returned in the count parameter.

Result codes	noErr	No error
	dskFulErr	Disk full
	fLckdErr	File locked
	fnOpnErr	File not open
	ioErr	I/O error
	paramErr	Negative count
	rfNumErr	Bad reference number
	vLckdErr	Software volume lock
	wPrErr	Hardware volume lock
	wrPermErr	Read/write permission doesn't allow writing

```
FUNCTION GetFPos (refNum: INTEGER; VAR filePos: LONGINT) : OSErr;
            [Not in ROM]
```

GetFPos returns, in filePos, the mark of the open file whose access path is specified by refNum.

Result codes	noErr	No error
	extFSErr	External file system
	fnOpnErr	File not open
	ioErr	I/O error
	rfNumErr	Bad reference number

```
FUNCTION SetFPos (refNum: INTEGER; posMode: INTEGER; posOff:
            LONGINT) : OSErr;    [Not in ROM]
```

SetFPos sets the mark of the open file whose access path is specified by refNum to the position specified by posMode and posOff (except when posMode is equal to fsAtMark, in which case posOff is ignored). PosMode indicates how to position the mark; it must contain one of the following values:

```
CONST fsAtMark    = 0;  {at current mark}
      fsFromStart = 1;  {set mark relative to beginning of file}
      fsFromLEOF  = 2;  {set mark relative to logical end-of-file}
      fsFromMark  = 3;  {set mark relative to current mark}
```

If you specify fsAtMark, posOffset is ignored and the mark is left wherever it's currently positioned. If you choose to set the mark (relative to either the beginning of the file, the logical end-of-file, or the current mark), posOffset specifies the byte offset from the chosen point (either positive or negative) where the mark should be set. If you try to set the mark past the logical end-of-file, SetFPos moves the mark to the end-of-file and returns eofErr as its function result.

Result codes	noErr	No error
	eofErr	End-of-file
	extFSErr	External file system
	fnOpnErr	File not open
	ioErr	I/O error
	posErr	Attempt to position before start of file
	rfNumErr	Bad reference number

```
FUNCTION GetEOF (refNum: INTEGER; VAR logEOF: LONGINT) : OSErr;
```
[Not in ROM]

GetEOF returns, in logEOF, the logical end-of-file of the open file whose access path is specified by refNum.

Result codes	noErr	No error
	extFSErr	External file system
	fnOpnErr	File not open
	ioErr	I/O error
	rfNumErr	Bad reference number

```
FUNCTION SetEOF (refNum: INTEGER; logEOF: LONGINT) : OSErr;
```
[Not in ROM]

SetEOF sets the logical end-of-file of the open file whose access path is specified by refNum to the position specified by logEOF. If you attempt to set the logical end-of-file beyond the physical end-of-file, the physical end-of-file is set to one byte beyond the end of the next free allocation block; if there isn't enough space on the volume, no change is made, and SetEOF returns dskFulErr as its function result. If logEOF is 0, all space occupied by the file on the volume is released.

Result codes	noErr	No error
	dskFulErr	Disk full
	extFSErr	External file system
	fLckdErr	File locked
	fnOpnErr	File not open
	ioErr	I/O error
	rfNumErr	Bad reference number

	vLckdErr	Software volume lock
	wPrErr	Hardware volume lock
	wrPermErr	Read/write permission doesn't allow writing

```
FUNCTION Allocate (refNum: INTEGER; VAR count: LONGINT) : OSErr;
```
[Not in ROM]

Allocate adds the number of bytes specified by the count parameter to the open file whose access path is specified by refNum, and sets the physical end-of-file to one byte beyond the last block allocated. The number of bytes actually allocated is rounded up to the nearest multiple of the allocation block size, and returned in the count parameter. If there isn't enough empty space on the volume to satisfy the allocation request, Allocate allocates the rest of the space on the volume and returns dskFulErr as its function result.

Result codes	noErr	No error
	dskFulErr	Disk full
	fLckdErr	File locked
	fnOpnErr	File not open
	ioErr	I/O error
	rfNumErr	Bad reference number
	vLckdErr	Software volume lock
	wPrErr	Hardware volume lock
	wrPermErr	Read/write permission doesn't allow writing

```
FUNCTION FSClose (refNum: INTEGER) : OSErr;
```
[Not in ROM]

FSClose removes the access path specified by refNum, writes the contents of the volume buffer to the volume, and updates the file's entry in the file directory.

Note: There's no guarantee that any bytes have been written until FlushVol is called.

Result codes	noErr	No error
	extFSErr	External file system
	fnfErr	File not found
	fnOpnErr	File not open
	ioErr	I/O error
	nsvErr	No such volume
	rfNumErr	Bad reference number

Creating and Deleting Files

```
FUNCTION Create (fileName: Str255; vRefNum: INTEGER; creator:
           OSType; fileType: OSType) : OSErr;
```
[Not in ROM]

Create creates a new file (both forks) with the specified name, file type, and creator on the specified volume. (File type and creator are discussed in the Finder Interface chapter.) The new file is unlocked and empty. The date and time of its creation and last modification are set to the current date and time.

Result codes	noErr	No error
	bdNamErr	Bad file name
	dupFNErr	Duplicate file name and version
	dirFulErr	File directory full
	extFSErr	External file system
	ioErr	I/O error
	nsvErr	No such volume
	vLckdErr	Software volume lock
	wPrErr	Hardware volume lock


```
FUNCTION FSDelete (fileName: Str255; vRefNum: INTEGER) : OSErr;
```
[Not in ROM]

FSDelete removes the closed file having the name fileName from the specified volume.

Note: This function will delete *both* forks of a file.

Result codes	noErr	No error
	bdNamErr	Bad file name
	extFSErr	External file system
	fBsyErr	File busy
	fLckdErr	File locked
	fnfErr	File not found
	ioErr	I/O error
	nsvErr	No such volume
	vLckdErr	Software volume lock
	wPrErr	Hardware volume lock

Changing Information About Files

All of the routines described in this section affect both forks of the file, and don't require the file to be open.

```
FUNCTION GetFInfo (fileName: Str255; vRefNum: INTEGER; VAR
            fndrInfo: FInfo) : OSErr;
```
[Not in ROM]

For the file having the name fileName on the specified volume, GetFInfo returns information used by the Finder in fndrInfo (see the section "Information Used by the Finder").

Result codes	noErr	No error
	bdNamErr	Bad file name
	extFSErr	External file system
	fnfErr	File not found
	ioErr	I/O error
	nsvErr	No such volume
	paramErr	No default volume

```
FUNCTION SetFInfo (fileName: Str255; vRefNum: INTEGER; fndrInfo:
          FInfo) : OSErr;    [Not in ROM]
```

For the file having the name fileName on the specified volume, SetFInfo sets information used by the Finder to fndrInfo (see the section "Information Used by the Finder").

Result codes	noErr	No error
	extFSErr	External file system
	fLckdErr	File locked
	fnfErr	File not found
	ioErr	I/O error
	nsvErr	No such volume
	vLckdErr	Software volume lock
	wPrErr	Hardware volume lock

```
FUNCTION SetFLock (fileName: Str255; vRefNum: INTEGER) : OSErr;
          [Not in ROM]
```

SetFLock locks the file having the name fileName on the specified volume. Access paths currently in use aren't affected.

Result codes	noErr	No error
	extFSErr	External file system
	fnfErr	File not found
	ioErr	I/O error
	nsvErr	No such volume
	vLckdErr	Software volume lock
	wPrErr	Hardware volume lock

```
FUNCTION RstFLock (fileName: Str255; vRefNum: INTEGER) : OSErr;
          [Not in ROM]
```

RstFLock unlocks the file having the name fileName on the specified volume. Access paths currently in use aren't affected.

Result codes	noErr	No error
	extFSErr	External file system
	fnfErr	File not found
	ioErr	I/O error
	nsvErr	No such volume
	vLckdErr	Software volume lock
	wPrErr	Hardware volume lock

```
FUNCTION Rename (oldName: Str255; vRefNum: INTEGER; newName:
          Str255) : OSErr;    [Not in ROM]
```

Given a file name in oldName, Rename changes the name of the file to newName. Access paths currently in use aren't affected. Given a volume name in oldName or a volume reference number in vRefNum, Rename changes the name of the specified volume to newName.

Warning: If you're renaming a volume, be sure that both names end with a colon.

Result codes		
	noErr	No error
	bdNamErr	Bad file name
	dirFulErr	Directory full
	dupFNErr	Duplicate file name
	extFSErr	External file system
	fLckdErr	File locked
	fnfErr	File not found
	fsRnErr	Problem during rename
	ioErr	I/O error
	nsvErr	No such volume
	paramErr	No default volume
	vLckdErr	Software volume lock
	wPrErr	Hardware volume lock

LOW-LEVEL FILE MANAGER ROUTINES

This section contains information for programmers using the low-level Pascal or assembly-language routines of the File Manager, and describes them in detail.

Most low-level File Manager routines can be executed either **synchronously** (meaning that the application can't continue until the routine is completed) or **asynchronously** (meaning that the application is free to perform other tasks while the routine is executing). Some, however, can only be executed synchronously because they use the Memory Manager to allocate and release memory.

When an application calls a File Manager routine asynchronously, an **I/O request** is placed in the **file I/O queue**, and control returns to the calling program—possibly even before the actual I/O is completed. Requests are taken from the queue one at a time, and processed; meanwhile, the calling program is free to work on other things.

The calling program may specify a **completion routine** to be executed at the end of an asynchronous operation.

At any time, you can clear all queued File Manager calls except the current one by using the InitQueue procedure. InitQueue is especially useful when an error occurs and you no longer want queued calls to be executed.

Parameter Blocks

Routine parameters passed by an application to the File Manager and returned by the File Manager to an application are contained in a **parameter block**, which is a data structure in the heap or stack. When there are a number of parameters to be passed to, or returned from, a routine, the parameters are grouped together in a block and a pointer to the block is passed instead.

Most low-level calls to the File Manager are of the form

```
FUNCTION PBCallName (paramBlock: PtrToParamBlk; async: BOOLEAN) :
      OSErr;
```

PBCallName is the name of the routine. ParamBlock points to the parameter block containing the parameters for the routine; its data type depends on the type of parameter block. If async is TRUE, the call is executed asynchronously; otherwise the call is executed synchronously. The routine returns an integer result code of type OSErr. Each routine description lists all of the applicable result codes, along with a short description of what the result code means. Lengthier explanations of all the result codes can be found in the summary at the end of this chapter.

Assembly-language note: When you call a File Manager routine, A0 must point to a parameter block containing the parameters for the routine. If you want the routine to be executed asynchronously, set bit 10 of the routine trap word. You can do this by supplying the word ASYNC as the second argument to the routine macro. For example:

```
        _Read   ,ASYNC
```

You can set or test bit 10 of a trap word by using the global constant asyncTrpBit. (This syntax applies to the Lisa Workshop Assembler; programmers using another development system should consult its documentation for the proper syntax.)

All File Manager routines except InitQueue return a result code in D0.

There are many parameters used in the File Manager routines. To group them all together in a single parameter block would be unmanageable, so several different parameter block records have been defined. Figure 6 gives an overview of the various parameter blocks.

```
ParamBlkType =       (ioParam,fileParam,
                      volumeParam,cntrlParam);
ParmBlkPtr =         ^ParamBlockRec;
ParamBlockRec =      RECORD
  qLink:             QElemPtr;
  qType:             INTEGER;
  ioTrap:            INTEGER;
  ioCmdAddr:         Ptr;
  ioCompletion:      ProcPtr;
  ioResult:          OSErr;
  ioNamePtr:         StringPtr;
  ioVRefNum:         INTEGER;
CASE ParamBlkType OF
ioParam:
  (ioRefNum:         INTEGER;
  ioVersNum:         SignedByte;
  ioPermssn:         SignedByte;
  ioMisc:            Ptr;
  ioBuffer:          Ptr;
  ioReqCount:        LONGINT;
  ioActCount:        LONGINT;
  ioPosMode:         INTEGER;
  ioPosOffset:       LONGINT);
fileParam:
  (ioFRefNum:        INTEGER;
  ioFVersNum:        SignedByte;
  filler1:           SignedByte;
  ioFDirIndex:       INTEGER;
  ioFlAttrib:        SignedByte;
  ioFlVersNum:       SignedByte;
  ioFlFndrInfo:      FInfo;
  ioFlNum:           LONGINT;
  ioFlStBlk:         INTEGER;
  ioFlLgLen:         LONGINT;
  ioFlPyLen:         LONGINT;
  ioFlRStBlk:        INTEGER;
  ioFlRLgLen:        LONGINT;
  ioFlRPyLen:        LONGINT;
  ioFlCrDat:         LONGINT;
  ioFlMdDat:         LONGINT);
volumeParam:
  (filler2:          LONGINT;
  ioVolIndex:        INTEGER;
  ioVCrDate:         LONGINT;
  ioVLsBkUp:         LONGINT;
  ioVAtrb:           INTEGER;
  ioVNmFls           INTEGER;
  ioVDirSt:          INTEGER;
  ioVBlLn:           INTEGER;
  ioVNmAlBlks:       INTEGER;
  ioVAlBlkSiz:       LONGINT;
  ioVClpSiz:         LONGINT;
  ioAlBlSt:          INTEGER;
  ioVNxtFNum:        LONGINT;
  ioVFrBlk:          INTEGER);
cntrlParam:
  {used by Device Manager}
END;

CMovePBPtr = ^CMovePBRec;
CMovePBRec = RECORD
  qLink:             QElemPtr;
  qType:             INTEGER;
  ioTrap:            INTEGER;
  ioCmdAddr:         Ptr;
  ioCompletion:      ProcPtr;
  ioResult:          OSErr;
  ioNamePtr:         StringPtr;
  ioVRefNum:         INTEGER;
  filler1:           LONGINT;
  ioNewName:         StringPtr;
  filler2:           LONGINT;
  ioNewDirID:        LONGINT;
  filler3:           ARRAY [1..2]
                       OF LONGINT;
  ioDirID:           LONGINT);
END;

HParmBlkPtr =        ^HParamBlockRec
HParamBlockRec =     RECORD
  qLink:             QElemPtr;
  qType:             INTEGER;
  ioTrap:            INTEGER;
  ioCmdAddr:         Ptr;
  ioCompletion:      ProcPtr;
  ioResult:          OSErr;
  ioNamePtr:         StringPtr;
  ioVRefNum:         INTEGER;
CASE ParamBlkType OF
ioParam:
  (ioRefNum:         INTEGER;
  ioVersNum:         SignedByte;
  ioPermssn:         SignedByte;
  ioMisc:            Ptr;
  ioBuffer:          Ptr;
  ioReqCount:        LONGINT;
  ioActCount:        LONGINT;
  ioPosMode:         INTEGER;
  ioPosOffset:       LONGINT);
fileParam:
  (ioFRefNum:        INTEGER;
  ioFVersNum:        SignedByte;
  filler1:           SignedByte;
  ioFDirIndex:       INTEGER;
  ioFlAttrib:        SignedByte;
  ioFlVersNum:       SignedByte;
  ioFlFndrInfo:      FInfo;
  ioDirID:           LONGINT;
  ioFlStBlk:         INTEGER;
  ioFlLgLen:         LONGINT;
  ioFlPyLen:         LONGINT;
  ioFlRStBlk:        INTEGER;
  ioFlRLgLen:        LONGINT;
  ioFlRPyLen:        LONGINT;
  ioFlCrDat:         LONGINT;
  ioFlMdDat:         LONGINT);
volumeParam:
  (filler2:          LONGINT;
  ioVolIndex:        INTEGER;
  ioVCrDate:         LONGINT;
  ioVLsMod:          LONGINT;
  ioVAtrb:           INTEGER;
  ioVNmFls:          INTEGER;
  ioVBitMap:         INTEGER;
  ioAllocPtr:        INTEGER;
  ioVNmAlBlks:       INTEGER;
  ioVAlBlkSiz:       LONGINT;
  ioVClpSiz:         LONGINT;
  ioAlBlSt:          INTEGER;
  ioVNxtCNID:        LONGINT;
  ioVFrBlk:          INTEGER;
  ioVSigWord:        INTEGER;
  ioVDrvInfo:        INTEGER;
  ioVDRefNum:        INTEGER;
  ioVFSID:           INTEGER;
  ioVBkUp:           LONGINT;
  ioVSeqNum:         INTEGER;
  ioVWrCnt           LONGINT;
  ioVFilCnt:         LONGINT;
  ioVDirCnt:         LONGINT;
  ioVFndrInfo:       ARRAY [1..8]
                       OF LONGINT);
END;

WDPBPtr = ^WDPBRec;
WDPBRec = RECORD
  qLink:             QElemPtr;
  qType:             INTEGER;
  ioTrap:            INTEGER;
  ioCmdAddr:         Ptr;
  ioCompletion:      ProcPtr;
  ioResult:          OSErr;
  ioNamePtr:         StringPtr;
  ioVRefNum:         INTEGER;
  filler1:           INTEGER;
  ioWDIndex:         INTEGER;
  ioWDProcID:        LONGINT;
  ioWDVRefNum:       INTEGER;
  filler2:           ARRAY[1..7]
                       OF INTEGER;
  ioWDDirID:         LONGINT);
END;

CInfoType   = (hfileInfo,dirInfo);
CInfoPBPtr  = ^cInfoPBRec;
CInfoPBRec  = RECORD
  qLink:             QElemPtr;
  qType:             INTEGER;
  ioTrap:            INTEGER;
  ioCmdAddr:         Ptr;
  ioCompletion:      ProcPtr;
  ioResult:          OSErr;
  ioNamePtr:         StringPtr;
  ioVRefNum:         INTEGER;
  ioFRefNum:         INTEGER;
  ioFVersNum         SignedByte;
  filler1:           SignedByte;
  ioFDirIndex:       INTEGER;
  ioFlAttrib:        SignedByte;
  filler2:           SignedByte;
CASE CInfoType OF
hFileInfo:
  (ioFlFndrInfo:     FInfo;
  ioDirID:           LONGINT;
  ioFlStBlk:         INTEGER;
  ioFlLgLen:         LONGINT;
  ioFlPyLen:         LONGINT;
  ioFlRStBlk:        INTEGER;
  ioFlRLgLen:        LONGINT;
  ioFlRPyLen:        LONGINT;
  ioFlCrDat:         LONGINT;
  ioFlMdDat:         LONGINT;
  ioFlBkDat:         LONGINT;
  ioFlXFndrInfo:     FInfo;
  ioFlParID:         LONGINT;
  ioFlClpSiz:        LONGINT);
dirInfo:
  (ioDrUsrWds:       ARRAY [1..8]
                       OF INTEGER;
  ioDrDirID:         LONGINT;
  ioDrNmFls:         INTEGER;
  filler3:           ARRAY [1..9]
                       OF INTEGER;
  ioDrCrDat:         LONGINT;
  ioDrMdDat:         LONGINT;
  ioDrBkDat:         LONGINT;
  ioDrFndrInfo:      ARRAY [1..8]
                       OF INTEGER;
  ioDrParID:         LONGINT);
END;

FCBPBPtr = ^FCBPBRec
FCBPBRec = RECORD
  qLink:             QElemPtr;
  qType:             INTEGER;
  ioTrap:            INTEGER;
  ioCmdAddr:         Ptr;
  ioCompletion:      ProcPtr;
  ioResult:          OSErr;
  ioNamePtr:         StringPtr;
  ioVRefNum:         INTEGER;
  ioRefNum:          INTEGER;
  filler:            INTEGER;
  ioFCBIndx:         LONGINT;
  ioFCBFlNm:         LONGINT;
  ioFCBFlags:        INTEGER;
  ioFCBStBlk:        INTEGER;
  ioFCBEOF:          LONGINT;
  ioFCBPLen:         LONGINT;
  ioFCBCrPs:         LONGINT;
  ioFCBVRefNum:      INTEGER;
  ioFCBClpSiz:       LONGINT;
  ioFCBParID:        LONGINT;
END;
```

Figure 6. File Manager Parameter Block Records

ParamBlockRec is the record used by all routines in the 64K ROM version of the File Manager; these routines include general I/O operations, as well as access to information about files and volumes. The RAM-based version of the File Manager provides additional calls that are slight extensions of certain basic routines, allowing you to take advantage of the hierarchical file directory. For instance, HOpen is an extension of the Open call that lets you use a directory ID and a pathname to specify the file to be opened. These hierarchical routines use the record HParamBlockRec, which, as you can see from Figure 6, is a superset of ParamBlockRec.

Assembly-language note: The hierarchical extensions of certain basic File Manager routines are actually not new calls. For instance, _Open and _HOpen both trap to the same routine. The trap word generated by the _HOpen macro is the same as the trap word that would be generated by invoking the _Open macro with bit 9 set. (Note that this is the same bit used in the Device Manager to indicate that a particular call should be executed immediately.) The setting of this bit tells the File Manager to expect a larger parameter block containing the additional fields (such as a directory ID) needed to handle a hierarchical directory volume. You can set or test bit 9 of a trap word by using the global contstant hfsBit.

Three parameter block records—CInfoPBRec, CMovePBRec, and WDPBRec—are used by routines that deal specifically with the hierarchical file directory. These routines work *only* with the 128K ROM version of the File Manager.

Finally, the record FCBPBRec is used by a single routine, PBGetFCBInfo, to gain access to the contents of a file's file control block; this routine also works *only* with the 128K ROM version of the File Manager.

Assembly-language note: You can invoke each of the routines that deal specifically with the hierarchical file directory with a macro that has the same name as the routine preceded by an underscore. These macros, however, aren't trap macros themselves; instead they expand to invoke the trap macro _HFSDispatch. The File Manager determines which routine to execute from the **routine selector**, an integer that's placed in register D0. The routine selectors are as follows:

Routine	Call number
OpenWD	1
CloseWD	2
CatMove	5
DirCreate	6
GetWDInfo	7
GetFCBInfo	8
GetCatInfo	9
SetCatInfo	10
SetVolInfo	11
LockRng	16
UnlockRng	17

Warning: Using these routines on a Macintosh equipped only with the 64K ROM will result in a system error.

Three of the records—ParamBlockRec, HParamBlockRec, and CInfoPBRec—have CASE statements that separate some of their parameters into functional subsections (also known as variants of the record). The other records—CMovePBRec, WDPBRec, and FCBPBRec—are not divided in this way.

All of the parameter block records used by the File Manager begin with eight fields of standard information:

```
qLink:         QElemPtr;    {next queue entry}
qType:         INTEGER;     {queue type}
ioTrap:        INTEGER;     {routine trap}
ioCmdAddr:     Ptr;         {routine address}
ioCompletion:  ProcPtr;     {completion routine}
ioResult:      OSErr;       {result code}
ioNamePtr:     StringPtr;   {pathname}
ioVRefNum:     INTEGER;     {volume reference number, drive number, }
                            { or working directory reference number}
```

The first four fields in each parameter block are handled entirely by the File Manager, and most programmers needn't be concerned with them; programmers who are interested in them should see the section "Data Structures in Memory".

IOCompletion contains a pointer to a completion routine to be executed at the end of an asynchronous call; it should be NIL for asynchronous calls with no completion routine, and is automatically set to NIL for all synchronous calls.

> **Warning:** Completion routines are executed at the interrupt level and must preserve all registers other than A0, A1, and D0–D2. Your completion routine must not make any calls to the Memory Manager, directly or indirectly, and can't depend on handles to unlocked blocks being valid. If it uses application globals, it must also ensure that register A5 contains the address of the boundary between the application globals and the application parameters; for details, see SetUpA5 and RestoreA5 in the Operating System Utilities chapter.

When your completion routine is called, register A0 points to the parameter block of the asynchronous call and register D0 contains the result code.

Routines that are executed asynchronously return control to the calling program with the result code noErr as soon as the call is placed in the file I/O queue. This isn't an indication of successful call completion, but simply indicates that the call was successfully queued. To determine when the call is actually completed, you can poll the ioResult field; this field is set to 1 when the call is made, and receives the actual result code upon completion of the call. Completion routines are executed after the result code is placed in ioResult.

IONamePtr *points* to a pathname (i.e. it does *not* itself contain the characters. It can be either a full or partial pathname. In other words, it can be a volume name (that is, the name of the root directory), a file name, or a concatenation of directory and file names. If ioNamePtr is NIL or points to an improper pathname, an error is returned. For routines that access directories, if a directory ID is specified, ioNamePtr can be NIL.

Note: Although ioNamePtr can be a full pathname, you should *not* require users to enter full pathnames.

IOVRefNum contains either a volume reference number, a drive number, or a working directory reference number.

The remainder of the parameters are presented below, organized by parameter block records.

IOParam Variant (ParamBlockRec and HParamBlockRec)

The ioParam variants of ParamBlockRec and HParamBlockRec are identical; the fields are presented below.

```
ioParam:
 (ioRefNum:     INTEGER;     {path reference number}
  ioVersNum:    SignedByte;  {version number}
  ioPermssn:    SignedByte;  {read/write permission}
  ioMisc:       Ptr;         {miscellaneous}
  ioBuffer:     Ptr;         {data buffer}
  ioReqCount:   LONGINT;     {requested number of bytes}
  ioActCount:   LONGINT;     {actual number of bytes}
  ioPosMode:    INTEGER;     {positioning mode and newline character}
  ioPosOffset:  LONGINT);    {positioning offset}
```

For routines that access open files, the File Manager determines which file to access by using the path reference number in ioRefNum.

64K ROM note: The 64K ROM version of the File Manager also allows the specification of a version number to distinguish between different files with the same name. Version numbers are generally set to 0, though, because the Resource Manager, Segment Loader, and Standard File Package won't operate on files with nonzero version numbers, and the Finder ignores version numbers.

IOPermssn requests permission to read or write via an access path, and must contain one of the following values:

```
CONST  fsCurPerm     = 0;  {whatever is currently allowed}
       fsRdPerm      = 1;  {request for read permission only}
       fsWrPerm      = 2;  {request for write permission}
       fsRdWrPerm    = 3;  {request for exclusive read/write }
                           { permission}
       fsRdWrShPerm  = 4;  {request for shared read/write permission}
```

This request is compared with the open permission of the file. If the open permission doesn't allow I/O as requested, a result code indicating the error is returned.

> **Warning:** To ensure data integrity be sure to lock the portion of the file you'll be using if you specify shared write permission.

The content of ioMisc depends on the routine called. It contains either a new logical end-of-file, a new version number, a pointer to an access path buffer, or a pointer to a new pathname. Since ioMisc is of type Ptr, you'll need to perform type coercion to correctly interpret the value of ioMisc when it contains an end-of-file (a LONGINT) or version number (a SignedByte).

IOBuffer points to a data buffer into which data is written by Read calls and from which data is read by Write calls. IOReqCount specifies the requested number of bytes to be read, written, or allocated. IOActCount contains the number of bytes actually read, written, or allocated.

IOPosMode and ioPosOffset specify the position of the mark for Read, Write, LockRng, UnlockRng, and SetFPos calls. IOPosMode contains the positioning mode; bits 0 and 1 indicate how to position the mark, and you can use the following predefined constants to set or test their value:

```
CONST fsAtMark     = 0;   {at current mark}
      fsFromStart  = 1;   {set mark relative to beginning of file}
      fsFromLEOF   = 2;   {set mark relative to logical end-of-file}
      fsFromMark   = 3;   {set mark relative to current mark}
```

If you specify fsAtMark, ioPosOffset is ignored and the operation begins wherever the mark is currently positioned. If you choose to set the mark (relative to either the beginning of the file, the logical end-of-file, or the current mark), ioPosOffset must specify the byte offset from the chosen point (either positive or negative) where the operation should begin.

> **Note:** Advanced programmers: Bit 7 of ioPosMode is the newline flag; it's set if read operations should terminate at a newline character. The ASCII code of the newline character is specified in the high-order byte of ioPosMode. If the newline flag is set, the data will be read one byte at a time until the newline character is encountered, ioReqCount bytes have been read, or the end-of-file is reached. If the newline flag is clear, the data will be read one byte at a time until ioReqCount bytes have been read or the end-of-file is reached.

To have the File Manager verify that all data written to a volume exactly matches the data in memory, make a Read call right after the Write call. The parameters for a read-verify operation are the same as for a standard Read call, except that the following constant must be added to the positioning mode:

```
CONST  rdVerify = 64;    {read-verify mode}
```

The result code ioErr is returned if any of the data doesn't match.

FileParam Variant (ParamBlockRec and HParamBlockRec)

The fileParam variants of ParamBlockRec and HParamBlockRec are identical, with one exception: The field ioDirID in HParamBlockRec is called ioFlNum in ParamBlockRec. The fields of the fileParam variant of HParamBlockRec are as follows:

```
fileParam:
 (ioFRefNum:     INTEGER;     {path reference number}
  ioFVersNum:    SignedByte;  {version number}
  filler1:       SignedByte;  {not used}
  ioFDirIndex:   INTEGER;     {index}
  ioFlAttrib:    SignedByte;  {file attributes}
  ioFlVersNum:   SignedByte;  {version number}
  ioFlFndrInfo:  FInfo;       {information used by the Finder}
  ioDirID:       LONGINT;     {directory ID or file number}
  ioFlStBlk:     INTEGER;     {first allocation block of data fork}
  ioFlLgLen:     LONGINT;     {logical end-of-file of data fork}
  ioFlPyLen:     LONGINT;     {physical end-of-file of data fork}
  ioFlRStBlk:    INTEGER;     {first allocation block of resource fork}
  ioFlRLgLen:    LONGINT;     {logical end-of-file of resource fork}
  ioFlRPyLen:    LONGINT;     {physical end-of-file of resource fork}
  ioFlCrDat:     LONGINT;     {date and time of creation}
  ioFlMdDat:     LONGINT);    {date and time of last modification}
```

IOFDirIndex can be used with the PBGetFInfo and PBHGetFInfo to index through the files in a given directory.

> **Warning**: When used with GetFileInfo, ioFDirIndex will index only the *files* in a directory. To index both files *and* directories, you can use ioFDirIndex with PBGetCatInfo.

IOFlAttrib contains the following file attributes:

Bit	**Meaning**
0	Set if file is locked
2	Set if resource fork is open
3	Set if data fork is open
4	Set if a directory
7	Set if file (either fork) is open

When passed to a routine, ioDirID contains a directory ID; it can be used to refer to a directory or, in conjuction with a partial pathname from that directory, to other files and directories. If both a directory ID and a working directory reference number are provided, the directory ID is used to identify the directory on the volume indicated by the working directory reference number. In other words, a directory ID specified by the caller will override the working directory referred to by the working directory reference number. If you don't want this to happen, you can set ioDirID to 0. (If no directory is specified through a working directory reference number, the root directory ID will be used.)

When returned from a routine, ioDirID contains the file number of a file; most programmers needn't be concerned with file numbers, but those interested can read the section "Data Organization on Volumes".

IOFlStBlk and ioFlRStBlk contain 0 if the file's data or resource fork is empty, respectively; they're used only with flat volumes. The date and time in the ioFlCrDat and ioFlMdDat fields are specified in seconds since midnight, January 1, 1904.

VolumeParam Variant (ParamBlockRec)

When you call GetVolInfo, you'll use the volumeParam variant of ParamBlockRec:


```
volumeParam:
 (filler2:       LONGINT;     {not used}
  ioVolIndex:    INTEGER;     {index}
  ioVCrDate:     LONGINT;     {date and time of initialization}
  ioVLsBkUp:     LONGINT;     {date and time of last modification}
  ioVAtrb:       INTEGER;     {volume attributes}
  ioVNmFls:      INTEGER;     {number of files in root directory}
  ioVDirSt:      INTEGER;     {first block of directory}
  ioVBlLn:       INTEGER;     {length of directory in blocks}
  ioVNmAlBlks:   INTEGER;     {number of allocation blocks}
  ioVAlBlkSiz:   LONGINT;     {size of allocation blocks}
  ioVClpSiz:     LONGINT;     {number of bytes to allocate}
  ioAlBlSt:      INTEGER;     {first block in volume block map}
  ioVNxtFNum:    LONGINT;     {next unused file number}
  ioVFrBlk:      INTEGER);    {number of unused allocation blocks}
```

IOVolIndex can be used to index through all the mounted volumes; using an index of 1 accesses the first volume mounted, and so on. (For more information on indexing, see the section "Indexing" above.)

IOVLsBkUp contains the date and time the volume information was last modified (this is not necessarily when it was flushed). (This field is not modified when information is written to a file.)

> **Note:** The name ioVLsBkUp is actually a misnomer; this field has always contained the date and time of the last modification to the volume, not the last backup.

Most programmers needn't be concerned with the remaining parameters, but interested programmers can read the section "Data Organization on Volumes".

VolumeParam Variant (HParamBlockRec)

When you call HGetVInfo and SetVolInfo, you'll use the volumeParam variant of HParamBlockRec. This is a superset of the volumeParam variant of ParamBlockRec; the names and functions of certain fields have been changed, and new fields have been added:

```
volumeParam:
 (filler2:       LONGINT;     {not used}
  ioVolIndex:    INTEGER;     {index}
  ioVCrDate:     LONGINT;     {date and time of initialization}
  ioVLsMod:      LONGINT;     {date and time of last modification}
  ioVAtrb:       INTEGER;     {volume attributes}
  ioVNmFls:      INTEGER;     {number of files in root directory}
  ioVBitMap:     INTEGER;     {first block of volume bit map}
  ioAllocPtr:    INTEGER;     {block at which next new file starts}
```

```
ioVNmAlBlks:   INTEGER;      {number of allocation blocks}
ioVAlBlkSiz:   LONGINT;      {size of allocation blocks}
ioVClpSiz:     LONGINT;      {number of bytes to allocate}
ioAlBlSt:      INTEGER;      {first block in volume block map}
ioVNxtCNID:    LONGINT;      {next unused file number}
ioVFrBlk:      INTEGER;      {number of unused allocation blocks}
ioVSigWord:    INTEGER;      {volume signature}
ioVDrvInfo:    INTEGER;      {drive number}
ioVDRefNum:    INTEGER;      {driver reference number}
ioVFSID:       INTEGER;      {file system handling this volume}
ioVBkUp:       LONGINT;      {date and time of last backup}
ioVSeqNum:     INTEGER;      {used internally}
ioVWrCnt       LONGINT;      {volume write count}
ioVFilCnt:     LONGINT;      {number of files on volume}
ioVDirCnt:     LONGINT;      {number of directories on volume}
ioVFndrInfo:   ARRAY[1..8] OF LONGINT); {information used by the }
                                        { Finder}
```

IOVolIndex can be used to index through all the mounted volumes; using an index of 1 accesses the first volume mounted, and so on. (For more information on indexing, see the section "Indexing" above.)

IOVLsMod contains the date and time the volume information was last modified (this is not necessarily when it was flushed). (This field is not modified when information is written to a file.)

> **Note:** IOVLsMod replaces the field ioVLsBkUp in ParamBlockRec. The name ioVLsBkUp was actually a misnomer; this field has always contained the date and time of the last modification, not the last backup. Another field, ioVBkUp, contains the date and time of the last backup.

IOVClpSiz can be used to set the volume **clump size** in bytes; it's used for files that don't have a clump size defined as part of their file information in the catalog. To promote file contiguity and avoid fragmentation, space is allocated to a file not in allocation blocks but in **clumps**. A clump is a group of contiguous allocation blocks. The clump size is always a multiple of the allocation block size; it's the minimum number of bytes to allocate each time the Allocate function is called or the end-of-file is reached during the Write routine.

IOVSigWord contains a signature word identifying the type of volume; it's $D2D7 for flat directory volumes and $4244 for hierarchical directory volumes. The drive number of the drive containing the volume is returned in ioDrvInfo. For on-line volumes, ioVDRefNum returns the reference number of the I/O driver for the drive identified by ioDrvInfo.

IOVFSID is the file-system identifier. It indicates which file system is servicing the volume; it's 0 for File Manager volumes and nonzero for volumes handled by an external file system.

IOVBkUp specifies the date and time the volume was last backed up (it's 0 if never backed up).

IOVNmFls contains the number of *files* in the root directory. IOVFilCnt contains the total number of files on the volume, while ioVDirCnt contains the total number of directories (not including the root directory).

Most programmers needn't be concerned with the other parameters, but interested programmers can read the section "Data Organization on Volumes".

CInfoPBRec

The routines GetCatInfo and SetCatInfo are used for getting and setting information about the files and directories within a directory. With files, you'll use the following 19 additional fields after the standard eight fields in the parameter block record CInfoPBRec:


```
    ioFRefNum:       INTEGER;      {path reference number}
    ioFVersNum:      SignedByte;   {version number}
    filler1:         SignedByte;   {not used}
    ioFDirIndex:     INTEGER;      {index}
    ioFlAttrib:      SignedByte;   {file attributes}
    filler2:         SignedByte;   {not used}
  hFileInfo:
   (ioFlFndrInfo:    FInfo;        {information used by the Finder}
    ioDirID:         LONGINT;      {directory ID or file number}
    ioFlStBlk:       INTEGER;      {first allocation block of data fork}
    ioFlLgLen:       LONGINT;      {logical end-of-file of data fork}
    ioFlPyLen:       LONGINT;      {physical end-of-file of data fork}
    ioFlRStBlk:      INTEGER;      {first allocation block of resource }
                                   { fork}
    ioFlRLgLen:      LONGINT;      {logical end-of-file of resource fork}
    ioFlRPyLen:      LONGINT;      {physical end-of-file of resource fork}
    ioFlCrDat:       LONGINT;      {date and time of creation}
    ioFlMdDat:       LONGINT;      {date and time of last modification}
    ioFlBkDat:       LONGINT;      {date and time of last backup}
    ioFlXFndrInfo:   FXInfo;       {additional information used by the }
                                   { Finder}
    ioFlParID:       LONGINT;      {file's parent directory ID (integer)}
    ioFlClpSiz:      LONGINT);     {file's clump size}
```

IOFDirIndex can be used with the function PBGetCatInfo to index through the files and directories in a given directory. For each iteration of the function, you can determine whether it's a file or a directory by testing bit 4 (the fifth least significant bit) of ioFlAttrib. You can test for a directory by using the Toolbox Utilities BitTst function in the following manner (remember, the Toolbox Utilities routines reverse the standard 68000 notation):

```
BitTst(@myCInfoRec.ioFlAttrib,3)
```

IOFlAttrib contains the following attributes:

Bit	Meaning
0	Set if file is locked
2	Set if resource fork is open
3	Set if data fork is open
4	Set if a directory
7	Set if file (either fork) is open

When passed to a routine, ioDirID contains a directory ID; it can be used to refer to a directory or, in conjuction with a partial pathname from that directory, to other files and directories. If both a directory ID and a working directory reference number are provided, the directory ID is used to identify the directory on the volume indicated by the working directory reference number. In other words, a directory ID specified by the caller will override the working directory referred to by the working directory reference number. If you don't want this to happen, you can set ioDirID to 0. (If no directory is specified through a working directory reference number, the root directory ID will be used.)

> **Warning:** With files, ioDirID returns the file number of the file; when indexing with GetCatInfo, you'll need to reset this field for each iteration.

IOFlStBlk and ioFlRStBlk contain 0 if the file's data or resource fork is empty, respectively; they're used only with flat volumes. The date and time in the ioFlCrDat, ioFlMdDat, and ioFlBkDat fields are specified in seconds since midnight, January 1, 1904.

IOFlParID contains the directory ID of the file's parent. IOFlClpSiz is the clump size to be used when writing the file; if it's 0, the volume's clump size is used when the file is opened.

With directories, you'll use the following 14 additional fields after the standard eight fields in the parameter block record CInfoPBRec:

```
    ioFRefNum:      INTEGER;        {file reference number}
    ioFVersNum      SignedByte;     {version number}
    filler1:        SignedByte;     {not used}
    ioFDirIndex:    INTEGER;        {index}
    ioFlAttrib:     SignedByte;     {file attributes}
    filler2:        SignedByte;     {not used}
  dirInfo:
   (ioDrUsrWds:     DInfo;          {information used by the Finder}
    ioDrDirID:      LONGINT;        {directory ID}
    ioDrNmFls:      INTEGER;        {number of files in directory}
    filler3:        ARRAY[1..9] OF INTEGER; {not used}
    ioDrCrDat:      LONGINT;        {date and time of creation}
    ioDrMdDat:      LONGINT;        {date and time of last modification}
    ioDrBkDat:      LONGINT;        {date and time of last backup}
    ioDrFndrInfo:   DXInfo;         {additional information used by the }
                                    { Finder}
    ioDrParID:      LONGINT);       {directory's parent directory ID }
                                    { (integer)}
```

IOFDirIndex can be used with the function PBGetCatInfo to index through the files and directories in a given directory. For each iteration of the function, you can determine whether it's a file or a directory by testing bit 4 of ioFlAttrib.

When passed to a routine, ioDrDirID contains a directory ID; it can be used to refer to a directory or, in conjuction with a partial pathname from that directory, to other files and directories. If both a directory ID and a working directory reference number are provided, the directory ID is used to identify the directory on the volume indicated by the working directory reference number. In other words, a directory ID specified by the caller will override the working directory referred to by the working directory reference number. If you don't want this to happen, you can set ioDirID to 0. (If no directory is specified through a working directory reference number, the root directory ID will be used.)

With directories, ioDrDirID returns the directory ID of the directory.

IODrNmFls is the number of files *and* directories contained in this directory (the valence of the directory).

The date and time in the ioDrCrDat, ioDrMdDat, and ioDrBkDat fields are specified in seconds since midnight, January 1, 1904.

IODrParID contains the directory ID of the directory's parent.

CMovePBRec

When you call CatMove to move files or directories into a different directory, you'll use the following six additional fields after the standard eight fields in the parameter block record CMovePBRec:

```
filler1:      LONGINT;    {not used}
ioNewName:    StringPtr;  {name of new directory}
filler2:      LONGINT;    {not used}
ioNewDirID:   LONGINT;    {directory ID of new directory}
filler3:      ARRAY[1..2] OF LONGINT; {not used}
ioDirID:      LONGINT);   {directory ID of current directory}
```

IONewName and ioNewDirID specify the name and directory ID of the directory to which the file or directory is to be moved. IODirID (used in conjuntion with the ioVRefNum and ioNamePtr) specifies the current directory ID of the file or directory to be moved.

WDPBRec

When you call the routines that open, close, and get information about working directories, you'll use the following six additional fields after the standard eight fields in the parameter block record WDPBRec:

```
filler1:      INTEGER;    {not used}
ioWDIndex:    INTEGER;    {index}
ioWDProcID:   LONGINT;    {working directory user identifier}
ioWDVRefNum: INTEGER;     {working directory's volume reference number}
filler2:      ARRAY[1..7] OF INTEGER;  {not used}
ioWDDirID:    LONGINT);   {working directory's directory ID}
```

IOWDIndex can be used with the function PBGetWDInfo to index through the current working directories.

IOWDProcID is an identifier that's used to distinguish between working directories set up by different users; you should use the application's signature (discussed in the Finder Interface chapter) as the ioWDProcID.

Routine Descriptions

Each routine description includes the low-level Pascal form of the call and the routine's assembly-language macro. A list of the parameter block fields used by the call is also given.

Assembly-language note: The field names given in these descriptions are those found in the Pascal parameter block records; see the summary at the end of this chapter for the names of the corresponding assembly-language offsets. (The names for some offsets differ from their Pascal equivalents, and in certain cases more than one name for the same offset is provided.)

The number next to each parameter name indicates the byte offset of the parameter from the start of the parameter block pointed to by register A0; only assembly-language programmers need be concerned with it. An arrow next to each parameter name indicates whether it's an input, output, or input/output parameter:

Arrow	**Meaning**
—>	Parameter is passed to the routine
<—	Parameter is returned by the routine
<->	Parameter is passed to and returned by the routine

Warning: You must pass something (even if it's NIL) for each of the parameters shown for a particular routine; if you don't, the File Manager may use garbage that's sitting at a particular offset.

Initializing the File I/O Queue

```
PROCEDURE FInitQueue;
```

Trap macro _InitQueue

FInitQueue clears all queued File Manager calls except the current one.

Accessing Volumes

To get the volume reference number of a volume, given the path reference number of a file on that volume, both Pascal and assembly-language programmers can call the high-level File Manager function GetVRefNum. Assembly-language programmers may prefer calling the function GetFCBInfo (described below in the section "Data Structures in Memory").

```
FUNCTION PBMountVol (paramBlock: ParmBlkPtr) : OSErr;
```

Trap macro _MountVol

Parameter block

<—	16	ioResult	word
<->	22	ioVRefNum	word

PBMountVol mounts the volume in the drive specified by ioVRefNum, and returns a volume reference number in ioVRefNum. If there are no volumes already mounted, this volume becomes the default volume. PBMountVol is always executed synchronously.

Note: When mounting hierarchical volumes, PBMountVol opens two files needed for maintaining file directory and file mapping information. PBMountVol can fail if there are no access paths available for these two files; it will return tmfoErr as its function result.

Result codes		
	noErr	No error
	badMDBErr	Bad master directory block
	extFSErr	External file system
	ioErr	I/O error
	memFullErr	Not enough room in heap zone
	noMacDskErr	Not a Macintosh disk
	nsDrvErr	No such drive
	paramErr	Bad drive number
	tmfoErr	Too many files open
	volOnLinErr	Volume already on-line

```
FUNCTION PBGetVInfo (paramBlock: ParmBlkPtr; async: BOOLEAN) :
     OSErr;
```

Trap macro _GetVolInfo

Parameter block

—>	12	ioCompletion	pointer
<—	16	ioResult	word
<->	18	ioNamePtr	pointer
<->	22	ioVRefNum	word
—>	28	ioVolIndex	word
<—	30	ioVCrDate	long word
<—	34	ioVLsBkUp	long word
<—	38	ioVAtrb	word
<—	40	ioVNmFls	word
<—	42	ioVDirSt	word
<—	44	ioVBlLn	word
<—	46	ioVNmAlBlks	word
<—	48	ioVAlBlkSiz	long word
<—	52	ioVClpSiz	long word
<—	56	ioAlBlSt	word
<—	58	ioVNxtFNum	long word
<—	62	ioVFrBlk	word

PBGetVInfo returns information about the specified volume. If ioVolIndex is positive, the File Manager attempts to use it to find the volume; for instance, if ioVolIndex is 2, the File Manager will attempt to access the second mounted volume. If ioVolIndex is negative, the File Manager uses ioNamePtr and ioVRefNum in the standard way (described in the section "Specifying Volumes, Directories, and Files") to determine which volume. If ioVolIndex is 0, the File Manager attempts to access the volume by using ioVRefNum only. The volume reference number is returned in ioVRefNum, and a pointer to the volume name is returned in ioNamePtr (unless ioNamePtr is NIL).

If a working directory reference number is passed in ioVRefNum (or if the default directory is a subdirectory), the number of files and directories in the specified directory (the directory's valence) will be returned in ioVNmFls. Also, the volume reference number won't be returned; ioVRefNum will still contain the working directory reference number.

Warning: IOVNmAlBlks and ioVFrBlks, which are actually unsigned integers, are clipped to 31744 ($7C00) regardless of the size of the volume.

Result codes	noErr	No error
	nsvErr	No such volume
	paramErr	No default volume

```
FUNCTION PBHGetVInfo (paramBlock: HParmBlkPtr; async: BOOLEAN) :
     OSErr;
```

Trap macro _HGetVInfo

Parameter block

—>	12	ioCompletion	pointer
<—	16	ioResult	word
<->	18	ioNamePtr	pointer
<->	22	ioVRefNum	word
—>	28	ioVolIndex	word
<—	30	ioVCrDate	long word
<—	34	ioVLsMod	long word
<—	38	ioVAtrb	word
<—	40	ioVNmFls	word
<—	42	ioVBitMap	word
<—	44	ioVAllocPtr	word
<—	46	ioVNmAlBlks	word
<—	48	ioVAlBlkSiz	long word
<—	52	ioVClpSiz	long word
<—	56	ioAlBlSt	word
<—	58	ioVNxtFNum	long word
<—	62	ioVFrBlk	word
<—	64	ioVSigWord	word
<—	66	ioVDrvInfo	word
<—	68	ioVDRefNum	word
<—	70	ioVFSID	word
<—	72	ioVBkUp	long word
<—	76	ioVSeqNum	word
<—	78	ioVWrCnt	long word
<—	82	ioVFilCnt	long word
<—	86	ioVDirCnt	long word
<—	90	ioVFndrInfo	32 bytes

PBHGetVInfo is similar in function to PBGetVInfo but returns a larger parameter block. In addition, PBHGetVInfo always returns the volume reference number in ioVRefNum (regardless of what was passed in). Also, ioVNmAlBlks and ioVFrBlks are not clipped as they are by PBGetVInfo.

Result codes	noErr	No error
	nsvErr	No such volume
	paramErr	No default volume

```
FUNCTION PBSetVInfo (paramBlock: HParmBlkPtr; async: BOOLEAN) :
     OSErr;
```

Trap macro _SetVolInfo

Parameter block

—>	12	ioCompletion	pointer
<—	16	ioResult	word
—>	18	ioNamePtr	pointer
—>	22	ioVRefNum	word
—>	30	ioVCrDate	long word
—>	34	ioVLsMod	long word
—>	38	ioVAtrb	word
—>	52	ioVClpSiz	long word
—>	72	ioVBkUp	long word
—>	76	ioVSeqNum	word
—>	90	ioVFndrInfo	32 bytes

PBSetVInfo lets you modify information about volumes. A pointer to a new name for the volume can be specified in ioNamePtr. The date and time of the volume's creation and modification can be set with ioVCrDate and ioVLsMod respectively. Only bit 15 of ioVAtrb can be changed; setting it locks the volume.

Note: The volume cannot be specified by name; you must use either the volume reference number or the drive number.

Warning: PBSetVInfo operates *only* with the hierarchical version of the File Manager; if used on a Macintosh equipped only with the 64K ROM version of the File Manager, it will generate a system error.

Result codes	noErr	No error
	nsvErr	No such volume
	paramErr	No default volume

```
FUNCTION PBGetVol (paramBlock: ParmBlkPtr; async: BOOLEAN) : OSErr;
```

Trap macro _GetVol

Parameter block

—>	12	ioCompletion	pointer
<—	16	ioResult	word
<—	18	ioNamePtr	pointer
<—	22	ioVRefNum	word

PBGetVol returns a pointer to the name of the default volume in ioNamePtr (unless ioNamePtr is NIL) and its volume reference number in ioVRefNum. If a default directory was set with a previous PBSetVol call, a pointer to its name will be returned in ioNamePtr and its working directory reference number in ioVRefNum.

Result codes	noErr	No error
	nsvErr	No default volume

```
FUNCTION PBHGetVol (paramBlock: WDPBPtr; async: BOOLEAN) : OSErr;
```

Trap macro _HGetVol

Parameter block

—>	12	ioCompletion	pointer
<—	16	ioResult	word
<—	18	ioNamePtr	pointer
<—	22	ioVRefNum	word
<—	28	ioWDProcID	long word
<—	32	ioWDVRefNum	word
<—	48	ioWDDirID	long word

PBHGetVol returns the default volume and directory last set by either a PBSetVol or a PBHSetVol call. The reference number of the default volume is returned in ioVRefNum.

Warning: IOVRefNum will return a working directory reference number (instead of the volume reference number) if, in the last call to PBSetVol or PBHSetVol, a working directory reference number was passed in this field.

The volume reference number of the volume on which the default directory exists is returned in ioWDVRefNum. The directory ID of the default directory is returned in ioWDDirID.

Result codes	noErr	No error
	nsvErr	No default volume

```
FUNCTION PBSetVol (paramBlock: ParmBlkPtr; async: BOOLEAN) : OSErr;
```

Trap macro _SetVol

Parameter block

—>	12	ioCompletion	pointer
<—	16	ioResult	word
—>	18	ioNamePtr	pointer
—>	22	ioVRefNum	word

PBSetVol sets the default volume to the mounted volume specified by ioNamePtr or ioVRefNum. On hierarchical volumes, PBSetVol also sets the root directory as the default directory.

Result codes	noErr	No error
	bdNamErr	Bad volume name
	nsvErr	No such volume
	paramErr	No default volume

```
FUNCTION PBHSetVol (paramBlock: WDPBPtr; async: BOOLEAN) : OSErr;
```

Trap macro _HSetVol

Parameter block

—>	12	ioCompletion	pointer
<—	16	ioResult	word
—>	18	ioNamePtr	pointer
—>	22	ioVRefNum	word
—>	48	ioWDDirID	long word

PBHSetVol sets both the default volume and the default directory. The default directory to be used can be specified by either a volume reference number or a working directory reference number in ioVRefNum, a directory ID in ioWDDirID, or a pointer to a pathname (possibly NIL) in ioNamePtr.

Note: Both the default volume *and* the default directory are used in calls made with no volume name and a volume reference number of zero.

Result codes		
	noErr	No error
	nsvErr	No default volume

```
FUNCTION PBFlushVol (paramBlock: ParmBlkPtr; async: BOOLEAN) :
     OSErr;
```

Trap macro _FlushVol

Parameter block

—>	12	ioCompletion	pointer
<—	16	ioResult	word
—>	18	ioNamePtr	pointer
—>	22	ioVRefNum	word

On the volume specified by ioNamePtr or ioVRefNum, PBFlushVol writes descriptive information about the volume, the contents of the associated volume buffer, and all access path buffers for the volume (if they've changed since the last time PBFlushVol was called).

Note: The date and time of the last modification to the volume are set when the modification is made, not when the volume is flushed.

Result codes		
	noErr	No error
	bdNamErr	Bad volume name
	extFSErr	External file system
	ioErr	I/O error
	nsDrvErr	No such drive
	nsvErr	No such volume
	paramErr	No default volume

```
FUNCTION PBUnmountVol (paramBlock: ParmBlkPtr) : OSErr;
```

Trap macro _UnmountVol

Parameter block

<—	16	ioResult	word
—>	18	ioNamePtr	pointer
—>	22	ioVRefNum	word

PBUnmountVol unmounts the volume specified by ioNamePtr or ioVRefNum, by calling PBFlushVol to flush the volume, closing all open files on the volume, and releasing the memory used for the volume. PBUnmountVol is always executed synchronously.

Warning: Don't unmount the startup volume.

Note: Unmounting a volume does not close working directories; to release the memory allocated to a working directory, call PBCloseWD.

Result codes		
	noErr	No error
	bdNamErr	Bad volume name
	extFSErr	External file system
	ioErr	I/O error
	nsDrvErr	No such drive
	nsvErr	No such volume
	paramErr	No default volume

```
FUNCTION PBOffLine (paramBlock: ParmBlkPtr) : OSErr;
```

Trap macro _OffLine

Parameter block

—>	12	ioCompletion	pointer
<—	16	ioResult	word
—>	18	ioNamePtr	pointer
—>	22	ioVRefNum	word

PBOffLine places off-line the volume specified by ioNamePtr or ioVRefNum, by calling PBFlushVol to flush the volume and releasing all the memory used for the volume except for the volume control block. PBOffLine is always executed synchronously.

Result codes		
	noErr	No error
	bdNamErr	Bad volume name
	extFSErr	External file system
	ioErr	I/O error
	nsDrvErr	No such drive
	nsvErr	No such volume
	paramErr	No default volume

```
FUNCTION PBEject (paramBlock: ParmBlkPtr) : OSErr;
```

Trap macro _Eject

Parameter block

—>	12	ioCompletion	pointer
<—	16	ioResult	word
—>	18	ioNamePtr	pointer
—>	22	ioVRefNum	word

PBEject flushes the volume specified by ioNamePtr or ioVRefNum, places it off-line, and then ejects the volume.

Assembly-language note: You may invoke the macro _Eject asynchronously; the first part of the call is executed synchronously, and the actual ejection is executed asynchronously.

Result codes		
	noErr	No error
	bdNamErr	Bad volume name
	extFSErr	External file system
	ioErr	I/O error
	nsDrvErr	No such drive
	nsvErr	No such volume
	paramErr	No default volume

Accessing Files

```
FUNCTION PBOpen (paramBlock: ParmBlkPtr; async: BOOLEAN) : OSErr;
```

Trap macro _Open

Parameter block

—>	12	ioCompletion	pointer
<—	16	ioResult	word
—>	18	ioNamePtr	pointer
—>	22	ioVRefNum	word
<—	24	ioRefNum	word
—>	26	ioVersNum	byte
—>	27	ioPermssn	byte
—>	28	ioMisc	pointer

PBOpen creates an access path to the file having the name pointed to by ioNamePtr (and on flat volumes, the version number ioVersNum) on the volume specified by ioVRefNum. A path reference number is returned in ioRefNum.

IOMisc either points to a portion of memory (522 bytes) to be used as the access path's buffer, or is NIL if you want the volume buffer to be used instead.

Warning: All access paths to a single file that's opened multiple times should share the same buffer so that they will read and write the same data.

IOPermssn specifies the path's read/write permission. A path can be opened for writing even if it accesses a file on a locked volume, and an error won't be returned until a PBWrite, PBSetEOF, or PBAllocate call is made.

If you attempt to open a locked file for writing, PBOpen will return permErr as its function result. If you request exclusive read/write permission but another access path already has write permission (whether write only, exclusive read/write, or shared read/write), PBOpen will return the reference number of the existing access path in ioRefNum and opWrErr as its function result. Similarly, if you request shared read/write permission but another access path already has exclusive read/write permission, PBOpen will return the reference number of the access path in ioRefNum and opWrErr as its function result.

Result codes		
	noErr	No error
	bdNamErr	Bad file name
	extFSErr	External file system
	fnfErr	File not found
	ioErr	I/O error
	nsvErr	No such volume
	opWrErr	File already open for writing
	permErr	Attempt to open locked file for writing
	tmfoErr	Too many files open

```
FUNCTION PBHOpen (paramBlock: HParmBlkPtr; async: BOOLEAN) : OSErr;
```

Trap macro _HOpen

Parameter block

—>	12	ioCompletion	pointer
<—	16	ioResult	word
—>	18	ioNamePtr	pointer
—>	22	ioVRefNum	word
<—	24	ioRefNum	word
—>	27	ioPermssn	byte
—>	28	ioMisc	pointer
—>	48	ioDirID	long word

PBHOpen is identical to PBOpen except that it accepts a directory ID in ioDirID.

Result codes		
	noErr	No error
	bdNamErr	Bad file name
	dirNFErr	Directory not found or incomplete pathname
	extFSErr	External file system
	fnfErr	File not found
	ioErr	I/O error
	nsvErr	No such volume
	opWrErr	File already open for writing
	permErr	Attempt to open locked file for writing
	tmfoErr	Too many files open

```
FUNCTION PBOpenRF (paramBlock: ParmBlkPtr; async: BOOLEAN) : OSErr;
```

Trap macro _OpenRF

Parameter block

—>	12	ioCompletion	pointer
<—	16	ioResult	word
—>	18	ioNamePtr	pointer
—>	22	ioVRefNum	word
<—	24	ioRefNum	word
—>	26	ioVersNum	byte
—>	27	ioPermssn	byte
—>	28	ioMisc	pointer

PBOpenRF is identical to PBOpen, except that it opens the file's resource fork instead of its data fork.

Note: Normally you should access a file's resource fork through the routines of the Resource Manager rather than the File Manager. PBOpenRF doesn't read the resource map into memory; it's really only useful for block-level operations such as copying files.

Result codes

noErr	No error
bdNamErr	Bad file name
extFSErr	External file system
fnfErr	File not found
ioErr	I/O error
nsvErr	No such volume
opWrErr	File already open for writing
permErr	Attempt to open locked file for writing
tmfoErr	Too many files open

```
FUNCTION PBHOpenRF (paramBlock: HParmBlkPtr; async: BOOLEAN) :
     OSErr;
```

Trap macro _HOpenRF

Parameter block

—>	12	ioCompletion	pointer
<—	16	ioResult	word
—>	18	ioNamePtr	pointer
—>	22	ioVRefNum	word
<—	24	ioRefNum	word
—>	27	ioPermssn	byte
—>	28	ioMisc	pointer
—>	48	ioDirID	long word

PBHOpenRF is identical to PBOpenRF except that it accepts a directory ID in ioDirID.

Result codes		
	noErr	No error
	bdNamErr	Bad file name
	dirNFErr	Directory not found or incomplete pathname
	extFSErr	External file system
	fnfErr	File not found
	ioErr	I/O error
	nsvErr	No such volume
	opWrErr	File already open for writing
	permErr	Attempt to open locked file for writing
	tmfoErr	Too many files open

```
FUNCTION PBLockRange (paramBlock: ParmBlkPtr; async: BOOLEAN) :
     OSErr;
```

Trap macro _LockRng

Parameter block

—>	12	ioCompletion	pointer
<—	16	ioResult	word
—>	24	ioRefNum	word
—>	36	ioReqCount	long word
—>	44	ioPosMode	word
—>	46	ioPosOffset	long word

On a file opened with a shared read/write permission, PBLockRange is used in conjunction with PBRead and PBWrite to lock a certain portion of the file. PBLockRange uses the same parameters as both PBRead and PBWrite; by calling it immediately before PBRead, you can use the information present in the parameter block for the PBRead call.

When you're finished with the data (typically after a call to PBWrite), be sure to call PBUnlockRange to free up that portion of the file for subsequent PBRead calls.

Warning: PBLockRange operates *only* with the hierarchical version of the File Manager; if used on a Macintosh equipped only with the 64K ROM version of the File Manager, it will generate a system error.

Result codes		
	noErr	No error
	eofErr	End-of-file
	extFSErr	External file system
	fnOpnErr	File not open
	ioErr	I/O error
	paramErr	Negative ioReqCount
	rfNumErr	Bad reference number

```
FUNCTION PBUnlockRange (paramBlock: ParmBlkPtr; async: BOOLEAN) :
    OSErr;
```

Trap macro _UnlockRng

Parameter block

—>	12	ioCompletion	pointer
<—	16	ioResult	word
—>	24	ioRefNum	word
—>	36	ioReqCount	long word
—>	44	ioPosMode	word
—>	46	ioPosOffset	long word

PBUnlockRange is used in conjunction with PBRead and PBWrite to unlock a certain portion of a file that you locked with PBLockRange.

Warning: PBUnlockRange operates *only* with the hierarchical version of the File Manager; if used on a Macintosh equipped only with the 64K ROM version of the File Manager, it will generate a system error.

Result codes

noErr	No error
eofErr	End-of-file
extFSErr	External file system
fnOpnErr	File not open
ioErr	I/O error
paramErr	Negative ioReqCount
rfNumErr	Bad reference number

```
FUNCTION PBRead (paramBlock: ParmBlkPtr; async: BOOLEAN) : OSErr;
```

Trap macro _Read

Parameter block

—>	12	ioCompletion	pointer
<—	16	ioResult	word
—>	24	ioRefNum	word
—>	32	ioBuffer	pointer
—>	36	ioReqCount	long word
<—	40	ioActCount	long word
—>	44	ioPosMode	word
<->	46	ioPosOffset	long word

PBRead attempts to read ioReqCount bytes from the open file whose access path is specified by ioRefNum, and transfer them to the data buffer pointed to by ioBuffer. The position of the mark is specified by ioPosMode and ioPosOffset. If you try to read past the logical end-of-file, PBRead moves the mark to the end-of-file and returns eofErr as its function result. After the read is completed, the mark is returned in ioPosOffset and the number of bytes actually read is returned in ioActCount.

Result codes	noErr	No error
	eofErr	End-of-file
	extFSErr	External file system
	fnOpnErr	File not open
	ioErr	I/O error
	paramErr	Negative ioReqCount
	rfNumErr	Bad reference number

```
FUNCTION PBWrite (paramBlock: ParmBlkPtr; async: BOOLEAN) : OSErr;
```

Trap macro _Write

Parameter block

—>	12	ioCompletion	pointer
<—	16	ioResult	word
—>	24	ioRefNum	word
—>	32	ioBuffer	pointer
—>	36	ioReqCount	long word
<—	40	ioActCount	long word
—>	44	ioPosMode	word
<–>	46	ioPosOffset	long word

PBWrite takes ioReqCount bytes from the buffer pointed to by ioBuffer and attempts to write them to the open file whose access path is specified by ioRefNum. The position of the mark is specified by ioPosMode and ioPosOffset. After the write is completed, the mark is returned in ioPosOffset and the number of bytes actually written is returned in ioActCount.

Result codes	noErr	No error
	dskFulErr	Disk full
	fLckdErr	File locked
	fnOpnErr	File not open
	ioErr	I/O error
	paramErr	Negative ioReqCount
	posErr	Attempt to position before start of file
	rfNumErr	Bad reference number
	vLckdErr	Software volume lock
	wPrErr	Hardware volume lock
	wrPermErr	Read/write permission doesn't allow writing

```
FUNCTION PBGetFPos (paramBlock: ParmBlkPtr; async: BOOLEAN) :
     OSErr;
```

Trap macro _GetFPos

Parameter block

—>	12	ioCompletion	pointer
<—	16	ioResult	word
—>	24	ioRefNum	word
<—	36	ioReqCount	long word
<—	40	ioActCount	long word
<—	44	ioPosMode	word
<—	46	ioPosOffset	long word

PBGetFPos returns, in ioPosOffset, the mark of the open file whose access path is specified by ioRefNum. It sets ioReqCount, ioActCount, and ioPosMode to 0.

Result codes		
	noErr	No error
	extFSErr	External file system
	fnOpnErr	File not open
	gfpErr	Error during GetFPos
	ioErr	I/O error
	rfNumErr	Bad reference number

```
FUNCTION PBSetFPos (paramBlock: ParmBlkPtr; async: BOOLEAN) : OSErr;
```

Trap macro _SetFPos

Parameter block

—>	12	ioCompletion	pointer
<—	16	ioResult	word
—>	24	ioRefNum	word
—>	44	ioPosMode	word
<—>	46	ioPosOffset	long word

PBSetFPos sets the mark of the open file whose access path is specified by ioRefNum to the position specified by ioPosMode and ioPosOffset. The position at which the mark is actually set is returned in ioPosOffset. If you try to set the mark past the logical end-of-file, PBSetFPos moves the mark to the end-of-file and returns eofErr as its function result.

Result codes		
	noErr	No error
	eofErr	End-of-file
	extFSErr	External file system
	fnOpnErr	File not open
	ioErr	I/O error
	posErr	Attempt to position before start of file
	rfNumErr	Bad reference number

```
FUNCTION PBGetEOF (paramBlock: ParmBlkPtr; async: BOOLEAN) : OSErr;
```

Trap macro _GetEOF

Parameter block

—>	12	ioCompletion	pointer
<—	16	ioResult	word
—>	24	ioRefNum	word
<—	28	ioMisc	long word

PBGetEOF returns, in ioMisc, the logical end-of-file of the open file whose access path is specified by ioRefNum.

Result codes		
	noErr	No error
	extFSErr	External file system
	fnOpnErr	File not open
	ioErr	I/O error
	rfNumErr	Bad reference number

```
FUNCTION PBSetEOF (paramBlock: ParmBlkPtr; async: BOOLEAN) : OSErr;
```

Trap macro _SetEOF

Parameter block

—>	12	ioCompletion	pointer
<—	16	ioResult	word
—>	24	ioRefNum	word
—>	28	ioMisc	long word

PBSetEOF sets the logical end-of-file of the open file, whose access path is specified by ioRefNum, to ioMisc. If you attempt to set the logical end-of-file beyond the physical end-of-file, another allocation block is added to the file; if there isn't enough space on the volume, no change is made, and PBSetEOF returns dskFulErr as its function result. If ioMisc is 0, all space occupied by the file on the volume is released.

Result codes		
	noErr	No error
	dskFulErr	Disk full
	extFSErr	External file system
	fLckdErr	File locked
	fnOpnErr	File not open
	ioErr	I/O error
	rfNumErr	Bad reference number
	vLckdErr	Software volume lock
	wPrErr	Hardware volume lock
	wrPermErr	Read/write permission doesn't allow writing

```
FUNCTION PBAllocate (paramBlock: ParmBlkPtr; async: BOOLEAN) :
     OSErr;
```

Trap macro _Allocate

Parameter block

—>	12	ioCompletion	pointer
<—	16	ioResult	word
—>	24	ioRefNum	word
—>	36	ioReqCount	long word
<—	40	ioActCount	long word

PBAllocate adds ioReqCount bytes to the open file whose access path is specified by ioRefNum, and sets the physical end-of-file to one byte beyond the last block allocated. The number of bytes actually allocated is rounded up to the nearest multiple of the allocation block size, and returned in ioActCount. If there isn't enough empty space on the volume to satisfy the allocation request, PBAllocate allocates the rest of the space on the volume and returns dskFulErr as its function result.

Note: Even if the total number of requested bytes is unavailable, PBAllocate will allocate whatever space, contiguous or not, is available. To force the allocation of the entire requested space as a contiguous piece, call PBAllocContig instead.

Result codes		
	noErr	No error
	dskFulErr	Disk full
	fLckdErr	File locked
	fnOpnErr	File not open
	ioErr	I/O error
	rfNumErr	Bad reference number
	vLckdErr	Software volume lock
	wPrErr	Hardware volume lock
	wrPermErr	Read/write permission doesn't allow writing

```
FUNCTION PBAllocContig (paramBlock: ParmBlkPtr; async: BOOLEAN) :
     OSErr;
```

Trap macro _AllocContig

Parameter block

—>	12	ioCompletion	pointer
<—	16	ioResult	word
—>	24	ioRefNum	word
—>	36	ioReqCount	long word
<—	40	ioActCount	long word

PBAllocContig is identical to PBAllocate except that if there isn't enough contiguous empty space on the volume to satisfy the allocation request, PBAllocContig will do nothing and will return dskFulErr as its function result. If you want to allocate whatever space is available, even when the entire request cannot be filled as a contiguous piece, call PBAllocate instead.

Result codes	noErr	No error
	dskFulErr	Disk full
	fLckdErr	File locked
	fnOpnErr	File not open
	ioErr	I/O error
	rfNumErr	Bad reference number
	vLckdErr	Software volume lock
	wPrErr	Hardware volume lock
	wrPermErr	Read/write permission doesn't allow writing

```
FUNCTION PBFlushFile (paramBlock: ParmBlkPtr; async: BOOLEAN) :
     OSErr;
```

Trap macro _FlushFile

Parameter block

—>	12	ioCompletion	pointer
<—	16	ioResult	word
—>	24	ioRefNum	word

PBFlushFile writes the contents of the access path buffer indicated by ioRefNum to the volume, and updates the file's entry in the file directory (or in the file catalog, in the case of hierarchical volumes).

Warning: Some information stored on the volume won't be correct until PBFlushVol is called.

Result codes	noErr	No error
	extFSErr	External file system
	fnfErr	File not found
	fnOpnErr	File not open
	ioErr	I/O error
	nsvErr	No such volume
	rfNumErr	Bad reference number

```
FUNCTION PBClose (paramBlock: ParmBlkPtr; async: BOOLEAN) : OSErr;
```

Trap macro _Close

Parameter block

—>	12	ioCompletion	pointer
<—	16	ioResult	word
—>	24	ioRefNum	word

PBClose writes the contents of the access path buffer specified by ioRefNum to the volume and removes the access path.

Warning: Some information stored on the volume won't be correct until PBFlushVol is called.

Result codes	noErr	No error
	extFSErr	External file system
	fnfErr	File not found
	fnOpnErr	File not open
	ioErr	I/O error
	nsvErr	No such volume
	rfNumErr	Bad reference number

Creating and Deleting Files and Directories

```
FUNCTION PBCreate (paramBlock: ParmBlkPtr; async: BOOLEAN) : OSErr;
```

Trap macro _Create

Parameter block

—>	12	ioCompletion	pointer
<—	16	ioResult	word
—>	18	ioNamePtr	pointer
—>	22	ioVRefNum	word
—>	26	ioFVersNum	byte

PBCreate creates a new file (both forks) having the name pointed to by ioNamePtr (and on flat volumes, the version number ioVersNum) on the volume specified by ioVRefNum. The new file is unlocked and empty. The date and time of its creation and last modification are set to the current date and time. If the file created isn't temporary (that is, if it will exist after the application terminates), the application should call PBSetFInfo (after PBCreate) to fill in the information needed by the Finder.

Assembly-language note: If a desk accessory creates a file, it should always create it in the directory containing the system folder. The working directory reference number for this directory is stored in the global variable BootDrive; you can pass it in ioVRefNum.

Result codes	noErr	No error
	bdNamErr	Bad file name
	dupFNErr	Duplicate file name and version
	dirFulErr	File directory full
	extFSErr	External file system
	ioErr	I/O error
	nsvErr	No such volume
	vLckdErr	Software volume lock
	wPrErr	Hardware volume lock

```
FUNCTION PBHCreate (paramBlock: HParmBlkPtr; async: BOOLEAN) :
     OSErr;
```

Trap macro _HCreate

Parameter block

—>	12	ioCompletion	pointer
<—	16	ioResult	word
—>	18	ioNamePtr	pointer
—>	22	ioVRefNum	word
—>	48	ioDirID	long word

PBHCreate is identical to PBCreate except that it accepts a directory ID in ioDirID.

Note: To create a directory instead of a file, call PBDirCreate.

Result codes		
	noErr	No error
	bdNamErr	Bad file name
	dupFNErr	Duplicate file name and version
	dirFulErr	File directory full
	dirNFErr	Directory not found or incomplete pathname
	extFSErr	External file system
	ioErr	I/O error
	nsvErr	No such volume
	vLckdErr	Software volume lock
	wPrErr	Hardware volume lock

```
FUNCTION PBDirCreate (paramBlock: HParmBlkPtr; async: BOOLEAN):
     OSErr;
```

Trap macro _DirCreate

Parameter block

—>	12	ioCompletion	pointer
<—	16	ioResult	word
<–>	18	ioNamePtr	pointer
—>	22	ioVRefNum	word
<–>	48	ioDirID	long word

PBDirCreate is identical to PBHCreate except that it creates a new directory instead of a file. You can specify the parent of the directory to be created in ioDirID; if it's 0, the new directory will be placed in the root directory. The directory ID of the new directory is returned in ioDirID.

Warning: PBDirCreate operates *only* with the hierarchical version of the File Manager; if used on a Macintosh equipped only with the 64K ROM version of the File Manager, it will generate a system error.

Result codes	noErr	No error
	bdNamErr	Bad file name
	dupFNErr	Duplicate file name and version
	dirFulErr	File directory full
	dirNFErr	Directory not found or incomplete pathname
	extFSErr	External file system
	ioErr	I/O error
	nsvErr	No such volume
	vLckdErr	Software volume lock
	wPrErr	Hardware volume lock

```
FUNCTION PBDelete (paramBlock: ParmBlkPtr; async: BOOLEAN) : OSErr;
```

Trap macro _Delete

Parameter block

—>	12	ioCompletion	pointer
<—	16	ioResult	word
—>	18	ioNamcPtr	pointer
—>	22	ioVRefNum	word
—>	26	ioFVersNum	byte

PBDelete removes the closed file having the name pointed to by ioNamePtr (and on flat volumes, the version number ioVersNum) from the volume pointed to by ioVRefNum. PBHDelete can be used to delete an empty directory as well.

Note: This function will delete *both* forks of the file.

Result codes	noErr	No error
	bdNamErr	Bad file name
	extFSErr	External file system
	fBsyErr	File busy, directory not empty, or working directory control block open
	fLckdErr	File locked
	fnfErr	File not found
	nsvErr	No such volume
	ioErr	I/O error
	vLckdErr	Software volume lock
	wPrErr	Hardware volume lock

```
FUNCTION PBHDelete (paramBlock: HParmBlkPtr; async: BOOLEAN) :
     OSErr;
```

Trap macro _HDelete

Parameter block

—>	12	ioCompletion	pointer
<—	16	ioResult	word
—>	18	ioNamePtr	pointer
—>	22	ioVRefNum	word
—>	48	ioDirID	long word

PBHDelete is identical to PBDelete except that it accepts a directory ID in ioDirID. PBHDelete can be used to delete an empty directory as well.

Result codes	noErr	No error
	bdNamErr	Bad file name
	dirNFErr	Directory not found or incomplete pathname
	extFSErr	External file system
	fBsyErr	File busy, directory not empty, or working directory control block open
	fLckdErr	File locked
	fnfErr	File not found
	nsvErr	No such volume
	ioErr	I/O error
	vLckdErr	Software volume lock
	wPrErr	Hardware volume lock

Changing Information About Files and Directories

```
FUNCTION PBGetFInfo (paramBlock: ParmBlkPtr; async: BOOLEAN) :
     OSErr;
```

Trap macro _GetFileInfo

Parameter block

—>	12	ioCompletion	pointer
<—	16	ioResult	word
<->	18	ioNamePtr	pointer
—>	22	ioVRefNum	word
<—	24	ioFRefNum	word
—>	26	ioFVersNum	byte
—>	28	ioFDirIndex	word
<—	30	ioFlAttrib	byte
<—	31	ioFlVersNum	byte
<—	32	ioFlFndrInfo	16 bytes
<—	48	ioFlNum	long word
<—	52	ioFlStBlk	word
<—	54	ioFlLgLen	long word
<—	58	ioFlPyLen	long word
<—	62	ioFlRStBlk	word
<—	64	ioFlRLgLen	long word
<—	68	ioFlRPyLen	long word
<—	72	ioFlCrDat	long word
<—	76	ioFlMdDat	long word

PBGetFInfo returns information about the specified file. If ioFDirIndex is positive, the File Manager returns information about the file whose directory index is ioFDirIndex on the volume specified by ioVRefNum. (See the section "Data Organization on Volumes" if you're interested in using this method.)

Note: If a working directory reference number is specified in ioVRefNum, the File Manager returns information about the file whose directory index is ioFDirIndex in the specified directory.

If ioFDirIndex is negative or 0, the File Manager returns information about the file having the name pointed to by ioNamePtr (and on flat volumes, the version number ioFVersNum) on the volume specified by ioVRefNum. If the file is open, the reference number of the first access path found is returned in ioFRefNum, and the name of the file is returned in ioNamePtr (unless ioNamePtr is NIL).

Result codes	noErr	No error
	bdNamErr	Bad file name
	extFSErr	External file system
	fnfErr	File not found
	ioErr	I/O error
	nsvErr	No such volume
	paramErr	No default volume

```
FUNCTION PBHGetFInfo (paramBlock: HParmBlkPtr; async: BOOLEAN) :
     OSErr;
```

Trap macro _HGetFileInfo

Parameter block

—>	12	ioCompletion	pointer
<—	16	ioResult	word
<->	18	ioNamePtr	pointer
—>	22	ioVRefNum	word
<—	24	ioFRefNum	word
—>	28	ioFDirIndex	word
<—	30	ioFlAttrib	byte
<—	32	ioFlFndrInfo	16 bytes
<->	48	ioDirID	long word
<—	52	ioFlStBlk	word
<—	54	ioFlLgLen	long word
<—	58	ioFlPyLen	long word
<—	62	ioFlRStBlk	word
<—	64	ioFlRLgLen	long word
<—	68	ioFlRPyLen	long word
<—	72	ioFlCrDat	long word
<—	76	ioFlMdDat	long word

PBHGetFInfo is identical to PBGetFInfo except that it accepts a directory ID in ioDirID.

Result codes	noErr	No error
	bdNamErr	Bad file name
	dirNFErr	Directory not found or incomplete pathname
	extFSErr	External file system
	fnfErr	File not found
	ioErr	I/O error
	nsvErr	No such volume
	paramErr	No default volume

```
FUNCTION PBSetFInfo (paramBlock: ParmBlkPtr; async: BOOLEAN) :
     OSErr;
```

Trap macro _SetFileInfo

Parameter block

—>	12	ioCompletion	pointer
<—	16	ioResult	word
—>	18	ioNamePtr	pointer
—>	22	ioVRefNum	word
—>	26	ioFVersNum	byte
—>	32	ioFlFndrInfo	16 bytes
—>	72	ioFlCrDat	long word
—>	76	ioFlMdDat	long word

PBSetFInfo sets information (including the date and time of creation and modification, and information needed by the Finder) about the file having the name pointed to by ioNamePtr (and on flat volumes, the version number ioFVersNum) on the volume specified by ioVRefNum. You should call PBGetFInfo just before PBSetFInfo, so the current information is present in the parameter block.

Result codes		
	noErr	No error
	bdNamErr	Bad file name
	extFSErr	External file system
	fLckdErr	File locked
	fnfErr	File not found
	ioErr	I/O error
	nsvErr	No such volume
	vLckdErr	Software volume lock
	wPrErr	Hardware volume lock

```
FUNCTION PBHSetFInfo (paramBlock: HParmBlkPtr; async: BOOLEAN) :
     OSErr;
```

Trap macro _HSetFileInfo

Parameter block

—>	12	ioCompletion	pointer
<—	16	ioResult	word
—>	18	ioNamePtr	pointer
—>	22	ioVRefNum	word
—>	32	ioFlFndrInfo	16 bytes
—>	48	ioDirID	long word
—>	72	ioFlCrDat	long word
—>	76	ioFlMdDat	long word

PBHSetFInfo is identical to PBSetFInfo except that it accepts a directory ID in ioDirID.

Result codes	noErr	No error
	bdNamErr	Bad file name
	dirNFErr	Directory not found or incomplete pathname
	extFSErr	External file system
	fLckdErr	File locked
	fnfErr	File not found
	ioErr	I/O error
	nsvErr	No such volume
	vLckdErr	Software volume lock
	wPrErr	Hardware volume lock


```
FUNCTION PBSetFLock (paramBlock: ParmBlkPtr; async: BOOLEAN) :
     OSErr;
```

Trap macro _SetFilLock

Parameter block

—>	12	ioCompletion	pointer
<—	16	ioResult	word
—>	18	ioNamePtr	pointer
—>	22	ioVRefNum	word
—>	26	ioFVersNum	byte

PBSetFLock locks the file having the name pointed to by ioNamePtr (and on flat volumes, the version number ioFVersNum) on the volume specified by ioVRefNum. Access paths currently in use aren't affected.

Result codes	noErr	No error
	extFSErr	External file system
	fnfErr	File not found
	ioErr	I/O error
	nsvErr	No such volume
	vLckdErr	Software volume lock
	wPrErr	Hardware volume lock

```
FUNCTION PBHSetFLock (paramBlock: HParmBlkPtr; async: BOOLEAN) :
     OSErr;
```

Trap macro _HSetFLock

Parameter block

—>	12	ioCompletion	pointer
<—	16	ioResult	word
—>	18	ioNamePtr	pointer
—>	22	ioVRefNum	word
—>	48	ioDirID	long word

PBHSetFLock is identical to PBSetFLock except that it accepts a directory ID in ioDirID.

Result codes	noErr	No error
	dirNFErr	Directory not found or incomplete pathname
	extFSErr	External file system
	fnfErr	File not found
	ioErr	I/O error
	nsvErr	No such volume
	vLckdErr	Software volume lock
	wPrErr	Hardware volume lock

```
FUNCTION PBRstFLock (paramBlock: ParmBlkPtr; async: BOOLEAN) :
     OSErr;
```

Trap macro _RstFilLock

Parameter block

—>	12	ioCompletion	pointer
<—	16	ioResult	word
—>	18	ioNamePtr	pointer
—>	22	ioVRefNum	word
—>	26	ioFVersNum	byte

PBRstFLock unlocks the file having the name pointed to by ioNamePtr (and on flat volumes, the version number ioFVersNum) on the volume specified by ioVRefNum. Access paths currently in use aren't affected.

Result codes	noErr	No error
	extFSErr	External file system
	fnfErr	File not found
	ioErr	I/O error
	nsvErr	No such volume
	vLckdErr	Software volume lock
	wPrErr	Hardware volume lock

```
FUNCTION PBHRstFLock (paramBlock: HParmBlkPtr; async: BOOLEAN) :
     OSErr;
```

Trap macro _HRstFLock

Parameter block

—>	12	ioCompletion	pointer
<—	16	ioResult	word
—>	18	ioNamePtr	pointer
—>	22	ioVRefNum	word
—>	48	ioDirID	long word

PBHRstFLock is identical to PBRstFLock except that it accepts a directory ID in ioDirID.

Result codes	noErr	No error
	dirNFErr	Directory not found or incomplete pathname
	extFSErr	External file system
	fnfErr	File not found
	ioErr	I/O error
	nsvErr	No such volume
	vLckdErr	Software volume lock
	wPrErr	Hardware volume lock


```
FUNCTION PBSetFVers (paramBlock: ParmBlkPtr; async: BOOLEAN) :
      OSErr;
```

Trap macro _SetFilType

Parameter block

—>	12	ioCompletion	pointer
<—	16	ioResult	word
—>	18	ioNamePtr	pointer
—>	22	ioVRefNum	word
—>	26	ioVersNum	byte
—>	28	ioMisc	byte

PBSetFVers has no effect on hierarchical volumes. On flat volumes, PBSetFVers changes the version number of the file having the name pointed to by ioNamePtr and version number ioVersNum, on the volume specified by ioVRefNum, to the version number stored in the high-order byte of ioMisc. Access paths currently in use aren't affected.

Result codes	noErr	No error
	bdNamErr	Bad file name
	dupFNErr	Duplicate file name and version
	extFSErr	External file system
	fLckdErr	File locked
	fnfErr	File not found
	nsvErr	No such volume
	ioErr	I/O error
	paramErr	No default volume
	vLckdErr	Software volume lock
	wPrErr	Hardware volume lock
	wrgVolTypErr	Attempt to perform hierarchical operation on a flat volume

```
FUNCTION PBRename (paramBlock: ParmBlkPtr; async: BOOLEAN) : OSErr;
```

Trap macro _Rename

Parameter block

—>	12	ioCompletion	pointer
<—	16	ioResult	word
—>	18	ioNamePtr	pointer
—>	22	ioVRefNum	word
—>	26	ioVersNum	byte
—>	28	ioMisc	pointer

Given a pointer to a file name in ioNamePtr (and on flat volumes, a version number in ioVersNum), PBRename changes the name of the file to the name pointed to by ioMisc. (If the name pointed to by ioNamePtr contains one or more colons, so must the name pointed to by ioMisc.) Access paths currently in use aren't affected. Given a pointer to a volume name in ioNamePtr or a volume reference number in ioVRefNum, it changes the name of the volume to the name pointed to by ioMisc. If a volume to be renamed is specified by its volume reference number, ioNamePtr can be NIL.

Warning: If a volume to be renamed is specified by its volume name, be sure that it ends with a colon, or Rename will consider it a file name.

Result codes	noErr	No error
	bdNamErr	Bad file name
	dirFulErr	File directory full
	dupFNErr	Duplicate file name and version
	extFSErr	External file system
	fLckdErr	File locked
	fnfErr	File not found
	fsRnErr	Problem during rename
	ioErr	I/O error
	nsvErr	No such volume
	paramErr	No default volume
	vLckdErr	Software volume lock
	wPrErr	Hardware volume lock

```
FUNCTION PBHRename (paramBlock: HParmBlkPtr; async: BOOLEAN) :
     OSErr;
```

Trap macro _HRename

Parameter block

—>	12	ioCompletion	pointer
<—	16	ioResult	word
—>	18	ioNamePtr	pointer
—>	22	ioVRefNum	word
—>	28	ioMisc	pointer
—>	48	ioDirID	long word

PBHRename is identical to PBRename except that it accepts a directory ID in ioDirID and can be used to rename directories as well as files and volumes. Given a pointer to the name of a file or directory in ioNamePtr, PBHRename changes it to the name pointed to by ioMisc. Given a pointer to a volume name in ioNamePtr or a volume reference number in ioVRefNum, it changes the name of the volume to the name pointed to by ioMisc.

Warning: PBHRename cannot be used to change the directory a file is in.

Result codes	noErr	No error
	bdNamErr	Bad file name
	dirFulErr	File directory full
	dirNFErr	Directory not found or incomplete pathname
	dupFNErr	Duplicate file name and version
	extFSErr	External file system
	fLckdErr	File locked

fnfErr	File not found
fsRnErr	Problem during rename
ioErr	I/O error
nsvErr	No such volume
paramErr	No default volume
vLckdErr	Software volume lock
wPrErr	Hardware volume lock

Hierarchical Directory Routines

Warning: The routines described in this section operate *only* with the hierarchical version of the File Manager; if used on a Macintosh equipped only with the 64K ROM version of the File Manager, they will generate a system error.

```
FUNCTION PBGetCatInfo (paramBlock: CInfoPBPtr; async: BOOLEAN):
     OSErr;
```

Trap macro _GetCatInfo

Parameter block

Files:				Directories:			
—>	12	ioCompletion	pointer	—>	12	ioCompletion	pointer
<—	16	ioResult	word	<—	16	ioResult	word
<->	18	ioNamePtr	pointer	<->	18	ioNamePtr	pointer
—>	22	ioVRefNum	word	—>	22	ioVRefNum	word
<—	24	ioFRefNum	word	<—	24	ioFRefNum	word
—>	28	ioFDirIndex	word	—>	28	ioFDirIndex	word
<—	30	ioFlAttrib	byte	<—	30	ioFlAttrib	byte
<—	32	ioFlFndrInfo	16 bytes	<—	32	ioDrUsrWds	16 bytes
<->	48	ioDirID	long word	<->	48	ioDrDirID	long word
<—	52	ioFlStBlk	word	<—	52	ioDrNmFls	word
<—	54	ioFlLgLen	long word				
<—	58	ioFlPyLen	long word				
<—	62	ioFlRStBlk	word				
<—	64	ioFlRLgLen	long word				
<—	68	ioFlRPyLen	long word				
<—	72	ioFlCrDat	long word	<—	72	ioDrCrDat	long word
<—	76	ioFlMdDat	long word	<—	76	ioDrMdDat	long word
<—	80	ioFlBkDat	long word	<—	80	ioDrBkDat	long word
<—	84	ioFlXFndrInfo	16 bytes	<—	84	ioDrFndrInfo	16 bytes
<—	100	ioFlParID	long word	<—	100	ioDrParID	long word
<—	104	ioFlClpSiz	long word				

PBGetCatInfo gets information about the files and directories in a file catalog. To determine whether the information is for a file or a directory, test bit 4 of ioFlAttrib, as described in the section "CInfoPBRec". The information that's returned for files is shown in the left column, and the corresponding information for directories is shown in the right column.

If ioFDirIndex is positive, the File Manager returns information about the file or directory whose directory index is ioFDirIndex in the directory specified by ioVRefNum (this will be the root directory if a volume reference number is provided).

If ioFDirIndex is 0, the File Manager returns information about the file or directory specified by ioNamePtr, in the directory specified by ioVRefNum (again, this will be the root directory if a volume reference number is provided).

If ioFDirIndex is negative, the File Manager ignores ioNamePtr and returns information about the directory specified by ioDirID.

With files, PBGetCatInfo is similar to PBHGetFileInfo but returns some additional information. If the file is open, the reference number of the first access path found is returned in ioFRefNum, and the name of the file is returned in ioNamePtr (unless ioNamePtr is NIL).

Result codes	noErr	No error
	bdNamErr	Bad file name
	dirNFErr	Directory not found or incomplete pathname
	extFSErr	External file system
	fnfErr	File not found
	ioErr	I/O error
	nsvErr	No such volume
	paramErr	No default volume

```
FUNCTION PBSetCatInfo (paramBlock: CInfoPBPtr; async: BOOLEAN) :
     OSErr;
```

Trap macro   _SetCatInfo

Parameter block

Files:

—>	12	ioCompletion	pointer
<—	16	ioResult	word
<—>	18	ioNamePtr	pointer
—>	22	ioVRefNum	word
—>	30	ioFlAttrib	byte
—>	32	ioFlFndrInfo	16 bytes
—>	48	ioDirID	long word
—>	72	ioFlCrDat	long word
—>	76	ioFlMdDat	long word
—>	80	ioFlBkDat	long word
—>	84	ioFlXFndrInfo	16 bytes
—>	104	ioFlClpSiz	long word

Directories:

—>	12	ioCompletion	pointer
<—	16	ioResult	word
<—>	18	ioNamePtr	pointer
—>	22	ioVRefNum	word
—>	30	ioFlAttrib	byte
—>	32	ioDrUsrWds	16 bytes
—>	48	ioDrDirID	long word
—>	72	ioDrCrDat	long word
—>	76	ioDrMdDat	long word
—>	80	ioDrBkDat	long word
—>	84	ioDrFndrInfo	16 bytes

PBSetCatInfo sets information about the files and directories in a catalog. With files, it's similar to PBHSetFileInfo but lets you set some additional information. The information that can be set for files is shown in the left column, and the corresponding information for directories is shown in the right column.

Result codes	noErr	No error
	bdNamErr	Bad file name
	dirNFErr	Directory not found or incomplete pathname
	extFSErr	External file system
	fnfErr	File not found
	ioErr	I/O error
	nsvErr	No such volume
	paramErr	No default volume

```
FUNCTION PBCatMove (paramBlock: CMovePBPtr; async: BOOLEAN) : OSErr;
```

Trap macro _CatMove

Parameter block

—>	12	ioCompletion	pointer
<—	16	ioResult	word
—>	18	ioNamePtr	pointer
—>	22	ioVRefNum	word
—>	28	ioNewName	pointer
—>	36	ioNewDirID	long word
—>	48	ioDirID	long word

PBCatMove moves files or directories from one directory to another. The name of the file or directory to be moved is pointed to by ioNamePtr; ioVRefNum contains either the volume reference number or working directory reference number. A directory ID can be specified in ioDirID. The name and directory ID of the directory to which the file or directory is to be moved are specified by ioNewName and ioNewDirID.

PBCatMove is strictly a file catalog operation; it does not actually change the location of the file or directory on the disk. PBCatMove cannot move a file or directory to another volume (that is, ioVRefNum is used in specifying both the source and the destination). It also cannot be used to rename files or directories; for that, use PBHRename.

Result codes	noErr	No error
	badMovErr	Attempt to move into offspring
	bdNamErr	Bad file name or attempt to move into a file
	dupFNErr	Duplicate file name and version
	fnfErr	File not found
	ioErr	I/O error
	nsvErr	No such volume
	paramErr	No default volume
	vLckdErr	Software volume lock
	wPrErr	Hardware volume lock

Working Directory Routines

Warning: The routines described in this section operate *only* with the hierarchical version of the File Manager; if used on a Macintosh equipped only with the 64K ROM version of the File Manager, they will generate a system error.

```
FUNCTION PBOpenWD (paramBlock: WDPBPtr; async: BOOLEAN) : OSErr;
```

Trap macro _OpenWD

Parameter block

—>	12	ioCompletion	pointer
<—	16	ioResult	word
—>	18	ioNamePtr	pointer
<->	22	ioVRefNum	word
—>	28	ioWDProcID	long word
—>	48	ioWDDirID	long word

PBOpenWD takes the directory specified by ioVRefNum, ioWDDirID, and ioWDProcID and makes it a working directory. (You can also specify the directory using a combination of partial pathname and directory ID.) It returns a working directory reference number in ioVRefNum that can be used in subsequent calls.

If a given directory has already been made a working directory using the same ioWDProcID, no new working directory will be opened; instead, the existing working directory reference number will be returned. If a given directory was already made a working directory using a different ioWDProcID, a new working directory reference number is returned.

Result codes	noErr	No error
	tmwdoErr	Too many working directories open

```
FUNCTION PBCloseWD (paramBlock: WDPBPtr; async: BOOLEAN) : OSErr;
```

Trap macro _CloseWD

Parameter block

—>	12	ioCompletion	pointer
<—	16	ioResult	word
—>	22	ioVRefNum	word

PBCloseWD releases the working directory whose working directory reference number is specified in ioVRefNum.

Note: If a volume reference number is specified in ioVRefNum, PBCloseWD does nothing.

Result codes	noErr	No error
	nsvErr	No such volume

```
FUNCTION PBGetWDInfo (paramBlock: WDPBPtr; async: BOOLEAN) : OSErr;
```

Trap macro _GetWDInfo

Parameter block

—>	12	ioCompletion	pointer
<—	16	ioResult	word
<—	18	ioNamePtr	pointer
<–>	22	ioVRefNum	word
—>	26	ioWDIndex	word
<–>	28	ioWDProcID	long word
<–>	32	ioWDVRefNum	word
<—	48	ioWDDirID	long word

PBGetWDInfo returns information about the specified working directory. The working directory can be specified either by its working directory reference number in ioVRefNum (in which case ioWDIndex should be 0), or by its index number in ioWDIndex. In the latter case, if ioVRefNum is nonzero, it's interpreted as a volume specification (volume reference number or drive number), and only working directories on that volume are indexed.

IOWDVRefNum always returns the volume reference number. IOVRefNum returns a working directory reference number when a working directory reference number is passed in that field; otherwise, it returns a volume reference number. The volume name is returned in ioNamePtr.

If IOWDProcID is nonzero, only working directories with that identifier are indexed; otherwise all working directories are indexed.

Result codes	noErr	No error
	nsvErr	No such volume

DATA ORGANIZATION ON VOLUMES

This section explains how information is organized on volumes. Most of the information is accessible only through assembly language, but may be of interest to some advanced Pascal programmers.

The File Manager communicates with device drivers that read and write data via block-level requests to devices containing Macintosh-initialized volumes. (Macintosh-initialized volumes are volumes initialized by the Disk Initialization Package.) The actual type of volume and device is unimportant to the File Manager; the only requirements are that the volume was initialized by the Disk Initialization Package and that the device driver is able to communicate via block-level requests.

The 3 1/2-inch built-in and optional external drives are accessed via the Disk Driver. The Hard Disk 20 is accessed via the Hard Disk 20 Driver. If you want to use the File Manager to access files on Macintosh-initialized volumes on other types of devices, you must write a device driver that can read and write data via block-level requests to the device on which the volume will be mounted. If you want to access files on volumes not initialized by the Macintosh, you must write your own external file system (see the section "Using an External File System").

The information on all block-formatted volumes is organized in **logical blocks** and allocation blocks. Logical blocks contain a number of bytes of standard information (512 bytes on Macintosh-initialized volumes), and an additional number of bytes of information specific to the device driver (12 bytes on Macintosh-initialized volumes; for details, see the Disk Driver chapter). Allocation blocks are composed of any integral number of logical blocks, and are simply a means of grouping logical blocks together in more convenient parcels. The allocation block size is a volume parameter whose value is set when the volume is initialized; it cannot be changed unless the volume is reinitialized.

The remainder of this section applies only to Macintosh-initialized volumes; the information may be different in future versions of Macintosh system software. There are two types of Macintosh-initialized volumes—flat directory volumes and hierarchical directory volumes. Other volumes must be accessed via an external file system, and the information on them must be organized by an external initializing program.

Flat Directory Volumes

A flat directory volume contains **system startup information** in logical blocks 0 and 1 (see Figure 7) that's read in at system startup. This information consists of certain configurable system parameters, such as the capacity of the event queue, the initial size of the system heap, and the number of open files allowed. The development system you're using may include a utility program for modifying the system startup blocks on a volume.

Logical block 2 of the volume begins the **master directory block**. The master directory block contains **volume information** and the **volume allocation block map**, which records whether each block on the volume is unused or what part of a file it contains data from.

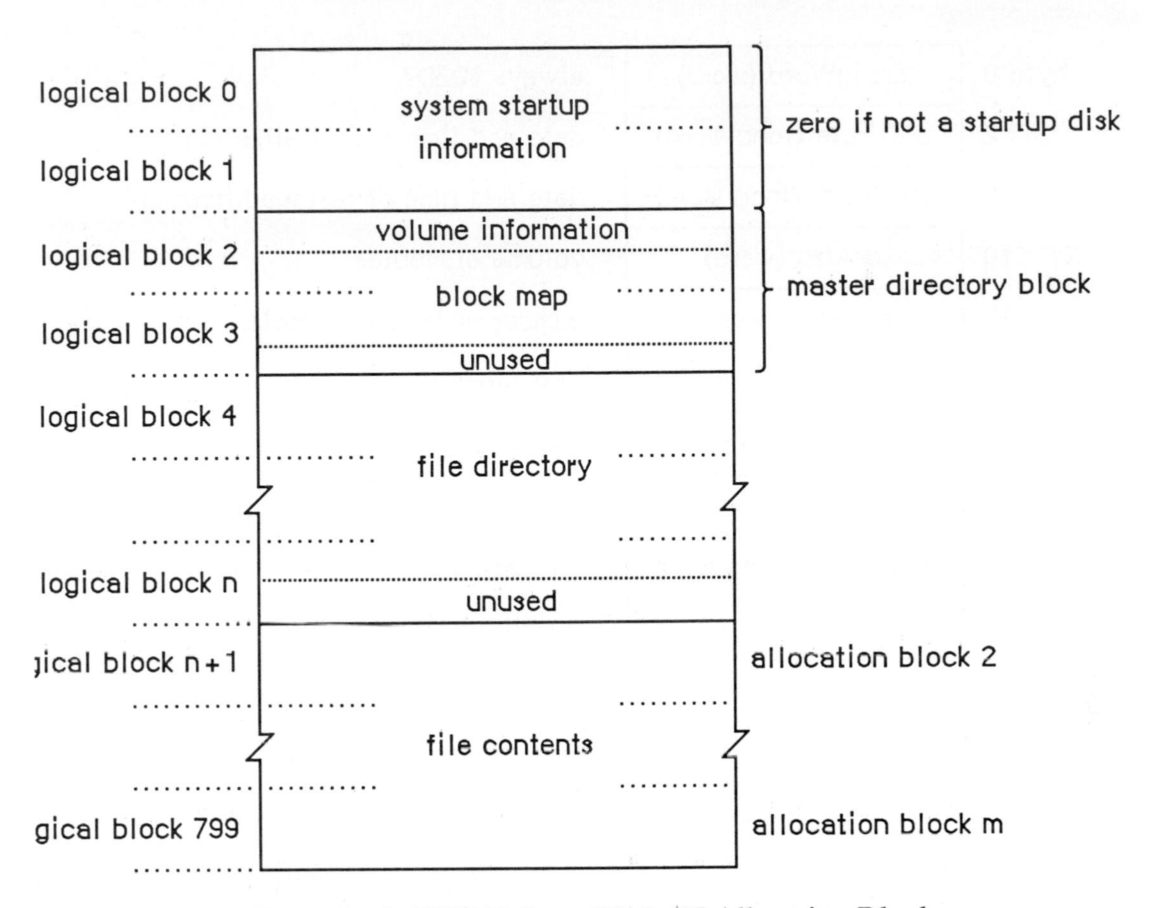

Figure 7. A 400K Volume With 1K Allocation Blocks

The master directory "block" always occupies two blocks—the Disk Initialization Package varies the allocation block size as necessary to achieve this constraint.

The file directory begins in the next logical block following the block map; it contains descriptions and locations of all the files on the volume. The rest of the logical blocks on the volume contain files or garbage (such as parts of deleted files). The exact format of the volume information, volume allocation block map, and file directory is explained in the following sections.

Volume Information

The volume information is contained in the first 64 bytes of the master directory block (see Figure 8). This information is written on the volume when it's initialized, and modified thereafter by the File Manager.

byte	field	description
0	drSigWord (word)	always $D2D7
2	drCrDate (long word)	date and time of initialization
6	drLsBkUp (long word)	date and time of last modification
10	drAtrb (word)	volume attributes
12	drNmFls (word)	number of files in directory
14	drDirSt (word)	first block of directory
16	drBlLen (word)	length of directory in blocks
18	drNmAlBlks (word)	number of allocation blocks
20	drAlBlkSiz (long word)	allocation block size
24	drClpSiz (long word)	number of bytes to allocate
28	drAlBlSt (word)	first allocation block in block map
30	drNxtFNum (long word)	next unused file number
34	drFreeBks (word)	number of unused allocation blocks
36	drVN (byte)	length of volume name
37	drVN+1 (bytes)	characters of volume name

Figure 8. Volume Information on Flat Directory Volumes

DrAtrb contains the **volume attributes**, as follows:

Bit	**Meaning**
7	Set if volume is locked by hardware
15	Set if volume is locked by software

DrClpSiz contains the minimum number of bytes to allocate each time the Allocate function is called, to minimize fragmentation of files; it's always a multiple of the allocation block size. DrNxtFNum contains the next unused file number (see the "File Directory" section below for an explanation of file numbers).

Volume Allocation Block Map

The volume allocation block map represents every allocation block on the volume with a 12-bit entry indicating whether the block is unused or allocated to a file. It begins in the master directory block at the byte following the volume information, and continues for as many logical blocks as needed.

The first entry in the block map is for block number 2; the block map doesn't contain entries for the system startup blocks. Each entry specifies whether the block is unused, whether it's the last block in the file, or which allocation block is next in the file:

Entry	Meaning
0	Block is unused
1	Block is the last block of the file
2–4095	Number of next block in the file

For instance, assume that there's one file on the volume, stored in allocation blocks 8, 11, 12, and 17; the first 16 entries of the block map would read

0 0 0 0 0 0 11 0 0 12 17 0 0 0 0 1

The first allocation block on a volume typically follows the file directory. It's numbered 2 because of the special meaning of numbers 0 and 1.

> **Note:** As explained below, it's possible to begin the allocation blocks immediately following the master directory block and place the file directory somewhere within the allocation blocks. In this case, the allocation blocks occupied by the file directory must be marked with $FFF's in the allocation block map.

Flat File Directory

The file directory contains an entry for each file. Each entry lists information about one file on the volume, including its name and location. Each file is listed by its own unique **file number**, which the File Manager uses to distinguish it from other files on the volume.

A file directory entry contains 51 bytes plus one byte for each character in the file name. If the file names average 20 characters, a directory can hold seven file entries per logical block. Entries are always an integral number of words and don't cross logical block boundaries. The length of a file directory depends on the maximum number of files the volume can contain; for example, on a 400K volume the file directory occupies 12 logical blocks.

The file directory conventionally follows the block map and precedes the allocation blocks, but a volume-initializing program could actually place the file directory anywhere within the allocation blocks as long as the blocks occupied by the file directory are marked with $FFF's in the block map.

The format of a file directory entry is shown in Figure 9.

byte	field	description
byte 0	flFlags (byte)	bit 7=1 if entry used; bit 0=1 if file locked
1	flTyp (byte)	version number
2	flUsrWds (16 bytes)	information used by the Finder
18	flFlNum (long word)	file number
22	flStBlk (word)	first allocation block of data fork
24	flLgLen (long word)	logical end-of-file of data fork
28	flPyLen (long word)	physical end-of-file of data fork
32	flRStBlk (word)	first allocation block of resource fork
34	flRLgLen (long word)	logical end-of-file of resource fork
38	flRPyLen (long word)	physical end-of-file of resource fork
42	flCrDat (long word)	date and time of creation
46	flMdDat (long word)	date and time of last modification
50	flNam (byte)	length of file name
51	flNam+1 (bytes)	characters of file name

Figure 9. A File Directory Entry

FlStBlk and flRStBlk are 0 if the data or resource fork doesn't exist. FlCrDat and flMdDat are given in seconds since midnight, January 1, 1904.

Each time a new file is created, an entry for the new file is placed in the file directory. Each time a file is deleted, its entry in the file directory is cleared, and all blocks used by that file on the volume are released.

Hierarchical Directory Volumes

A hierarchical directory volume contains **system startup information** in logical blocks 0 and 1 (see Figure 10) that's read in at system startup. This information is similar to the system startup information for flat directory volumes; it consists of certain configurable system parameters, such as the capacity of the event queue, the initial size of the system heap, and the number of open files allowed.

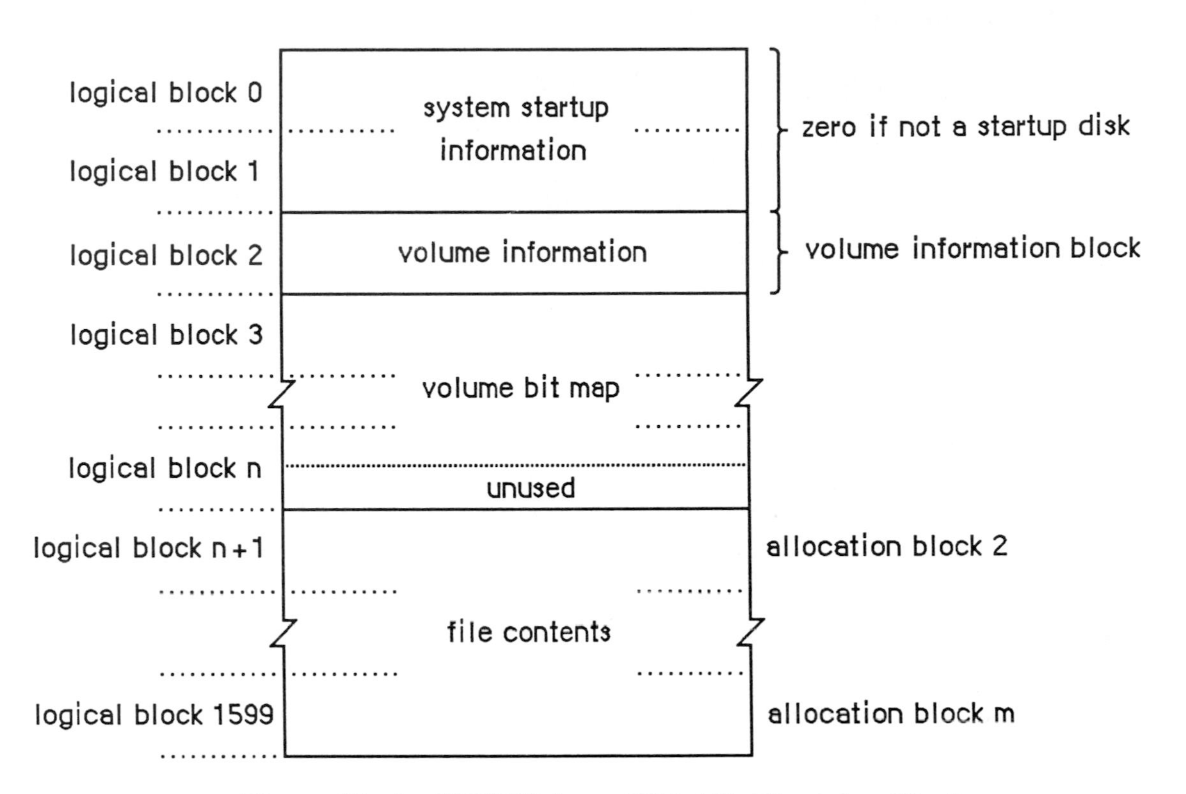

Figure 10. An 800K Volume With 1K Allocation Blocks

Logical block 2 of the volume (also known as the **volume information block**) contains the **volume information.** This volume information is a superset of the volume information found on flat directory volumes. Logical block 3 of the volume begins the **volume bit map**, which records whether each block on the volume is used or unused. The rest of the logical blocks on the volume contain files or garbage (such as parts of deleted files).

The volume bit map on hierarchical directory volumes replaces the volume allocation block map used on flat directory volumes. While the bit map does handle volume space management (as does the block map), it does not handle file mapping. A separate file, known as the **extents tree file**, performs this function. Finally, a file known as the **catalog tree file** is responsible for maintaining the hierarchical directory structure; it corresponds in function to the file directory found on flat directory volumes.

The exact format of the volume information, volume bit map, extents tree file, and catalog tree file is explained in the following sections. The discussion of the extents tree and catalog tree files is preceded by a short introduction to a data structure known as a B*-tree that's used to organize and access the information in these files.

Volume Information

The volume information is contained in the first 104 bytes of the volume information block (see Figure 11). This information is written on the volume when it's initialized, and modified thereafter by the File Manager.

byte	field	description
0	drSigWord (word)	always $4244
2	drCrDate (long word)	date and time of initialization
6	drLsMod (long word)	date and time of last modification
10	drAtrb (word)	volume attributes
12	drNmFls (word)	number of files in directory
14	drVBMSt (word)	first block of volume bit map
16	drAllocPtr (word)	used internally
18	drNmAlBlks (word)	number of allocation blocks
20	drAlBlkSiz (long word)	allocation block size
24	drClpSiz (long word)	default clump size
28	drAlBlSt (word)	first block in bit map
30	drNxtCNID (long word)	next unused directory ID or file number
34	drFreeBks (word)	number of unused allocation blocks
36	drVN (byte)	length of volume name
37	drVN+1 (bytes)	characters of volume name
64	drVolBkUp (long word)	date and time of last backup
68	drVSeqNum (word)	used internally
70	drWrCnt (long word)	volume write count
74	drXTClpSiz (long word)	clump size of extents tree file
78	drCTClpSiz (long word)	clump size of catalog tree file
82	drNmRtDirs (word)	number of directories in root
84	drFilCnt (long word)	number of files on volume
88	drDirCnt (long word)	number of directories on volume
92	drFndrInfo (32 bytes)	information used by the Finder
124	drVCSize (word)	used internally
126	drVCBMSize (word)	used internally
128	drCtlCSize (word)	used internally
130	drXTFlSize (long word)	length of extents tree (LEOF and PEOF)
134	drXTExtRec (12 bytes)	extent record for extents tree
146	drCTFlSize (long word)	length of catalog tree (LEOF and PEOF)
150	drCTExtRec (12 bytes)	first extent record for catalog tree

Figure 11. Volume Information on Hierarchical Directory Volumes

64K ROM note: The volume information on a flat directory volume is a subset of the hierarchical volume information. The flat directory volume information contains only the fields up to and including drVN+1. In addition, the names of several fields have been changed in the hierarchical volume information to reflect their new function: drLsBkUp, drDirSt, drBlLn, and drNxtFNum have been changed to drLsMod, drVBMSt, drAllocPtr, and drNxtCNID respectively. All of the offsets of the flat directory volume information, however, have been preserved to maintain compatibility.

DrLsMod contains the date and time that the volume was last modified (this is not necessarily when it was flushed).

64K ROM note: DrLsMod replaces the field drLsBkUp from flat directory volumes. The name drLsBkUp was actually a misnomer; this field has always contained the date and time of the last modification, not the last backup. Another field, drVolBkUp, contains the date and time of the last backup.

DrVBMSt replaces the field drDirSt; it contains the number of the first block in the volume bit map.

DrAtrb contains the **volume attributes**, as follows:

Bit	Meaning
7	Set if volume is locked by hardware
15	Set if volume is locked by software

DrClpSiz contains the default **clump size** for the volume. To promote file contiguity and avoid fragmentation, space is allocated to a file not in allocation blocks but in **clumps**. A clump is a group of contiguous allocation blocks. The clump size is always a multiple of the allocation block size; it's the minimum number of bytes to allocate each time the Allocate function is called or the end-of-file is reached during the Write routine. A clump size can be set when a particular file is opened, and can also be changed subsequently. If no clump size is specified, the value found in drClpSiz will be used.

DrNxtCNID replaces the field drNxtFNum; it's either the next file number or the next directory ID to be assigned.

Warning: The format of the volume information may be different in future versions of Macintosh system software.

Volume Bit Map

The flat directory file system uses the volume allocation block map to provide both volume space management and file mapping; the hierarchical file system instead uses a volume bit map. The block map contains a 12-bit entry for each allocation block. If an entry is 0, the corresponding allocation block is unused. If an allocation block is allocated to a file, its block map entry is nonzero, and can be used to find the next allocation block used by that file.

The File Manager keeps the entire block map in memory. The size of the block map is obviously a function of the number of allocation blocks on the volume. Similarly, the number of allocation blocks depends on the allocation block size. For larger volumes, the allocation block size must be increased in order to keep the block map to a reasonable size.

A tradeoff occurs between waste of space and speed of file access in this situation. Obviously, the use of large allocation blocks can waste disk space, particularly with small files. On the other hand, using smaller allocation blocks increases the size of the block map; this means the entire block map cannot be kept in memory at one time, resulting in a time-consuming sector-caching scheme.

The hierarchical file system discards the block map concept entirely, and instead uses a structure known as the **volume bit map**. The bit map has one bit for each allocation block on the volume; if a particular block is in use, its bit is set.

With extremely large volumes, the same space/time tradeoff can become an issue. In general, it's desirable to set the allocation block size such that the entire bit map can be kept in memory at all times.

B*-Trees

This section describes the B*-tree implementation used in the extents tree and catalog tree files. The data structures described in this section are accessible only through assembly language; an understanding of the B*-tree data structure is also assumed.

The nodes of a B*-tree contain records; each record consists of certain information (either pointers or data) and a key associated with that information (see Figure 12). A basic feature of the B*-tree is that data is stored only in the leaf nodes. The internal nodes (also known as index nodes) contain pointers to other nodes; they provide an index, used in conjunction with a search key, for accessing the data records stored in the leaf nodes.

key length (1 byte)	key (up to 255 bytes)	data or pointer (limited only by size of node)

Figure 12. A B*-Tree Node Record

Within each node, the records are maintained so that their keys are in ascending order. Figure 13 shows a sample B*-tree; hypothetical keys have been inserted to illustrate the structure of the tree and the relationship between index and leaf nodes.

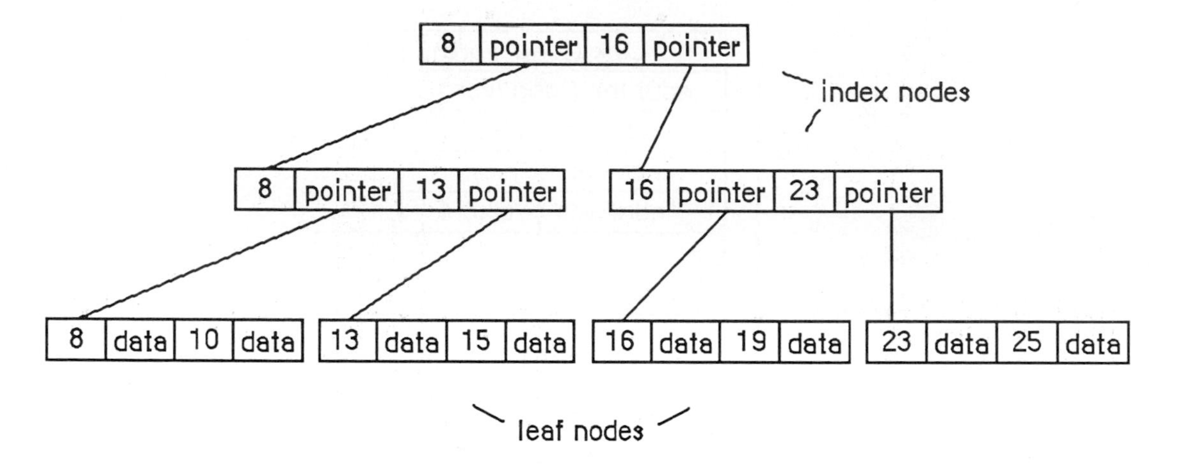

Figure 13. A Sample B*-Tree

When a data record is needed, the key of the desired record (the search key) is provided. The search begins at the root node (which is an index node, unless the tree has only one level), moving from one record to the next until the record with the highest key that's less than or equal to the search key is reached. The pointer of that record leads to another node, one level down in the tree. This process continues until a leaf node is reached; its records are examined until the desired key is found. (The desired key may not be found; in this case, the search stops when a key larger than the search key is reached.) Figure 14 shows a sample B*-tree search path; the arrows indicate the path to the second record in the second leaf node.

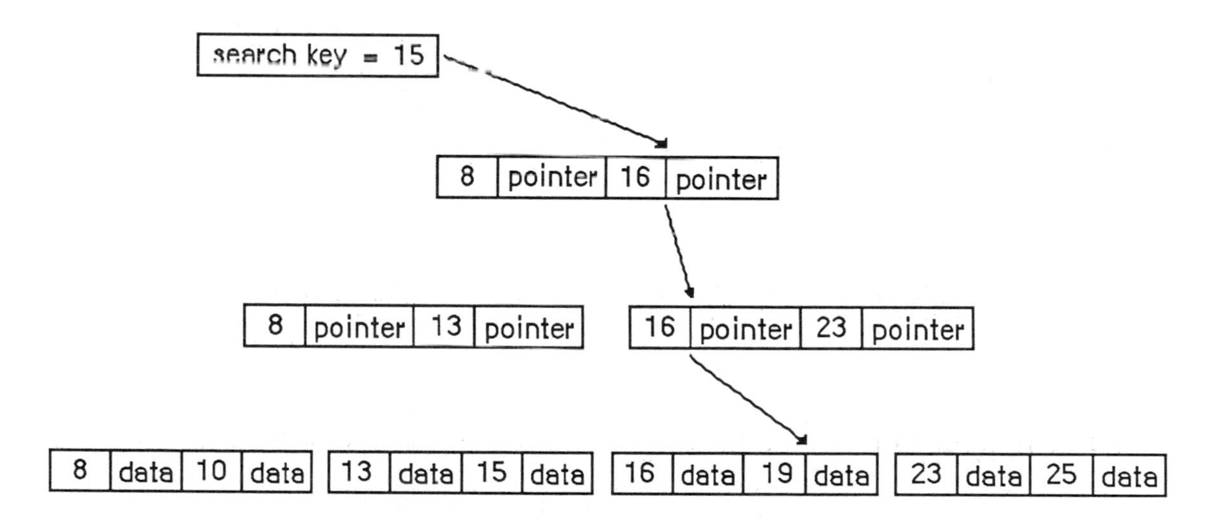

Figure 14. A Sample B*-Tree Search Path

All nodes in the B*-tree are of the same fixed size; the structure of a node is shown in Figure 15.

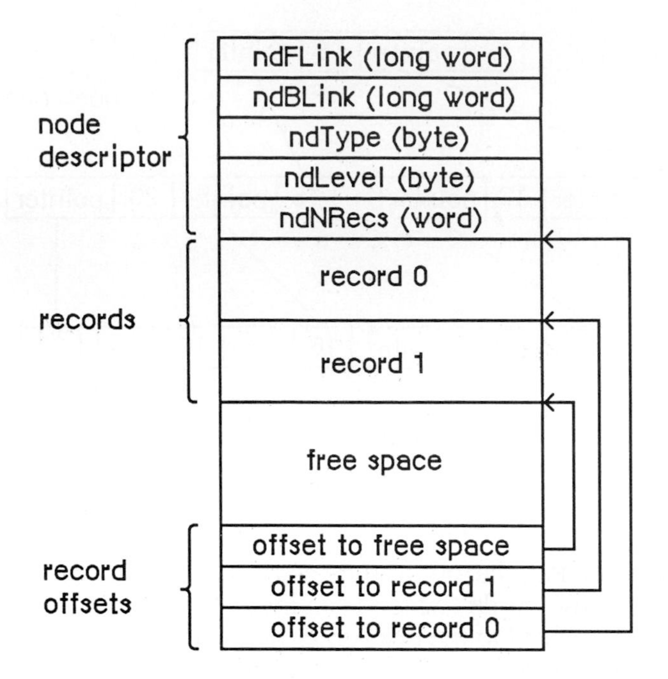

Figure 15. Structure of a B*-Tree Node

Each node begins with the node descriptor. NDNRecs contains the number of records currently in the node. NDType indicates the type of node; it contains $FF if it's a leaf node and 0 if it's an index node. NDLevel indicates the level of the node in the tree; leaf nodes are always at level 1, the first level of index nodes above them are at level 2, and so on.

NDBLink and ndFLink are used only with leaf nodes as a way of quickly moving through the data records; for each leaf node, they contain pointers to the previous and subsequent leaf nodes respectively.

The records in a node can be of variable length; for this reason, offsets to the beginning of each record are needed. The records begin after the field ndNRecs; they're followed by the unused space. The offsets to the records begin at the end of the node and work backwards; they're followed by an offset to the unused space.

Extents Tree File

File mapping information (or the location of a file's data on the volume) is contained in the extents tree file. A file **extent** is a series of contiguous allocation blocks. Ideally, a file would be stored in a single extent. Except in the case of preallocated or small files, however, the contents of a particular file are usually stored in more than one extent on different parts of a given volume. The extents tree file, organized as a B*-tree, records the volume location and size of the various extents that comprise a file.

Each extent on a volume is identified by an **extent descriptor**; each descriptor consists of the number of the first allocation block of the extent followed by the length of the extent in blocks (see Figure 16).

number of extent's first allocation block (word)
number of allocation blocks in extent (word)

Figure 16. Extent Descriptor

The extent descriptors are stored in **extent records** in the leaf nodes of the tree. Each extent record consists of a key followed by three extent descriptors. The extent records are kept sorted by the key, which has the format shown in Figure 18.

byte	field	description
0	xkrKeyLen (byte)	key length in bytes
1	xkrFkType (byte)	$00 for data fork; $FF for resource fork
2	xkrFNum (long word)	file number
6	xkrFABN (word)	allocation block number within file

Figure 17. Extents Key

Catalog Tree File

The catalog tree file corresponds in function to the flat file directory found on volumes formatted by the 64K ROM. Whereas a flat file directory contains entries for files only, the catalog tree file contains three types of records—file records, directory records, and thread records. (Threads can be viewed as the branches connecting the nodes of a catalog tree.) The catalog tree file is organized as a B*-tree; all three types of records are stored in the leaf nodes. The index nodes contain the index records used to search through the tree.

The catalog tree records consist of a key followed by the file, directory, or thread record. The records are kept sorted by key. The exact format of the key is shown in Figure 18.

byte	field	description
0	ckrKeyLen (byte)	key length in bytes
1	ckrResrv1 (byte)	used internally
2	ckrParID (long word)	parent ID
6	ckrCName (bytes)	file or directory name

Figure 18. Catalog Key

A file record is a superset of the file directory entry found on volumes formatted by the 64K ROM; its contents are shown in Figure 19.

byte	field	description
byte 0	cdrType (byte)	always 2 for file records
1	cdrResrv2 (byte)	used internally
2	filFlags (byte)	bit 7=1 if record used; bit 0=1 if file locked
3	filTyp (byte)	file type
4	filUsrWds (16 bytes)	information used by the Finder
20	filFlNum (long word)	file number
24	filStBlk (word)	first allocation block of data fork
26	filLgLen (long word)	logical end-of-file of data fork
30	filPyLen (long word)	physical end-of-file of data fork
34	filRStBlk (word)	first allocation block of resource fork
36	filRLgLen (long word)	logical end-of-file of resource fork
40	filRPyLen (long word)	physical end-of-file of resource fork
44	filCrDat (long word)	date and time of creation
48	filMdDat (long word)	date and time of last modification
52	filBkDat (long word)	date and time of last backup
56	filFndrInfo (16 bytes)	additional information used by the Finder
72	filClpSize (word)	file clump size
74	filExtRec (12 bytes)	first extent record for data fork
86	filRExtRec (12 bytes)	first extent record for resource fork
98	filResrv (long word)	used internally

Figure 19. File Record

A directory record records information about a single directory; the format of a directory record is shown in Figure 20.

byte	field	description
0	cdrType (byte)	always 1 for directory records
1	cdrResrv2 (byte)	used internally
2	dirFlags (word)	flags
4	dirVal (word)	valence
6	dirDirID (long word)	directory ID
10	dirCrDat (long word)	date and time of creation
14	dirMdDat (long word)	date and time of last modification
18	dirBkDat (long word)	date and time of last backup
22	dirUsrInfo (16 bytes)	information used by the Finder
38	dirFndrInfo (16 bytes)	additional information used by the Finder
54	dirResrv (16 bytes)	used internally

Figure 20. Directory Record

Thread records are used in conjunction with directory records to provide a link between a given directory and its parent. For any given directory, the records describing all of its offspring are stored contiguously. A thread record precedes each set of offspring; it contains the directory ID and name of the parent and provides a path to the parent's directory record. The format of a thread record is shown in Figure 21.

byte	field	description
0	cdrType (byte)	always 3 for thread records
1	cdrResrv2 (byte)	used internally
2	thdResrv (8 bytes)	used internally
10	thdParID (long word)	parent ID of associated directory
14	thdCName (bytes)	name of associated directory

Figure 21. Thread Record

A portion of a sample tree, along with the corresponding file, directory, and thread records, is shown in Figure 22.

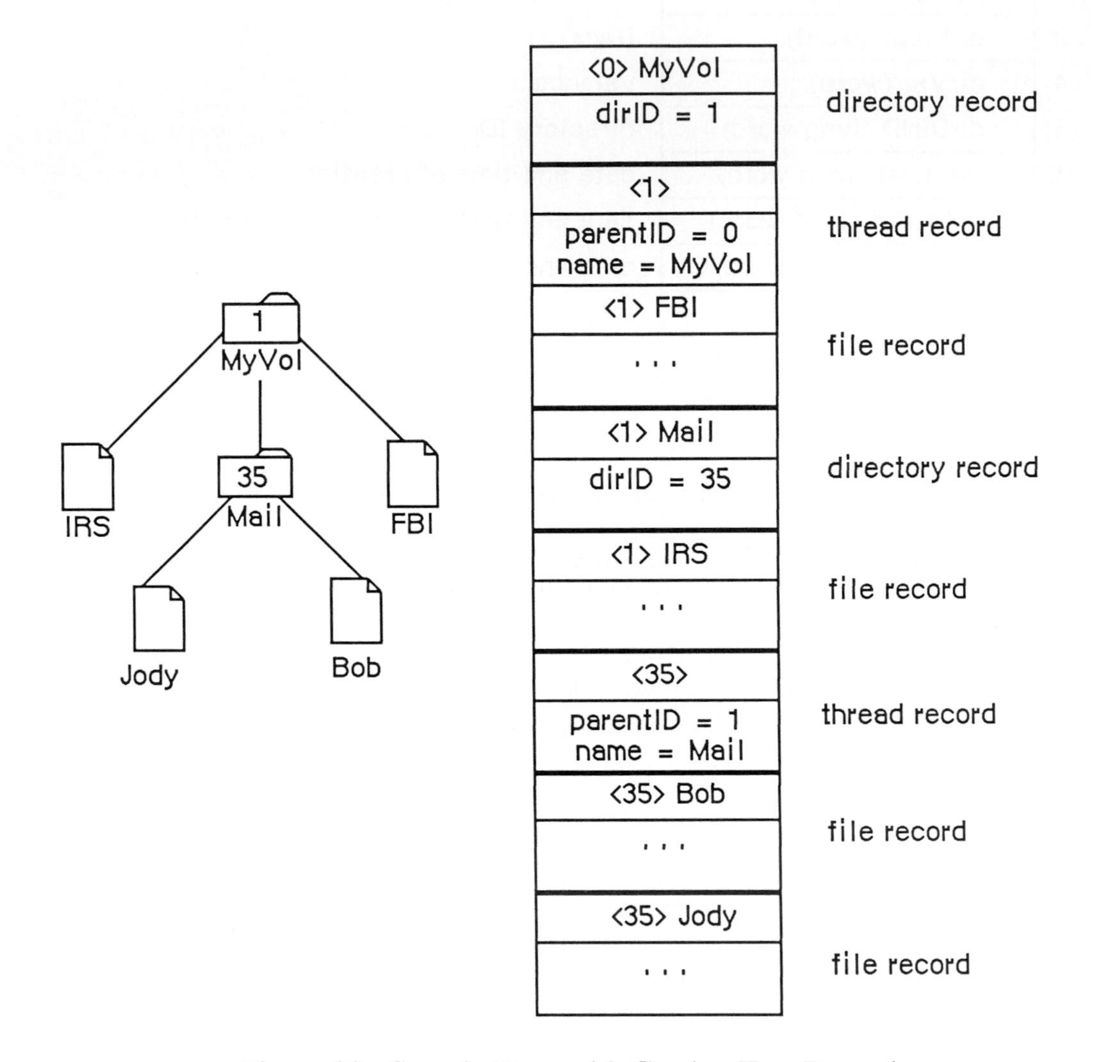

Figure 22. Sample Tree, with Catalog Tree Records

DATA STRUCTURES IN MEMORY

This section describes the memory data structures used by the File Manager and any external file system that accesses files on Macintosh-initialized volumes. Some of this data is accessible only through assembly language.

The data structures in memory used by the File Manager and all external file systems include:

- the file I/O queue, listing all asynchronous routines awaiting execution (including the currently executing routine, if any)
- the volume-control-block queue, listing information about each mounted volume
- a copy of the volume bit map for each on-line volume (volume allocation block map for flat directory volumes)
- the file-control-block buffer, listing information about each access path
- volume buffers (one for each on-line volume)
- optional access path buffers (one for each access path)
- the drive queue, listing information about each drive connected to the Macintosh

The File I/O Queue

The file I/O queue is a standard Operating System queue (described in the Operating System Utilities chapter) that contains parameter blocks for all asynchronous routines awaiting execution. Each time a routine is called, an entry is placed in the queue; each time a routine is completed, its entry is removed from the queue.

Each entry in the file I/O queue consists of a parameter block for the routine that was called. Most of the fields of this parameter block contain information needed by the specific File Manager routines; these fields are explained above in the section "Low-Level File Manager Routines". The first four fields of the parameter block, shown below, are used by the File Manager in processing the I/O requests in the queue.

```
TYPE ParamBlockRec = RECORD
                       qLink:      QElemPtr; {next queue entry}
                       qType:      INTEGER;  {queue type}
                       ioTrap:     INTEGER;  {routine trap}
                       ioCmdAddr:  Ptr;      {routine address}
                       . . .                 {rest of block}
                     END;
```

QLink points to the next entry in the queue, and qType indicates the queue type, which must always be ORD(ioQType). IOTrap and ioCmdAddr contain the trap word and address of the File Manager routine that was called.

You can get a pointer to the header of the file I/O queue by calling the File Manager function GetFSQHdr.

`FUNCTION GetFSQHdr : QHdrPtr;` [Not in ROM]

GetFSQHdr returns a pointer to the header of the file I/O queue.

Assembly-language note: The global variable FSQHdr contains the header of the file I/O queue.

Volume Control Blocks

Each time a volume is mounted, its volume information is read from it and is used to build a new **volume control block** in the **volume-control-block queue** (unless an ejected or off-line volume is being remounted). A copy of the volume block map is also read from the volume and placed in the system heap, and a volume buffer is created in the system heap.

The volume-control-block queue is a standard Operating System queue that's maintained in the system heap. It contains a volume control block for each mounted volume. A volume control block is a 178-byte nonrelocatable block that contains volume-specific information. It has the following structure:

```
TYPE VCB =
  RECORD
    qLink:        QElemPtr;     {next queue entry}
    qType:        INTEGER;      {queue type}
    vcbFlags:     INTEGER;      {bit 15=1 if dirty}
    vcbSigWord:   INTEGER;      {$4244 for hierarchical, $D2D7 for flat}
    vcbCrDate:    LONGINT;      {date and time of  initialization}
    vcbLsMod:     LONGINT;      {date and time of last modification}
    vcbAtrb:      INTEGER;      {volume attributes}
    vcbNmFls:     INTEGER;      {number of files in directory}
    vcbVBMSt:     INTEGER;      {first block of volume bit map}
    vcbAllocPtr:  INTEGER;      {used internally}
    vcbNmAlBlks:  INTEGER;      {number of allocation blocks}
    vcbAlBlkSiz:  LONGINT;      {allocation block size}
    vcbClpSiz:    LONGINT;      {default clump size}
    vcbAlBlSt:    INTEGER;      {first block in block map}
    vcbNxtCNID:   LONGINT;      {next unused directory ID or file number}
    vcbFreeBks:   INTEGER;      {number of unused allocation blocks}
    vcbVN:        STRING[27];   {volume name}
    vcbDrvNum:    INTEGER;      {drive number}
    vcbDRefNum:   INTEGER;      {driver reference number}
    vcbFSID:      INTEGER;      {file-system identifier}
    vcbVRefNum:   INTEGER;      {volume reference number}
    vcbMAdr:      Ptr;          {pointer to block map}
    vcbBufAdr:    Ptr;          {pointer to volume buffer}
    vcbMLen:      INTEGER;      {number of bytes in block map}
    vcbDirIndex:  INTEGER;      {used internally}
    vcbDirBlk:    INTEGER;      {used internally}
    vcbVolBkUp:   LONGINT;      {date and time of last backup}
    vcbVSeqNum:   INTEGER;      {used internally}
    vcbWrCnt:     LONGINT;      {volume write count}
    vcbXTClpSiz:  LONGINT;      {clump size of extents tree file}
    vcbCTClpSiz:  LONGINT;      {clump size of catalog tree file}
    vcbNmRtDirs:  INTEGER;      {number of directories in root}
    vcbFilCnt:    LONGINT;      {number of files on volume}
    vcbDirCnt:    LONGINT;      {number of directories on volume}
```

```
  vcbFndrInfo: ARRAY[1..8] OF LONGINT;  {information used by the }
                           { Finder}
  vcbVCSize:   INTEGER;    {used internally}
  vcbVBMCSiz:  INTEGER;    {used internally}
  vcbCtlCSiz:  INTEGER;    {used internally}
  vcbXTAlBks:  INTEGER;    {size in blocks of extents tree file}
  vcbCTAlBks:  INTEGER;    {size in blocks of catalog tree file}
  vcbXTRef:    INTEGER;    {path reference number for extents tree }
                           { file}
  vcbCTRef:    INTEGER;    {path reference number for catalog tree }
                           { file}
  vcbCtlBuf:   Ptr;        {pointer to extents and catalog tree }
                           { caches}
  vcbDirIDM:   LONGINT;    {directory last searched}
  vcbOffsM:    INTEGER     {offspring index at last search}
END;
```


64K ROM note: A volume control block created for a flat volume is a subset of the above structure. It's actually smaller and contains only the fields up to and including vcbDirBlk. In addition, the names of several fields have been changed to reflect the fact that they contain different information on hierarchical volumes: vcbLsBkUp, vcbDirSt, vcbBlLn, vcbNmBlks, and vcbNxtFNum have been changed to vcbLsMod, vcbVBMSt, vcbAllocPtr, vcbNmAlBlks, and vcbNxtCNID respectively.

QLink points to the next entry in the queue, and qType indicates the queue type, which must always be ORD(fsQType). Bit 15 of vcbFlags is set if the volume information has been changed by a routine call since the volume was last affected by a FlushVol call.

VCBLsMod contains the date and time that the volume was last modified (this is not necessarily when it was flushed).

64K ROM note: VCBLsMod replaces the field vcbLsBkUp from flat directory volumes. The name vcbLsBkUp was actually a misnomer; this field has always contained the date and time of the last modification, not the last backup. Another field, vcbVolBkUp, contains the date and time of the last backup.

VCBAtrb contains the volume attributes, as follows:

Bit	Meaning
0–4	Set if inconsistencies were found between the volume information and the file directory when the volume was mounted
6	Set if volume is busy (one or more files are open)
7	Set if volume is locked by hardware
15	Set if volume is locked by software

VCBVBMSt contains the number of the first block in the volume bit map; on flat volumes, it contains the first block of the file directory. VCBNmAlBlks contains the number of allocation blocks on the volume, and vcbFreeBks specifies how many of those blocks are unused. VCBAlBlSt is used only with flat volumes; it contains the number of the first block in the block map.

VCBDrvNum contains the drive number of the drive on which the volume is mounted; vcbDRefNum contains the driver reference number of the driver used to access the volume. When a mounted volume is placed off-line, vcbDrvNum is cleared. When a volume is ejected, vcbDrvNum is cleared and vcbDRefNum is set to the negative of vcbDrvNum (becoming a positive number). VCBFSID identifies the file system handling the volume; it's 0 for volumes handled by the File Manager, and nonzero for volumes handled by other file systems.

When a volume is placed off-line, its buffer and bit map (or block map, in the case of flat directory volumes) are released. When a volume is unmounted, its volume control block is removed from the volume-control-block queue.

You can get a pointer to the header of the volume-control-block queue by calling the File Manager function GetVCBQHdr.

`FUNCTION GetVCBQHdr : QHdrPtr;` [Not in ROM]

GetVCBQHdr returns a pointer to the header of the volume-control-block queue.

Assembly-language note: The global variable VCBQHdr contains the header of the volume-control-block-queue. The default volume's volume control block is pointed to by the global variable DefVCBPtr.

File Control Blocks

Each time a file is opened, the file's directory entry is used to build a **file control block** in the **file-control-block buffer**, which contains information about all access paths. The file-control-block-buffer is a nonrelocatable block in the system heap; the first word contains the length of the buffer.

The number of file control blocks is contained in the system startup information on a volume. With the 64K ROM, the standard number is 12 file control blocks on a Macintosh 128K and 48 file control blocks on the Macintosh 512K. With the 128K ROM, there's a standard of 40 file control blocks per volume.

Each open fork of a file requires one access path. Two access paths are used for the system and application resource files (whose resource forks are always open). On hierarchical directory volumes, two access paths are also needed for the extents and catalog trees. You should keep such files in mind when calculating the number of files that can be opened by your application.

Note: The size of the file-control-block buffer is determined by the system startup information stored on a volume.

You can get information from the file control block allocated for an open file by calling the File Manager function PBGetFCBInfo. When you call PBGetFCBInfo, you'll use the following 12 additional fields after the standard eight fields in the parameter block record FCBPBRec:

```
ioRefNum:      INTEGER;   {path reference number}
filler:        INTEGER;   {not used}
ioFCBIndx:     LONGINT;   {FCB index}
ioFCBFlNm:     LONGINT;   {file number}
ioFCBFlags:    INTEGER;   {flags}
ioFCBStBlk:    INTEGER;   {first allocation block of file}
ioFCBEOF:      LONGINT;   {logical end-of-file}
ioFCBPLen:     LONGINT;   {physical end-of-file}
ioFCBCrPs:     LONGINT;   {mark}
ioFCBVRefNum:  INTEGER;   {volume reference number}
ioFCBClpSiz:   LONGINT;   {file clump size}
ioFCBParID:    LONGINT;   {parent directory ID}
```

```
FUNCTION PBGetFCBInfo (paramBlock: FCBPBPtr; async: BOOLEAN) :
      OSErr;
```

Trap macro _GetFCBInfo

Parameter block

```
—>   12  ioCompletion   pointer
<—   16  ioResult       word
<—   18  ioNamePtr      pointer
<->  22  ioVRefNum      word
<->  24  ioRefNum       word
—>   28  ioFCBIndx      long word
<—   32  ioFCBFlNm      long word
<—   36  ioFCBFlags     word
<—   38  ioFCBStBlk     word
<—   40  ioFCBEOF       long word
<—   44  ioFCBPLen      long word
<—   48  ioFCBCrPs      long word
<—   52  ioFCBVRefNum   word
<—   54  ioFCBClpSiz    long word
<—   58  ioFCBParID     long word
```

PBGetFCBInfo returns information about the specified open file. If ioFCBIndx is positive, the File Manager returns information about the file whose file number is ioFCBIndx on the volume specified by ioVRefNum (which may contain a drive number, volume reference number, or working directory reference number). If ioVRefNum is 0, all open files are indexed; otherwise, only open files on the specified volume are indexed.

If ioFCBIndx is 0, the File Manager returns information about the file whose access path is specified by ioRefNum.

Assembly-language note: The global variable FCBSPtr points to the length word of the file-control-block buffer.

Each file control block contains 94 bytes of information about an access path; Figure 23 shows its structure (using the assembly-language offsets).

byte	field	description
byte 0	fcbFlNum (long word)	file number
4	fcbMdRByt (byte)	flags
5	fcbTypByt (byte)	version number
6	fcbSBlk (word)	first allocation block of file
8	fcbEOF (long word)	logical end-of-file
12	fcbPLen (long word)	physical end-of-file
16	fcbCrPs (long word)	mark
20	fcbVPtr (pointer)	pointer to volume control block
24	fcbBfAdr (pointer)	pointer to access path buffer
28	fcbFlPos (word)	used internally
30	fcbClmpSize (long word)	file clump size
34	fcbBTCBPtr (long word)	pointer to B*-tree control block
38	fcbExtRec (12 bytes)	first three file extents
50	fcbFType (long word)	file's finder type bytes
54	fcbCatPos (long word)	used internally
58	fcbDirID (long word)	file's parent ID
62	fcbCName (bytes)	name of open file

Figure 23. A File Control Block

64K ROM note: The structure of a file control block in the 64K ROM version of the File Manager is a subset of the above structure. The old file control block contained only the fields up to and including fcbFlPos.

FCBMdRByt (which corresponds to ioFCBFlags in the parameter block for PBGetFCBInfo) contains flags that describe the status of the file, as follows:

Bit	**Meaning**
0	Set if data can be written to the file
1	Set if the entry describes a resource fork
7	Set if the file has been changed since it was last flushed

Warning: The size and structure of a file control block may be different in future versions of Macintosh system software.

The Drive Queue

Disk drives connected to the Macintosh are opened when the system starts up, and information describing each is placed in the **drive queue**. This is a standard Operating System queue, and each entry in it has the following structure:


```
TYPE DrvQEl = RECORD
                qLink:       QElemPtr;  {next queue entry}
                qType:       INTEGER;   {queue type}
                dQDrive:     INTEGER;   {drive number}
                dQRefNum:    INTEGER;   {driver reference number}
                dQFSID:      INTEGER;   {file-system identifier}
                dQDrvSz:     INTEGER;   {number of logical blocks}
                                        { on drive}
                dQDrvSz2:    INTEGER;   {additional field to handle}
                                        { large drive size}
              END;
```

QLink points to the next entry in the queue. If qType is 0, this means the number of logical blocks on the drive is contained in the dQDrvSz field alone. If qType is 1, both dQDrvSz and dQDrvSz2 are used to store the number of blocks; dqDrvSz2 contains the high-order word of this number and dQDrvSz contains the low-order word.

DQDrive contains the drive number of the drive on which the volume is mounted; dQRefNum contains the driver reference number of the driver controlling the device on which the volume is mounted. DQFSID identifies the file system handling the volume in the drive; it's 0 for volumes handled by the File Manager, and nonzero for volumes handled by other file systems.

Four bytes of flags precede each drive queue entry; they're accessible only from assembly language.

Assembly-language note: These bytes contain the following:

Byte	Contents
0	Bit 7=1 if volume is locked
1	0 if no disk in drive; 1 or 2 if disk in drive; 8 if nonejectable disk in drive; $FC-$FF if disk was ejected within last 1.5 seconds; $48 if disk in drive is nonejectable but driver wants a call
2	Used internally during system startup
3	Bit 7=0 if disk is single-sided

You can get a pointer to the header of the drive queue by calling the File Manager function GetDrvQHdr.

`FUNCTION GetDrvQHdr : QHdrPtr;` [Not in ROM]

GetDrvQHdr returns a pointer to the header of the drive queue.

Assembly-language note: The global variable DrvQHdr contains the header of the drive queue.

The drive queue can support any number of drives, limited only by memory space.

USING AN EXTERNAL FILE SYSTEM

Due to the complexity of writing an external file system for the 128K ROM version of the File Manager, this subject is covered in a separate document. To receive a copy, write to:

Developer Technical Support
Mail Stop 3-T
Apple Computer, Inc.
20525 Mariani Avenue
Cupertino, CA 95014

SUMMARY OF THE FILE MANAGER

Constants

```
CONST { Flags in file information used by the Finder }

      fOnDesk     =  1;      {set if file is on desktop (hierarchical }
                             { volumes only)}
      fHasBundle  =  8192;   {set if file has a bundle}
      fInvisible  =  16384;  {set if file's icon is invisible}
      fTrash      = -3;      {file is in Trash window}
      fDesktop    = -2;      {file is on desktop}
      fDisk       =  0;      {file is in disk window}

      { Values for requesting read/write permission}

      fsCurPerm    = 0;  {whatever is currently allowed}
      fsRdPerm     = 1;  {request for read permission only}
      fsWrPerm     = 2;  {request for write permission only}
      fsRdWrPerm   = 3;  {request for exclusive read/write permission}
      fsRdWrShPerm = 4;  {request for shared read/write permission}

      { Positioning modes }

      fsAtMark    = 0;  {at current mark}
      fsFromStart = 1;  {set mark relative to beginning of file}
      fsFromLEOF  = 2;  {set mark relative to logical end-of-file}
      fsFromMark  = 3;  {set mark relative to current mark}
      rdVerify    = 64; {add to above for read-verify}
```

Data Types

```
TYPE FInfo = RECORD
               fdType:     OSType;  {file type}
               fdCreator:  OSType;  {file's creator}
               fdFlags:    INTEGER; {flags}
               fdLocation: Point;   {file's location}
               fdFldr:     INTEGER  {file's window}
             END;

     FXInfo = RECORD
               fdIconID:  INTEGER; {icon ID}
               fdUnused:  ARRAY[1..4] OF INTEGER; {reserved}
               fdComment: INTEGER; {comment ID}
               fdPutAway: LONGINT; {home directory ID}
             END;
```

```
DInfo = RECORD
          frRect:     Rect;    {folder's rectangle}
          frFlags:    INTEGER; {flags}
          frLocation: Point;   {folder's location}
          frView:     INTEGER; {folder's view}
        END;

DXInfo = RECORD
          frScroll:    Point;   {scroll position}
          frOpenChain: LONGINT; {directory ID chain of open }
                                { folders}
          frUnused:    INTEGER; {reserved}
          frComment:   INTEGER; {comment ID}
          frPutAway:   LONGINT; {directory ID}
        END;

ParamBlkType  =  (ioParam,fileParam,volumeParam,cntrlParam);

ParmBlkPtr    =  ^ParamBlockRec;
ParamBlockRec =  RECORD
  qLink:         QElemPtr;    {next queue entry}
  qType:         INTEGER;     {queue type}
  ioTrap:        INTEGER;     {routine trap}
  ioCmdAddr:     Ptr;         {routine address}
  ioCompletion:  ProcPtr;     {completion routine}
  ioResult:      OSErr;       {result code}
  ioNamePtr:     StringPtr;   {pathname}
  ioVRefNum:     INTEGER;     {volume reference number, drive }
                              { number, or working directory }
                              { reference number}
CASE ParamBlkType OF
ioParam:
 (ioRefNum:      INTEGER;     {path reference number}
  ioVersNum:     SignedByte;  {version number}
  ioPermssn:     SignedByte;  {read/write permission}
  ioMisc:        Ptr;         {miscellaneous}
  ioBuffer:      Ptr;         {data buffer}
  ioReqCount:    LONGINT;     {requested number of bytes}
  ioActCount:    LONGINT;     {actual number of bytes}
  ioPosMode:     INTEGER;     {positioning mode and newline }
                              { character}
  ioPosOffset:   LONGINT);    {positioning offset}
fileParam:
 (ioFRefNum:     INTEGER;     {path reference number}
  ioFVersNum:    SignedByte;  {version number}
  filler1:       SignedByte;  {not used}
  ioFDirIndex:   INTEGER;     {directory index}
  ioFlAttrib:    SignedByte;  {file attributes}
  ioFlVersNum:   SignedByte;  {version number}
  ioFlFndrInfo:  FInfo;       {information used by the Finder}
  ioFlNum:       LONGINT;     {file number}
  ioFlStBlk:     INTEGER;     {first allocation block of data fork}
  ioFlLgLen:     LONGINT;     {logical end-of-file of data fork}
  ioFlPyLen:     LONGINT;     {physical end-of-file of data fork}
  ioFlRStBlk:    INTEGER;     {first allocation block of resource }
                              { fork}
  ioFlRLgLen:    LONGINT;     {logical end-of-file of resource fork}
```

```
    ioFlRPyLen:    LONGINT;       {physical end-of-file of resource }
                                  { fork}
    ioFlCrDat:     LONGINT;       {date and time of creation}
    ioFlMdDat:     LONGINT);      {date and time of last modification}
 volumeParam:
   (filler2:       LONGINT;       {not used}
    ioVolIndex:    INTEGER;       {volume index}
    ioVCrDate:     LONGINT;       {date and time of initialization}
    ioVLsBkUp:     LONGINT;       {date and time of last modification}
    ioVAtrb:       INTEGER;       {volume attributes}
    ioVNmFls       INTEGER;       {number of files in directory}
    ioVDirSt:      INTEGER;       {first block of directory}
    ioVBlLn:       INTEGER;       {length of directory in blocks}
    ioVNmAlBlks:   INTEGER;       {number of allocation blocks}
    ioVAlBlkSiz:   LONGINT;       {size of allocation blocks}
    ioVClpSiz:     LONGINT;       {number of bytes to allocate}
    ioAlBlSt:      INTEGER;       {first block in block map}
    ioVNxtFNum:    LONGINT;       {next unused file number}
    ioVFrBlk:      INTEGER);      {number of unused allocation blocks}
 cntrlParam:
    . . .  {used by Device Manager}
 END;

 HParmBlkPtr    = ^HParamBlockRec;
 HParamBlockRec = RECORD
    qLink:         QElemPtr;      {queue link}
    qType:         INTEGER;       {queue type}
    ioTrap:        INTEGER;       {routine trap}
    ioCmdAddr:     Ptr;           {routine address}
    ioCompletion:  ProcPtr;       {completion routine}
    ioResult:      OSErr;         {result code}
    ioNamePtr:     StringPtr;     {pathname}
    ioVRefNum:     INTEGER;       {volume reference number, drive }
                                  { number, or working directory }
                                  { reference number}
 CASE ParamBlkType OF
 ioParam:
   (ioRefNum:      INTEGER;       {path reference number}
    ioVersNum:     SignedByte;    {version number}
    ioPermssn:     SignedByte;    {read/write permission}
    ioMisc:        Ptr;           {miscellaneous}
    ioBuffer:      Ptr;           {data buffer}
    ioReqCount:    LONGINT;       {requested number of bytes}
    ioActCount:    LONGINT;       {actual number of bytes}
    ioPosMode:     INTEGER;       {positioning mode and newline }
                                  { character}
    ioPosOffset:   LONGINT);      {positioning offset}
 fileParam:
   (ioFRefNum:     INTEGER;       {path reference number}
    ioFVersNum:    SignedByte;    {version number}
    filler1:       SignedByte;    {not used}
    ioFDirIndex:   INTEGER;       {directory index}
    ioFlAttrib:    SignedByte;    {file attributes}
    ioFlVersNum:   SignedByte;    {version number}
    ioFlFndrInfo:  FInfo;         {information used by the Finder}
    ioDirID:       LONGINT;       {directory ID or file number}
    ioFlStBlk:     INTEGER;       {first allocation block of data fork}
```

```
    ioFlLgLen:     LONGINT;     {logical end-of-file of data fork}
    ioFlPyLen:     LONGINT;     {physical end-of-file of data fork}
    ioFlRStBlk:    INTEGER;     {first allocation block of resource }
                                { fork}
    ioFlRLgLen:    LONGINT;     {logical end-of-file of resource fork}
    ioFlRPyLen:    LONGINT;     {physical end-of-file of resource }
                                { fork}
    ioFlCrDat:     LONGINT;     {date and time of creation}
    ioFlMdDat:     LONGINT);    {date and time of last modification}
volumeParam:
   (filler2:       LONGINT;     {not used}
    ioVolIndex:    INTEGER;     {volume index}
    ioVCrDate:     LONGINT;     {date and time of initialization}
    ioVLsMod:      LONGINT;     {date and time of last modification}
    ioVAtrb:       INTEGER;     {volume attributes}
    ioVNmFls:      INTEGER;     {number of files in directory}
    ioVBitMap:     INTEGER;     {first block of volume bitmap}
    ioAllocPtr:    INTEGER;     {used internally}
    ioVNmAlBlks:   INTEGER;     {number of allocation blocks}
    ioVAlBlkSiz:   LONGINT;     {size of allocation blocks}
    ioVClpSiz:     LONGINT;     {default clump size}
    ioAlBlSt:      INTEGER;     {first block in volume block map}
    ioVNxtCNID:    LONGINT;     {next unused node ID}
    ioVFrBlk:      INTEGER;     {number of unused allocation blocks}
    ioVSigWord:    INTEGER;     {volume signature}
    ioVDrvInfo:    INTEGER;     {drive number}
    ioVDRefNum:    INTEGER;     {driver reference number}
    ioVFSID:       INTEGER;     {file-system identifier}
    ioVBkUp:       LONGINT;     {date and time of last backup}
    ioVSeqNum:     INTEGER;     {used internally}
    ioVWrCnt       LONGINT;     {volume write count}
    ioVFilCnt:     LONGINT;     {number of files on volume}
    ioVDirCnt:     LONGINT;     {number of directories on volume}
    ioVFndrInfo:   ARRAY[1..8] OF LONGINT);  {information used by }
                                              { the Finder}
END;

CInfoType  = (hfileInfo,dirInfo);

CInfoPBPtr = ^CInfoPBRec;
CInfoPBRec = RECORD
    qLink:         QElemPtr;    {next queue entry}
    qType:         INTEGER;     {queue type}
    ioTrap:        INTEGER;     {routine trap}
    ioCmdAddr:     Ptr;         {routine address}
    ioCompletion:  ProcPtr;     {completion routine}
    ioResult:      OSErr;       {result code}
    ioNamePtr:     StringPtr;   {pathname}
    ioVRefNum:     INTEGER;     {volume reference number, drive }
                                { number, or working directory }
                                { reference number}
    ioFRefNum:     INTEGER;     {file reference number}
    ioFVersNum:    SignedByte;  {version number}
    filler1:       SignedByte;  {not used}
    ioFDirIndex:   INTEGER;     {directory index}
    ioFlAttrib:    SignedByte;  {file attributes}
    filler2:       SignedByte;  {not used}
```

```
CASE CInfoType OF
hFileInfo:
  (ioFlFndrInfo: FInfo;        {information used by the Finder}
   ioDirID:       LONGINT;     {directory ID or file number}
   ioFlStBlk:     INTEGER;     {first allocation block of data fork}
   ioFlLgLen:     LONGINT;     {logical end-of-file of data fork}
   ioFlPyLen:     LONGINT;     {physical end-of-file of data fork}
   ioFlRStBlk:    INTEGER;     {first allocation block of resource }
                               { fork}
   ioFlRLgLen:    LONGINT;     {logical end-of-file of resource fork}
   ioFlRPyLen:    LONGINT;     {physical end-of-file of resource }
                               { fork}
   ioFlCrDat:     LONGINT;     {date and time of creation}
   ioFlMdDat:     LONGINT;     {date and time of last modification}
   ioFlBkDat:     LONGINT;     {date and time of last back-up}
   ioFlXFndrInfo: FXInfo;      {additional information used by the }
                               { Finder}
   ioFlParID:     LONGINT;     {file parent directory ID (integer)}
   ioFlClpSiz:    LONGINT);    {file's clump size}
dirInfo:
  (ioDrUsrWds:   DInfo;        {information used by the }
                               { Finder}
   ioDrDirID:     LONGINT;     {directory ID}
   ioDrNmFls:     INTEGER;     {number of files in directory}
   filler3:       ARRAY[1..9] OF INTEGER;
   ioDrCrDat:     LONGINT;     {date and time of creation}
   ioDrMdDat:     LONGINT;     {date and time of last modification}
   ioDrBkDat:     LONGINT;     {date and time of last back-up}
   ioDrFndrInfo:  DXInfo;      {additional information used by the }
                               { Finder}
   ioDrParID:     LONGINT);    {directory's parent directory ID}
END;

CMovePBPtr = ^CMovePBRec;
CMovePBRec = RECORD
   qLink:         QElemPtr;    {next queue entry}
   qType:         INTEGER;     {queue type}
   ioTrap:        INTEGER;     {routine trap}
   ioCmdAddr:     Ptr;         {routine address}
   ioCompletion:  ProcPtr;     {completion routine}
   ioResult:      OSErr;       {result code}
   ioNamePtr:     StringPtr;   {pathname}
   ioVRefNum:     INTEGER;     {volume reference number, drive }
                               { number, or working directory }
                               { reference number}
   filler1:       LONGINT;     {not used}
   ioNewName:     StringPtr;   {name of new directory}
   filler2:       LONGINT;     {not used}
   ioNewDirID:    LONGINT;     {directory ID of new directory}
   filler3:       ARRAY[1..2] OF LONGINT;  {not used}
   ioDirID:       LONGINT);    {directory ID of current directory}
END;
```

```
WDPBPtr = ^WDPBRec;
WDPBRec = RECORD
  qLink:         QElemPtr;    {next queue entry}
  qType:         INTEGER;     {queue type}
  ioTrap:        INTEGER;     {routine trap}
  ioCmdAddr:     Ptr;         {routine address}
  ioCompletion:  ProcPtr;     {completion routine}
  ioResult:      OSErr;       {result code}
  ioNamePtr:     StringPtr;   {pathname}
  ioVRefNum:     INTEGER;     {volume reference number, drive }
                              { number, or working directory }
                              { reference number}
  filler1:       INTEGER;     {not used}
  ioWDIndex:     INTEGER;     {working directory index}
  ioWDProcID:    LONGINT;     {working directory user identifier}
  ioWDVRefNum:   INTEGER;     {working directory's volume }
                              { reference number}
  filler2:       ARRAY[1..7] OF INTEGER;   {not used}
  ioWDDirID:     LONGINT);    {working directory's directory ID}
END;

FCBPBPtr = ^FCBPBRec;
FCBPBRec = RECORD
  qLink:         QElemPtr;    {next queue entry}
  qType:         INTEGER;     {queue type}
  ioTrap:        INTEGER;     {routine trap}
  ioCmdAddr:     Ptr;         {routine address}
  ioCompletion:  ProcPtr;     {completion routine}
  ioResult:      OSErr;       {result code}
  ioNamePtr:     StringPtr;   {pathname}
  ioVRefNum:     INTEGER;     {volume reference number, drive }
                              { number, or working directory }
                              { reference number}
  ioRefNum:      INTEGER;     {path reference number}
  filler:        INTEGER;     {not used}
  ioFCBIndx:     LONGINT;     {FCB index}
  ioFCBFlNm:     LONGINT;     {file number}
  ioFCBFlags:    INTEGER;     {flags }
  ioFCBStBlk:    INTEGER;     {first allocation block of file}
  ioFCBEOF:      LONGINT;     {logical end-of-file}
  ioFCBPLen:     LONGINT;     {physical end-of-file}
  ioFCBCrPs:     LONGINT;     {mark}
  ioFCBVRefNum:  INTEGER;     {volume reference number}
  ioFCBClpSiz:   LONGINT;     {file's clump size}
  ioFCBParID:    LONGINT;     {parent directory ID}
END;

VCB = RECORD
        qLink:        QElemPtr;    {next queue entry}
        qType:        INTEGER;     {queue type}
        vcbFlags:     INTEGER;     {bit 15=1 if dirty}
        vcbSigWord:   INTEGER;     {$4244 for hierarchical, }
                                   {$D2D7 for flat}
        vcbCrDate:    LONGINT;     {date and time of initialization}
        vcbLsMod:     LONGINT;     {date and time of last }
                                   { modification}
        vcbAtrb:      INTEGER;     {volume attributes}
        vcbNmFls:     INTEGER;     {number of files in directory}
```

```
        vcbVBMSt:    INTEGER;      {first block of volume bit map}
        vcbAllocPtr: INTEGER;      {used internally}
        vcbNmAlBlks: INTEGER;      {number of allocation blocks}
        vcbAlBlkSiz: LONGINT;      {allocation block size}
        vcbClpSiz:   LONGINT;      {default clump size}
        vcbAlBlSt:   INTEGER;      {first block in bit map}
        vcbNxtCNID:  LONGINT;      {next unused node ID}
        vcbFreeBks:  INTEGER;      {number of unused allocation }
                                   { blocks}
        vcbVN:       STRING[27]; {volume name}
        vcbDrvNum:   INTEGER;      {drive number}
        vcbDRefNum:  INTEGER;      {driver reference number}
        vcbFSID:     INTEGER;      {file-system identifier}
        vcbVRefNum:  INTEGER;      {volume reference number}
        vcbMAdr:     Ptr;          {pointer to block map}
        vcbBufAdr:   Ptr;          {pointer to volume buffer}
        vcbMLen:     INTEGER;      {number of bytes in block map}
        vcbDirIndex: INTEGER;      {used internally}
        vcbDirBlk:   INTEGER;      {used internally}
        vcbVolBkUp:  LONGINT;      {date and time of last backup}
        vcbVSeqNum:  INTEGER;      {used internally}
        vcbWrCnt:    LONGINT;      {volume write count}
        vcbXTClpSiz: LONGINT;      {clump size of extents tree file}
        vcbCTClpSiz: LONGINT;      {clump size of catalog tree file}
        vcbNmRtDirs: INTEGER;      {number of directories in root}
        vcbFilCnt:   LONGINT;      {number of files on volume}
        vcbDirCnt:   LONGINT;      {number of directories on volume}
        vcbFndrInfo: ARRAY[1..8] OF LONGINT; {information used }
                                   { by the Finder}
        vcbVCSize:   INTEGER;      {used internally}
        vcbVBMCSiz:  INTEGER;      {used internally}
        vcbCtlCSiz:  INTEGER;      {used internally}
        vcbXTAlBlks: INTEGER;      {size in blocks of extents tree }
                                   { file}
        vcbCTAlBlks: INTEGER;      {size in blocks of catalog tree }
                                   { file}
        vcbXTRef:    INTEGER;      {path reference number for }
                                   { extents tree file}
        vcbCTRef:    INTEGER;      {path reference number for }
                                   { catalog tree file}
        vcbCtlBuf:   Ptr;          {pointer to extents and catalog }
                                   { caches}
        vcbDirIDM:   LONGINT;      {directory last searched}
        vcbOffsM:    INTEGER       {offspring index at last search}
      END;

DrvQEl = RECORD
           qLink:      QElemPtr; {next queue entry}
           qType:      INTEGER;  {queue type}
           dQDrive:    INTEGER;  {drive number}
           dQRefNum:   INTEGER;  {driver reference number}
           dQFSID:     INTEGER;  {file-system identifier}
           dQDrvSz:    INTEGER   {number of logical blocks}
           dQDrvSz2:   INTEGER   {additional field to handle }
                                 { large drive}
         END;
```

High-Level Routines [Not in ROM]

Accessing Volumes

```
FUNCTION GetVInfo     (drvNum: INTEGER; volName: StringPtr; VAR vRefNum:
                       INTEGER; VAR freeBytes: LONGINT) : OSErr;
FUNCTION GetVRefNum (pathRefNum: INTEGER; VAR vRefNum: INTEGER) :
                       OSErr;
FUNCTION GetVol       (volName: StringPtr; VAR vRefNum: INTEGER) : OSErr;
FUNCTION SetVol       (volName: StringPtr; vRefNum: INTEGER) : OSErr;
FUNCTION FlushVol     (volName: StringPtr; vRefNum: INTEGER) : OSErr;
FUNCTION UnmountVol (volName: StringPtr; vRefNum: INTEGER) : OSErr;
FUNCTION Eject        (volName: StringPtr; vRefNum: INTEGER) : OSErr;
```

Accessing Files

```
FUNCTION FSOpen       (fileName: Str255; vRefNum: INTEGER; VAR refNum:
                       INTEGER) : OSErr;
FUNCTION OpenRF       (fileName: Str255; vRefNum: INTEGER; VAR refNum:
                       INTEGER) : OSErr;
FUNCTION FSRead       (refNum: INTEGER; VAR count: LONGINT; buffPtr: Ptr)
                       : OSErr;
FUNCTION FSWrite      (refNum: INTEGER; VAR count: LONGINT; buffPtr: Ptr)
                       : OSErr;
FUNCTION GetFPos      (refNum: INTEGER; VAR filePos: LONGINT) : OSErr;
FUNCTION SetFPos      (refNum: INTEGER; posMode: INTEGER; posOff:
                       LONGINT) : OSErr;
FUNCTION GetEOF       (refNum: INTEGER; VAR logEOF: LONGINT) : OSErr;
FUNCTION SetEOF       (refNum: INTEGER; logEOF: LONGINT) : OSErr;
FUNCTION Allocate     (refNum: INTEGER; VAR count: LONGINT) : OSErr;
FUNCTION FSClose      (refNum: INTEGER) : OSErr;
```

Creating and Deleting Files

```
FUNCTION Create       (fileName: Str255; vRefNum: INTEGER; creator:
                       OSType; fileType: OSType) : OSErr;
FUNCTION FSDelete     (fileName: Str255; vRefNum: INTEGER) : OSErr;
```

Changing Information About Files

```
FUNCTION GetFInfo     (fileName: Str255; vRefNum: INTEGER; VAR fndrInfo:
                       FInfo) : OSErr;
FUNCTION SetFInfo     (fileName: Str255; vRefNum: INTEGER; fndrInfo:
                       FInfo) : OSErr;
FUNCTION SetFLock     (fileName: Str255; vRefNum: INTEGER) : OSErr;
FUNCTION RstFLock     (fileName: Str255; vRefNum: INTEGER) : OSErr;
FUNCTION Rename       (oldName: Str255; vRefNum: INTEGER; newName:
                       Str255) : OSErr;
```

Low-Level Routines

Initializing the File I/O Queue

```
PROCEDURE FInitQueue;

FUNCTION PBMountVol (paramBlock: ParmBlkPtr) : OSErr;
        <—   16   ioResult      word
        <->  22   ioVRefNum     word
```

Accessing Volumes

```
FUNCTION PBGetVInfo (paramBlock: ParmBlkPtr; async: BOOLEAN) : OSErr;
        —>   12   ioCompletion  pointer
        <—   16   ioResult      word
        <->  18   ioNamePtr     pointer
        <->  22   ioVRefNum     word
        —>   28   ioVolIndex    word
        <—   30   ioVCrDate     long word
        <—   34   ioVLsBkUp     long word
        <—   38   ioVAtrb       word
        <—   40   ioVNmFls      word
        <—   42   ioVDirSt      word
        <—   44   ioVBlLn       word
        <—   46   ioVNmAlBlks   word
        <—   48   ioVAlBlkSiz   long word
        <—   52   ioVClpSiz     long word
        <—   56   ioAlBlSt      word
        <—   58   ioVNxtFNum    long word
        <—   62   ioVFrBlk      word

FUNCTION PBHGetVInfo (paramBlock: HParmBlkPtr; async: BOOLEAN) : OSErr;
        —>   12   ioCompletion  pointer
        <—   16   ioResult      word
        <->  18   ioNamePtr     pointer
        <->  22   ioVRefNum     word
        —>   28   ioVolIndex    word
        <—   30   ioVCrDate     long word
        <—   34   ioVLsMod      long word
        <—   38   ioVAtrb       word
        <—   40   ioVNmFls      word
        <—   42   ioVBitMap     word
        <—   44   ioVAllocPtr   word
        <—   46   ioVNmAlBlks   word
        <—   48   ioVAlBlkSiz   long word
        <—   52   ioVClpSiz     long word
        <—   56   ioAlBlSt      word
        <—   58   ioVNxtFNum    long word
        <—   62   ioVFrBlk      word
        <—   64   ioVSigWord    word
        <—   66   ioVDrvInfo    word
        <—   68   ioVDRefNum    word
        <—   70   ioVFSID       word
        <—   72   ioVBkUp       long word
```

<—	76	ioVSeqNum	word
<—	78	ioVWrCnt	long word
<—	82	ioVFilCnt	long word
<—	86	ioVDirCnt	long word
<—	90	ioVFndrInfo	32 bytes

```
FUNCTION PBSetVInfo (paramBlock: HParmBlkPtr; async: BOOLEAN) : OSErr;
```

—>	12	ioCompletion	pointer
<—	16	ioResult	word
—>	18	ioNamePtr	pointer
—>	22	ioVRefNum	word
—>	30	ioVCrDate	long word
—>	34	ioVLsMod	long word
—>	38	ioVAtrb	word
—>	52	ioVClpSiz	long word
—>	72	ioVBkUp	long word
—>	76	ioVSeqNum	word
—>	90	ioVFndrInfo	32 bytes

```
FUNCTION PBGetVol (paramBlock: ParmBlkPtr; async: BOOLEAN) : OSErr;
```

—>	12	ioCompletion	pointer
<—	16	ioResult	word
<—	18	ioNamePtr	pointer
<—	22	ioVRefNum	word

```
FUNCTION PBHGetVol (paramBlock: WDPBPtr; async: BOOLEAN): OsErr;
```

—>	12	ioCompletion	pointer
<—	16	ioResult	word
<—	18	ioNamePtr	pointer
<—	22	ioVRefNum	word
<—	28	ioWDProcID	long word
<—	32	ioWDVRefNum	word
<—	48	ioWDDirID	long word

```
FUNCTION PBSetVol (paramBlock: ParmBlkPtr; async: BOOLEAN) : OSErr;
```

—>	12	ioCompletion	pointer
<—	16	ioResult	word
—>	18	ioNamePtr	pointer
—>	22	ioVRefNum	word

```
FUNCTION PBHSetVol (paramBlock: WDPBPtr; async: BOOLEAN) : OSErr;
```

—>	12	ioCompletion	pointer
<—	16	ioResult	word
—>	18	ioNamePtr	pointer
—>	22	ioVRefNum	word
—>	48	ioWDDirID	long word

```
FUNCTION PBFlushVol (paramBlock: ParmBlkPtr; async: BOOLEAN) : OSErr;
```

—>	12	ioCompletion	pointer
<—	16	ioResult	word
—>	18	ioNamePtr	pointer
—>	22	ioVRefNum	word

```
FUNCTION PBUnmountVol (paramBlock: ParmBlkPtr) : OSErr;
```

<—	16	ioResult	word
—>	18	ioNamePtr	pointer
—>	22	ioVRefNum	word

```
FUNCTION PBOffLine (paramBlock: ParmBlkPtr) : OSErr;
```

—>	12	ioCompletion	pointer
<—	16	ioResult	word
—>	18	ioNamePtr	pointer
—>	22	ioVRefNum	word

```
FUNCTION PBEject (paramBlock: ParmBlkPtr) : OSErr;
```

—>	12	ioCompletion	pointer
<—	16	ioResult	word
—>	18	ioNamePtr	pointer
—>	22	ioVRefNum	word

Accessing Files

```
FUNCTION PBOpen (paramBlock: ParmBlkPtr; async: BOOLEAN) : OSErr;
```

—>	12	ioCompletion	pointer
<—	16	ioResult	word
—>	18	ioNamePtr	pointer
—>	22	ioVRefNum	word
<—	24	ioRefNum	word
—>	26	ioVersNum	byte
—>	27	ioPermssn	byte
—>	28	ioMisc	pointer

```
FUNCTION PBHOpen (paramBlock: HParmBlkPtr; async: BOOLEAN) : OSErr;
```

—>	12	ioCompletion	pointer
<—	16	ioResult	word
—>	18	ioNamePtr	pointer
—>	22	ioVRefNum	word
<—	24	ioRefNum	word
—>	27	ioPermssn	byte
—>	28	ioMisc	pointer
—>	48	ioDirID	long word

```
FUNCTION PBOpenRF (paramBlock: ParmBlkPtr; async: BOOLEAN) : OSErr;
```

—>	12	ioCompletion	pointer
<—	16	ioResult	word
—>	18	ioNamePtr	pointer
—>	22	ioVRefNum	word
<—	24	ioRefNum	word
—>	26	ioVersNum	byte
—>	27	ioPermssn	byte
—>	28	ioMisc	pointer

```
FUNCTION PBHOpenRF (paramBlock: HParmBlkPtr; async: BOOLEAN) : OSErr;
```

—>	12	ioCompletion	pointer
<—	16	ioResult	word
—>	18	ioNamePtr	pointer
—>	22	ioVRefNum	word
<—	24	ioRefNum	word
—>	27	ioPermssn	byte
—>	28	ioMisc	pointer
—>	48	ioDirID	long word

```
FUNCTION PBLockRange (paramBlock: ParmBlkPtr; async: BOOLEAN) : OSErr;
```

—>	12	ioCompletion	pointer
<—	16	ioResult	word
—>	24	ioRefNum	word
—>	36	ioReqCount	long word
—>	44	ioPosMode	word
—>	46	ioPosOffset	long word

```
FUNCTION PBUnlockRange (paramBlock: ParmBlkPtr; async: BOOLEAN) : OSErr
```

—>	12	ioCompletion	pointer
<—	16	ioResult	word
—>	24	ioRefNum	word
—>	36	ioReqCount	long word
—>	44	ioPosMode	word
—>	46	ioPosOffset	long word

```
FUNCTION PBRead (paramBlock: ParmBlkPtr; async: BOOLEAN) : OSErr;
```

—>	12	ioCompletion	pointer
<—	16	ioResult	word
—>	24	ioRefNum	word
—>	32	ioBuffer	pointer
—>	36	ioReqCount	long word
<—	40	ioActCount	long word
—>	44	ioPosMode	word
<—>	46	ioPosOffset	long word

```
FUNCTION PBWrite (paramBlock: ParmBlkPtr; async: BOOLEAN) : OSErr;
```

—>	12	ioCompletion	pointer
<—	16	ioResult	word
—>	24	ioRefNum	word
—>	32	ioBuffer	pointer
—>	36	ioReqCount	long word
<—	40	ioActCount	long word
—>	44	ioPosMode	word
<—>	46	ioPosOffset	long word

```
FUNCTION PBGetFPos (paramBlock: ParmBlkPtr; async: BOOLEAN) : OSErr;
```

—>	12	ioCompletion	pointer
<—	16	ioResult	word
—>	24	ioRefNum	word
<—	36	ioReqCount	long word
<—	40	ioActCount	long word
<—	44	ioPosMode	word
<—	46	ioPosOffset	long word

```
FUNCTION PBSetFPos (paramBlock: ParmBlkPtr; async: BOOLEAN) : OSErr;
```

—>	12	ioCompletion	pointer
<—	16	ioResult	word
—>	24	ioRefNum	word
—>	44	ioPosMode	word
<->	46	ioPosOffset	long word

```
FUNCTION PBGetEOF (paramBlock: ParmBlkPtr; async: BOOLEAN) : OSErr;
```

—>	12	ioCompletion	pointer
<—	16	ioResult	word
—>	24	ioRefNum	word
<—	28	ioMisc	long word

```
FUNCTION PBSetEOF (paramBlock: ParmBlkPtr; async: BOOLEAN) : OSErr;
```

—>	12	ioCompletion	pointer
<—	16	ioResult	word
—>	24	ioRefNum	word
—>	28	ioMisc	long word

```
FUNCTION PBAllocate (paramBlock: ParmBlkPtr; async: BOOLEAN) : OSErr;
```

—>	12	ioCompletion	pointer
<—	16	ioResult	word
—>	24	ioRefNum	word
—>	36	ioReqCount	long word
<—	40	ioActCount	long word

```
FUNCTION PBAllocContig (paramBlock: ParmBlkPtr; async: BOOLEAN) : OSErr;
```

—>	12	ioCompletion	pointer
<—	16	ioResult	word
—>	24	ioRefNum	word
—>	36	ioReqCount	long word
<—	40	ioActCount	long word

```
FUNCTION PBFlushFile (paramBlock: ParmBlkPtr; async: BOOLEAN) : OSErr;
```

—>	12	ioCompletion	pointer
<—	16	ioResult	word
—>	24	ioRefNum	word

```
FUNCTION PBClose (paramBlock: ParmBlkPtr; async: BOOLEAN) : OSErr;
```

—>	12	ioCompletion	pointer
<—	16	ioResult	word
—>	24	ioRefNum	word

Creating and Deleting Files and Directories

```
FUNCTION PBCreate (paramBlock: ParmBlkPtr; async: BOOLEAN) : OSErr;
```

—>	12	ioCompletion	pointer
<—	16	ioResult	word
—>	18	ioNamePtr	pointer
—>	22	ioVRefNum	word
—>	26	ioFVersNum	byte

```
FUNCTION PBHCreate (paramBlock: HParmBlkPtr; async: BOOLEAN) : OSErr;
        —>    12   ioCompletion    pointer
        <—    16   ioResult        word
        —>    18   ioNamePtr       pointer
        —>    22   ioVRefNum       word
        —>    48   ioDirID         long word
```

```
FUNCTION PBDirCreate (paramBlock: HParmBlkPtr; async: BOOLEAN) : OSErr;
        —>    12   ioCompletion    pointer
        <—    16   ioResult        word
        <->   18   ioNamePtr       pointer
        —>    22   ioVRefNum       word
        <->   48   ioDirID         long word
```

```
FUNCTION PBDelete (paramBlock: ParmBlkPtr; async: BOOLEAN) : OSErr;
        —>    12   ioCompletion    pointer
        <—    16   ioResult        word
        —>    18   ioNamePtr       pointer
        —>    22   ioVRefNum       word
        —>    26   ioFVersNum      byte
```

```
FUNCTION PBHDelete (paramBlock: HParmBlkPtr; async: BOOLEAN) : OSErr;
        —>    12   ioCompletion    pointer
        <—    16   ioResult        word
        —>    18   ioNamePtr       pointer
        —>    22   ioVRefNum       word
        —>    48   ioDirID         long word
```

Changing Information About Files and Directories

```
FUNCTION PBGetFInfo (paramBlock: ParmBlkPtr; async: BOOLEAN) : OSErr;
        —>    12   ioCompletion    pointer
        <—    16   ioResult        word
        <->   18   ioNamePtr       pointer
        —>    22   ioVRefNum       word
        <—    24   ioFRefNum       word
        —>    26   ioFVersNum      byte
        —>    28   ioFDirIndex     word
        <—    30   ioFlAttrib      byte
        <—    31   ioFlVersNum     byte
        <—    32   ioFlFndrInfo    16 bytes
        <—    48   ioFlNum         long word
        <—    52   ioFlStBlk       word
        <—    54   ioFlLgLen       long word
        <—    58   ioFlPyLen       long word
        <—    62   ioFlRStBlk      word
        <—    64   ioFlRLgLen      long word
        <—    68   ioFlRPyLen      long word
        <—    72   ioFlCrDat       long word
        <—    76   ioFlMdDat       long word
```

```
FUNCTION PBHGetFInfo (paramBlock: HParmBlkPtr; async: BOOLEAN) : OSErr;
```

—>	12	ioCompletion	pointer
<—	16	ioResult	word
<->	18	ioNamePtr	pointer
—>	22	ioVRefNum	word
<—	24	ioFRefNum	word
—>	28	ioFDirIndex	word
<—	30	ioFlAttrib	byte
<—	32	ioFlFndrInfo	16 bytes
<->	48	ioDirID	long word
<—	52	ioFlStBlk	word
<—	54	ioFlLgLen	long word
<—	58	ioFlPyLen	long word
<—	62	ioFlRStBlk	word
<—	64	ioFlRLgLen	long word
<—	68	ioFlRPyLen	long word
<—	72	ioFlCrDat	long word
<—	76	ioFlMdDat	long word

```
FUNCTION PBSetFInfo (paramBlock: ParmBlkPtr; async: BOOLEAN) : OSErr;
```

—>	12	ioCompletion	pointer
<—	16	ioResult	word
—>	18	ioNamePtr	pointer
—>	22	ioVRefNum	word
—>	26	ioFVersNum	byte
—>	32	ioFlFndrInfo	16 bytes
—>	72	ioFlCrDat	long word
—>	76	ioFlMdDat	long word

```
FUNCTION PBHSetFInfo (paramBlock: HParmBlkPtr; async: BOOLEAN) : OSErr;
```

—>	12	ioCompletion	pointer
<—	16	ioResult	word
—>	18	ioNamePtr	pointer
—>	22	ioVRefNum	word
—>	32	ioFlFndrInfo	16 bytes
—>	48	ioDirID	long word
—>	72	ioFlCrDat	long word
—>	76	ioFlMdDat	long word

```
FUNCTION PBSetFLock (paramBlock: ParmBlkPtr; async: BOOLEAN) : OSErr;
```

—>	12	ioCompletion	pointer
<—	16	ioResult	word
—>	18	ioNamePtr	pointer
—>	22	ioVRefNum	word
—>	26	ioFVersNum	byte

```
FUNCTION PBHSetFLock (paramBlock: HParmBlkPtr; async: BOOLEAN) : OSErr;
```

—>	12	ioCompletion	pointer
<—	16	ioResult	word
—>	18	ioNamePtr	pointer
—>	22	ioVRefNum	word
—>	48	ioDirID	long word

```
FUNCTION PBRstFLock (paramBlock: ParmBlkPtr; async: BOOLEAN) : OSErr;
    —>   12  ioCompletion   pointer
    <—   16  ioResult       word
    —>   18  ioNamePtr      pointer
    —>   22  ioVRefNum      word
    —>   26  ioFVersNum     byte
```

```
FUNCTION PBHRstFLock (paramBlock: HParmBlkPtr; async: BOOLEAN) : OSErr;
    —>   12  ioCompletion   pointer
    <—   16  ioResult       word
    —>   18  ioNamePtr      pointer
    —>   22  ioVRefNum      word
    —>   48  ioDirID        long word
```

```
FUNCTION PBSetFVers (paramBlock: ParmBlkPtr; async: BOOLEAN) : OSErr;
    —>   12  ioCompletion   pointer
    <—   16  ioResult       word
    —>   18  ioNamePtr      pointer
    —>   22  ioVRefNum      word
    —>   26  ioVersNum      byte
    —>   28  ioMisc         byte
```

```
FUNCTION PBRename (paramBlock: ParmBlkPtr; async: BOOLEAN) : OSErr;
    —>   12  ioCompletion   pointer
    <—   16  ioResult       word
    —>   18  ioNamePtr      pointer
    —>   22  ioVRefNum      word
    —>   26  ioVersNum      byte
    —>   28  ioMisc         pointer
```

```
FUNCTION PBHRename (paramBlock: HParmBlkPtr; async: BOOLEAN) : OSErr;
    —>   12  ioCompletion   pointer
    <—   16  ioResult       word
    —>   18  ioNamePtr      pointer
    —>   22  ioVRefNum      word
    —>   28  ioMisc         pointer
    —>   48  ioDirID        long word
```

Hierarchical Directory Routines

```
FUNCTION PBGetCatInfo (paramBlock: CInfoPBPtr; async: BOOLEAN) : OSErr;
    —>   12  ioCompletion   pointer
    <—   16  ioResult       word
    <->  18  ioNamePtr      pointer
    —>   22  ioVRefNum      word
    <—   24  ioFRefNum      word
    —>   28  ioFDirIndex    word
    <—   30  ioFlAttrib     byte
    <—   32  ioFlFndrInfo   16 bytes
    <—   32  ioDrUsrWds     16 bytes
    <->  48  ioDirID        long word
    <->  48  ioDrDirID      long word
    <—   52  ioFlStBlk      word
```

<—	52	ioDrNmFls	word
<—	54	ioFlLgLen	long word
<—	58	ioFlPyLen	long word
<—	62	ioFlRStBlk	word
<—	64	ioFlRLgLen	long word
<—	68	ioFlRPyLen	long word
<—	72	ioFlCrDat	long word
<—	72	ioDrCrDat	long word
<—	76	ioFlMdDat	long word
<—	76	ioDrMdDat	long word
<—	80	ioFlBkDat	long word
<—	80	ioDrBkDat	long word
<—	84	ioFlXFndrInfo	16 bytes
<—	84	ioDrFndrInfo	16 bytes
<—	100	ioFlParID	long word
<—	100	ioDrParID	long word
<—	104	ioFlClpSiz	long word


```
FUNCTION PBSetCatInfo (paramBlock: CInfoPBPtr; async: BOOLEAN) : OSErr;
```

—>	12	ioCompletion	pointer
<—	16	ioResult	word
<->	18	ioNamePtr	pointer
—>	22	ioVRefNum	word
—>	28	ioFDirIndex	word
—>	30	ioFlAttrib	byte
—>	32	ioFlFndrInfo	16 bytes
—>	32	ioDrUsrWds	16 bytes
—>	48	ioDirID	long word
—>	48	ioDrDirID	long word
—>	72	ioFlCrDat	long word
—>	72	ioDrCrDat	long word
—>	76	ioFlMdDat	long word
—>	76	ioDrMdDat	long word
—>	80	ioFlBkDat	long word
—>	80	ioDrBkDat	long word
—>	84	ioFlXFndrInfo	16 bytes
—>	84	ioDrFndrInfo	16 bytes
—>	104	ioFlClpSiz	long word

```
FUNCTION PBCatMove (paramBlock: CMovePBPtr; async: BOOLEAN) : OSErr;
```

—>	12	ioCompletion	pointer
<—	16	ioResult	word
—>	18	ioNamePtr	pointer
—>	22	ioVRefNum	word
—>	28	ioNewName	pointer
—>	36	ioNewDirID	long word
—>	48	ioDirID	long word

Working Directory Routines

```
FUNCTION PBOpenWD (paramBlock: WDPBPtr; async: BOOLEAN) : OSErr;
```

—>	12	ioCompletion	pointer
<—	16	ioResult	word
—>	18	ioNamePtr	pointer
<->	22	ioVRefNum	word
—>	28	ioWDProcID	long word
—>	48	ioWDDirID	long word

```
FUNCTION PBCloseWD (paramBlock: WDPBPtr; async: BOOLEAN) : OSErr;
```

—>	12	ioCompletion	pointer
<—	16	ioResult	word
—>	22	ioVRefNum	word

```
FUNCTION PBGetWDInfo (paramBlock: WDPBPtr; async: BOOLEAN) : OSErr;
```

—>	12	ioCompletion	pointer
<—	16	ioResult	word
<—	18	ioNamePtr	pointer
<->	22	ioVRefNum	word
—>	26	ioWDIndex	word
<->	28	ioWDProcID	long word
<->	32	ioWDVRefNum	word
<—	48	ioWDDirID	long word

Advanced Routines

```
FUNCTION GetFSQHdr   : QHdrPtr;   [Not in ROM]
FUNCTION GetVCBQHdr : QHdrPtr;   [Not in ROM]
FUNCTION GetDrvQHdr : QHdrPtr;   [Not in ROM]
```

```
FUNCTION PBGetFCBInfo (paramBlock: FCBPBPtr; async: BOOLEAN) : OSErr;
```

—>	12	ioCompletion	pointer
<—	16	ioResult	word
<—	18	ioNamePtr	pointer
<->	22	ioVRefNum	word
<->	24	ioRefNum	word
—>	28	ioFCBIndx	long word
<—	32	ioFCBFlNm	long word
<—	36	ioFCBFlags	word
<—	38	ioFCBStBlk	word
<—	40	ioFCBEOF	long word
<—	44	ioFCBPLen	long word
<—	48	ioFCBCrPs	long word
<—	52	ioFCBVRefNum	word
<—	54	ioFCBClpSiz	long word
<—	58	ioFCBParID	long word

Result Codes

Name	Value	Meaning
badMDBErr	–60	Master directory block is bad; must reinitialize volume
badMovErr	–122	Attempted to move into offspring
bdNamErr	–37	Bad file name or volume name (perhaps zero-length); attempt to move into a file
dirFulErr	–33	File directory full
dirNFErr	–120	Directory not found
dskFulErr	–34	All allocation blocks on the volume are full
dupFNErr	–48	A file with the specified name and version number already exists
eofErr	–39	Logical end-of-file reached during read operation
extFSErr	–58	External file system; file-system identifier is nonzero, or path reference number is greater than 1024
fBsyErr	–47	File is busy; one or more files are open; directory not empty or working directory control block is open
fLckdErr	–45	File locked
fnfErr	–43	File not found
fnOpnErr	–38	File not open
fsDSIntErr	–127	Internal file system error
fsRnErr	–59	Problem during rename
gfpErr	–52	Error during GetFPos
ioErr	–36	I/O error
memFullErr	–108	Not enough room in heap zone
noErr	0	No error
noMacDskErr	–57	Volume lacks Macintosh-format directory
nsDrvErr	–56	Specified drive number doesn't match any number in the drive queue
nsvErr	–35	Specified volume doesn't exist
opWrErr	–49	The read/write permission of only one access path to a file can allow writing
paramErr	–50	Parameters don't specify an existing volume, and there's no default volume
permErr	–54	Attempt to open locked file for writing
posErr	–40	Attempt to position before start of file
rfNumErr	–51	Reference number specifies nonexistent access path
tmfoErr	–42	Too many files open
tmwdoErr	–121	Too many working directories open
volOffLinErr	–53	Volume not on-line
volOnLinErr	–55	Specified volume is already mounted and on-line
vLckdErr	–46	Volume is locked by a software flag
wrgVolTypErr	–123	Attempt to do hierarchical operation on nonhierarchical volume
wrPermErr	–61	Read/write permission doesn't allow writing
wPrErr	–44	Volume is locked by a hardware setting

Assembly-Language Information

Constants

```
; Flags in file information used by the Finder

fOnDesk        .EQU  1   ;set if file is on desktop (hierarchical
                         ; volumes only)
fHasBundle     .EQU  13  ;set if file has a bundle
fInvisible     .EQU  14  ;set if file's icon is invisible
fTrash         .EQU  -3  ;file is in Trash window
fDesktop       .EQU  -2  ;file is on desktop
fDisk          .EQU  0   ;file is in disk window

; Flags in trap words

asnycTrpBit    .EQU  10  ;set for an asynchronous call

; Values for requesting read/write permission

fsCurPerm      .EQU  0   ;whatever is currently allowed
fsRdPerm       .EQU  1   ;request for read permission only
fsWrPerm       .EQU  2   ;request for write permission only
fsRdWrPerm     .EQU  3   ;request for exclusive read/write permission
fsRdWrShPerm   .EQU  4   ;request for shared read/write permission

; Positioning modes

fsAtMark       .EQU    0    ;at current mark
fsFromStart    .EQU    1    ;set mark relative to beginning of file
fsFromLEOF     .EQU    2    ;set mark relative to logical end-of-file
fsFromMark     .EQU    3    ;set mark relative to current mark
rdVerify       .EQU    64   ;add to above for read-verify
```

Structure of File Information Used by the Finder

fdType	File type (long)
fdCreator	File's creator (long)
fdFlags	Flags (word)
fdLocation	File's location (point; long)
fdFldr	File's window (word)
fdIconID	File's icon ID (word)
fdUnused	Reserved (8 bytes)
fdComment	File's comment ID (word)
fdPutAway	File's home directory ID (long word)

Structure of Directory Information Used by the Finder

frRect	Folder's rectangle (8 bytes)
frFlags	Flags (word)
frLocation	Folder's location (point; long)

frView	Folder's view (word)
frScroll	Folder's scroll position (point; long)
frOpenChain	Directory ID chain of open folders (long word)
frUnused	Reserved (word)
frComment	Folder's comment ID (word)
frPutAway	Folders's home directory ID (long word)

Standard Parameter Block Data Structure

qLink	Pointer to next queue entry
qType	Queue type (word)
ioTrap	Routine trap (word)
ioCmdAddr	Routine address
ioCompletion	Address of completion routine
ioResult	Result code (word)
ioFileName	Pointer to pathname (preceded by length byte)
ioVNPtr	Pointer to volume name (preceded by length byte)
ioVRefNum	Volume reference number or working directory reference number (word)
ioDrvNum	Drive number (word)

Structure of I/O Parameter Block

ioRefNum	Path reference number (word)
ioFileType	Version number (byte)
ioPermssn	Read/write permission (byte)
ioNewName	Pointer to new pathname (preceded by length byte)
ioLEOF	Logical end-of-file for SetEOF (long)
ioOwnBuf	Pointer to access path buffer
ioNewType	New version number for SetFilType (byte)
ioBuffer	Pointer to data buffer
ioReqCount	Requested number of bytes (long)
ioActCount	Actual number of bytes (long)
ioPosMode	Positioning mode and newline character (word)
ioPosOffset	Positioning offset (long)
ioQElSize	Size in bytes of I/O parameter block

Structure of File Parameter Block

ioRefNum	Path reference number (word)
ioFileType	Version number (byte)
ioFDirIndex	Directory index (word)
ioFlAttrib	File attributes (byte)
ioFFlType	Version number (byte)
ioFlUsrWds	Information used by the Finder (16 bytes)
ioDirID	Directory ID (long)
ioFFlNum	File number (long)
ioFlStBlk	First allocation block of data fork (word)
ioFlLgLen	Logical end-of-file of data fork (long)

ioFlPyLen	Physical end-of-file of data fork (long)
ioFlRStBlk	First allocation block of resource fork (word)
ioFlRLgLen	Logical end-of-file of resource fork (long)
ioFlRPyLen	Physical end-of-file of resource fork (long)
ioFlCrDat	Date and time of creation (long)
ioFlMdDat	Date and time of last modification (long)
ioFQElSize	Size in bytes of file information parameter block

Structure of Volume Information Parameter Block (Flat Directory)

ioVolIndex	Volume index (word)
ioVCrDate	Date and time of initialization (long)
ioVLsBkUp	Date and time of last modification (long)
ioVAtrb	Volume attributes; bit 15=1 if volume locked (word)
ioVNmFls	Number of files in directory (word)
ioVDirSt	First block of directory (word)
ioVBlLn	Length of directory in blocks (word)
ioVNmAlBlks	Number of allocation blocks on volume (word)
ioVAlBlkSiz	Size of allocation blocks (long)
ioVClpSiz	Number of bytes to allocate (long)
ioAlBlSt	First block in block map (word)
ioVNxtFNum	Next unused file number (long)
ioVFrBlk	Number of unused allocation blocks (word)
ioVQElSize	Size in bytes of volume information parameter block

Structure of Volume Information Parameter Block (Hierarchical Directory)

ioVolIndex	Volume index (word)
ioVCrDate	Date and time of initialization (long)
ioVLsMod	Date and time of last modification (long)
ioVAtrb	Volume attributes (word)
ioVNmFls	Number of files in directory (word)
ioVCBVBMSt	First block of volume bit map (word)
ioVNmAlBlks	Number of allocation blocks (word)
ioVAlBlkSiz	Size of allocation blocks (long)
ioVClpSiz	Default clump size (long)
ioAlBlSt	First block in block map (word)
ioVNxtCNID	Next unused node ID (long)
ioVFrBlk	Number of unused allocation blocks (word)
ioVSigWord	Volume signature (word)
ioVDrvInfo	Drive number (word)
ioVDRefNum	Driver reference number (word)
ioVFSID	File-system identifier (word)
ioVBkUp	Date and time of last backup (long)
ioVWrCnt	Volume write count (long)
ioVFilCnt	Number of files on volume (long)
ioVDirCnt	Number of directories on volume (long)
ioVFndrInfo	Information used by the Finder (32 bytes)
ioHVQElSize	Size in bytes of hierarchical volume information parameter block

Structure of Catalog Information Parameter Block (Files)

ioRefNum	Path reference number (word)
ioFileType	Version number (byte)
ioFDirIndex	Directory index (word)
ioFlAttrib	File attributes
ioFlUsrWds	Information used by the Finder (16 bytes)
ioFFlNum	File number (long)
ioFlStBlk	First allocation block of data fork (word)
ioFlLgLen	Logical end-of-file of data fork (long)
ioFlPyLen	Physical end-of-file of data fork (long)
ioFlRStBlk	First allocation block of resource fork (word)
ioFlRLgLen	Logical end-of-file of resource fork (long)
ioFlRPyLen	Physical end-of-file of resource fork (long)
ioFlCrDat	Date and time of creation (long)
ioFlMdDat	Date and time of last modification (long)
ioFlBkDat	Date and time of last backup (long)
ioFlXFndrInfo	Additional information used by the Finder (16 bytes)
ioFlParID	File parent directory ID (long)
ioFlClpSiz	File's clump size (long)

Structure of Catalog Information Parameter Block (Directories)

ioRefNum	Path reference number (word)
ioFDirIndex	Catalog index (word)
ioFlAttrib	File attributes
ioDrUsrWds	Information used by the Finder (16 bytes)
ioDrDirID	Directory ID (long)
ioDrNmFls	Number of files in directory (word)
ioDrCrDat	Date and time of creation (long)
ioDrMdDat	Date and time of last modification (long)
ioDrBkDat	Date and time of last backup (long)
ioDrFndrInfo	Additional information used by the Finder (16 bytes)
ioDrParID	Directory's parent directory ID (long)

Structure of Catalog Move Parameter Block

ioNewName	Pointer to name of new directory (preceded by length byte)
ioNewDirID	Directory ID of new directory (long)
ioDirID	Directory ID of current directory (long)

Structure of Working Directory Parameter Block

ioWDIndex	Working directory index (word)
ioWDProcID	Working directory's user identifier (long)
ioWDVRefNum	Working directory's volume reference number (word)
ioWDDirID	Working directory's directory ID (long)

Structure of File Control Block Information Parameter Block

ioFCBIndx	FCB index (long)
ioFCBFlNm	File number (long)
ioFCBFlags	Flags (word)
ioFCBStBlk	First allocation block of file (word)
ioFCBEOF	Logical end-of-file (long)
ioFCBPLen	Physical end-of-file (long)
ioFCBCrPs	Mark (long)
ioFCBVRefNum	Volume reference number (word)
ioFCBClpSiz	File's clump size (long)
ioFCBParID	Parent directory ID (long)

Volume Information Data Structure (Flat Directory)

drSigWord	Always $D2D7 (word)
drCrDate	Date and time of initialization (long)
drLsBkUp	Date and time of last modification (long)
drAtrb	Volume attributes (word)
drNmFls	Number of files in directory (word)
drDirSt	First block of directory (word)
drBlLn	Length of directory in blocks (word)
drNmAlBlks	Number of allocation blocks (word)
drAlBlkSiz	Allocation block size (long)
drClpSiz	Number of bytes to allocate (long)
drAlBlSt	First allocation block in block map (word)
drNxtFNum	Next unused file number (long)
drFreeBks	Number of unused allocation blocks (word)
drVN	Volume name preceded by length byte (28 bytes)

Volume Information Data Structure (Hierarchical Directory)

drSigWord	Always $4244 (word)
drCrDate	Date and time of initialization (long)
drLsMod	Date and time of last modification (long)
drAtrb	Volume attributes (word)
drNmFls	Number of files in directory (word)
drVBMSt	First block of volume bit map (word)
drNmAlBlks	Number of allocation blocks (word)
drAlBlkSiz	Allocation block size (long)
drClpSiz	Default clump size (long)
drAlBlSt	First block in block map (word)
drNxtCNID	Next unused directory ID (long)
drFreeBks	Number of unused allocation blocks (word)
drVN	Volume name (28 bytes)
drVolBkUp	Date and time of last backup (long)
drWrCnt	Volume write count (long)
drXTClpSiz	Clump size of extents tree file (long)
drCTClpSize	Clump size of catalog tree file (long)

drNmRtDirs	Number of directories in root (word)
drFilCnt	Number of files on volume (long)
drDirCnt	Number of directories on volume (long)
drFndrInfo	Information used by the Finder (32 bytes)
drXTFlSize	Length of extents tree (LEOF and PEOF) (long)
drXTExtRec	Extent record for extents tree file (12 bytes)
drCTFlSize	Length of catalog tree file (LEOF and PEOF) (long)
drCTExtRec	First extent record for catalog tree file (12 bytes)

File Directory Entry Data Structure (Flat Directory)

flFlags	Bit 7=1 if entry used; bit 0=1 if file locked (byte)
flTyp	Version number (byte)
flUsrWds	Information used by the Finder (16 bytes)
flFlNum	File number (long)
flStBlk	First allocation block of data fork (word)
flLgLen	Logical end-of-file of data fork (long)
flPyLen	Physical end-of-file of data fork (long)
flRStBlk	First allocation block of resource fork (word)
flRLgLen	Logical end-of-file of resource fork (long)
flRPyLen	Physical end-of-file of resource fork (long)
flCrDat	Date and time file of creation (long)
flMdDat	Date and time of last modification (long)
flNam	File name preceded by length byte

Extents Key Data Structure (Hierarchical Directory)

xkrKeyLen	Key length (byte)
xkrFkType	$00 for data fork; $FF for resource fork (byte)
xkrFNum	File number (long)
xkrFABN	Allocation block number within file (word)

Catalog Key Data Structure (Hierarchical Directory)

ckrKeyLen	Key length (byte)
ckrParID	Parent ID (long)
ckrCName	File or directory name preceded by length byte

File Record Data Structure (Hierarchical Directory)

cdrType	Always 2 for file records (byte)
filFlags	Bit 7=1 if entry used; bit 0=1 if file locked (byte)
filTyp	Version number (byte)
filUsrWds	Information used by the Finder (16 bytes)
filFlNum	File number (long)
filStBlk	First allocation block of data fork (word)
filLgLen	Logical end-of-file of data fork (long)
filPyLen	Physical end-of-file of data fork (long)
filRStBlk	First allocation block of resource fork (word)

filRLgLen	Logical end-of-file of resource fork (long)
filRPyLen	Physical end-of-file of resource fork (long)
filCrDat	Date and time of creation (long)
filMdDat	Date and time of last modification (long)
filBkDat	Date and time of last backup (long)
filFndrInfo	Additional information used by the Finder (16 bytes)
filClpSize	File's clump size (word)
filExtRec	First extent record for data fork (12 bytes)
filRExtRec	First extent record for resource fork (12 bytes)

Directory Record Data Structure (Hierarchical Directory)

cdrType	Always 1 for directory records (byte)
dirFlags	Flags (word)
dirVal	Valence (word)
dirDirID	Directory ID (long)
dirCrDat	Date and time of creation (long)
dirMdDat	Date and time of last modification (long)
dirBkDat	Date and time of last backup (long)
dirUsrInfo	Information used by the Finder (16 bytes)
dirFndrInfo	Additional information used by the Finder (16 bytes)

Thread Record Data Structure (Hierarchical Directory)

cdrType	Always 3 for thread records (byte)
thdParID	Parent ID of associated directory (long)
thdCName	Name of associated directory preceded by length byte

Volume Control Block Data Structure (Flat Directory)

qLink	Pointer to next queue entry
qType	Queue type (word)
vcbFlags	Bit 15=1 if volume control block is dirty (word)
vcbSigWord	Always $D2D7 (word)
vcbCrDate	Date and time of initialization (word)
vcbLsBkUp	Date and time of last modification (long)
vcbAtrb	Volume attributes (word)
vcbNmFls	Number of files in directory (word)
vcbDirSt	First block of directory (word)
vcbBlLn	Length of directory in blocks (word)
vcbNmBlks	Number of allocation blocks (word)
vcbAlBlkSiz	Allocation block size (long)
vcbClpSiz	Number of bytes to allocate (long)
vcbAlBlSt	First allocation block in block map (word)
vcbNxtFNum	Next unused file number (long)
vcbFreeBks	Number of unused allocation blocks (word)
vcbVN	Volume name preceded by length byte (28 bytes)
vcbDrvNum	Drive number (word)
vcbDRefNum	Driver reference number (word)
vcbFSID	File-system identifier (word)

vcbVRefNum	Volume reference number (word)
vcbMAdr	Pointer to block map
vcbBufAdr	Pointer to volume buffer
vcbMLen	Number of bytes in block map (word)

Volume Control Block Data Structure (Hierarchical Directory)

qLink	Pointer to next queue entry
qType	Queue type (word)
vcbFlags	Bit 15=1 if volume control block is dirty (word)
vcbSigWord	$4244 for hierarchical, $D2D7 for flat (word)
vcbCrDate	Date and time of initialization (word)
vcbLsMod	Date and time of last modification (long)
vcbAtrb	Volume attributes (word)
vcbNmFls	Number of files in directory (word)
vcbVBMSt	First block of volume bit map (word)
vcbNmAlBlks	Number of allocation blocks (word)
vcbAlBlkSiz	Allocation block size (long)
vcbClpSiz	Default clump size (long)
vcbAlBlSt	First block in bit map (word)
vcbNxtCNID	Next unused node ID (long)
vcbFreeBks	Number of unused allocation blocks (word)
vcbVN	Volume name preceded by length byte (28 bytes)
vcbDrvNum	Drive number (word)
vcbDRefNum	Driver reference number (word)
vcbFSID	File-system identifier (word)
vcbVRefNum	Volume reference number (word)
vcbMAdr	Pointer to block map
vcbBufAdr	Pointer to volume buffer
vcbMLen	Number of bytes in block map (word)
vcbVolBkUp	Date and time of last backup (long)
vcbVSeqNum	Index of volume in backup set (word)
vcbWrCnt	Volume write count (long)
vcbXTClpSiz	Clump size of extents tree file (long)
vcbCTClpSiz	Clump size of catalog tree file (long)
vcbNmRtDirs	Number of directories in root (word)
vcbFilCnt	Number of files on volume (long)
vcbDirCnt	Number of directories on volume (long)
vcbFndrInfo	Information used by the Finder (32 bytes)
vcbXTAlBks	Size in blocks of extents tree file (word)
vcbCTAlBks	Size in blocks of catalog tree file (word)
vcbXTRef	Path reference number for extents tree file (word)
vcbCTRef	Path reference number for catalog tree file (word)
vcbCtlBuf	Pointer to extents and catalog tree caches (long)
vcbDirIDM	Directory last searched (long)
vcbOffsM	Offspring index at last search (word)

File Control Block Data Structure (Flat Directory)

fcbFlNum	File number (long)
fcbMdRByt	Flags (byte)
fcbTypByt	Version number (byte)
fcbSBlk	First allocation block of file (word)
fcbEOF	Logical end-of-file (long)
fcbPLen	Physical end-of-file (long)
fcbCrPs	Mark (long)
fcbVPtr	Pointer to volume control block (long)
fcbBfAdr	Pointer to access path buffer (long)

File Control Block Data Structure (Hierarchical Directory)

fcbFlNum	File number (long)
fcbMdRByt	Flags (byte)
fcbTypByt	Version number (byte)
fcbSBlk	First allocation block of file (word)
fcbEOF	Logical end-of-file (long)
fcbPLen	Physical end-of-file (long)
fcbCrPs	Mark (long)
fcbVPtr	Pointer to volume control block (long)
fcbBfAdr	Pointer to access path buffer (long)
fcbClmpSize	File's clump size (long)
fcbBTCBPtr	Pointer to B*-tree control block (long)
fcbExtRec	First three file extents (12 bytes)
fcbFType	File's four Finder type bytes (long)
fcbDirID	File's parent ID (long)
fcbCName	Name of open file, preceded by length byte (32 bytes)

Drive Queue Entry Data Structure

qLink	Pointer to next queue entry
qType	Queue type (word)
dQDrive	Drive number (word)
dQRefNum	Driver reference number (word)
dQFSID	File-system identifier (word)
dQDrvSz	Number of logical blocks on drive (word)
dQDrvSz2	Additional field to handle large drive size (word)

Macro Names

Pascal name	Macro name
FInitQueue	_InitQueue
PBMountVol	_MountVol
PBGetVInfo	_GetVolInfo
PBHGetVInfo	_HGetVInfo
PBSetVInfo	_SetVolInfo

Pascal name	Macro name
PBGetVol	_GetVol
PBHGetVol	_HGetVol
PBSetVol	_SetVol
PBHSetVol	_HSetVol
PBFlushVol	_FlushVol
PBUnmountVol	_UnmountVol
PBOffLine	_OffLine
PBEject	_Eject
PBOpen	_Open
PBHOpen	_HOpen
PBOpenRF	_OpenRF
PBHOpenRF	_HOpenRF
PBLockRange	_LockRng
PBUnlockRange	_UnlockRng
PBRead	_Read
PBWrite	_Write
PBGetFPos	_GetFPos
PBSetFPos	_SetFPos
PBGetEOF	_GetEOF
PBSetEOF	_SetEOF
PBAllocate	_Allocate
PBAllocContig	_AllocContig
PBFlushFile	_FlushFile
PBClose	_Close
PBCreate	_Create
PBHCreate	_HCreate
PBDirCreate	_DirCreate
PBGetFInfo	_GetFileInfo
PBHGetFInfo	_HGetFileInfo
PBSetFInfo	_SetFileInfo
PBHSetFInfo	_HSetFileInfo
PBSetFLock	_SetFilLock
PBHSetFLock	_HSetFLock
PBRstFLock	_RstFilLock
PBHRstFLock	_HRstFLock
PBSetFVers	_SetFilType
PBRename	_Rename
PBHRename	_HRename
PBDelete	_Delete
PBHDelete	_HDelete
PBGetCatInfo	_GetCatInfo
PBSetCatInfo	_SetCatInfo
PBCatMove	_CatMove
PBOpenWD	_OpenWD
PBCloseWD	_CloseWD
PBGetWDInfo	_GetWDInfo
PBGetFCBInfo	_GetFCBInfo

Special Macro Name

_HFSDispatch

Variables

BootDrive	Working directory reference number for system startup volume (word)
FSQHdr	File I/O queue header (10 bytes)
VCBQHdr	Volume-control-block queue header (10 bytes)
DefVCBPtr	Pointer to default volume control block
FCBSPtr	Pointer to file-control-block buffer
DrvQHdr	Drive queue header (10 bytes)
ToExtFS	Pointer to external file system
FSFCBLen	Size of a file control block; on 64K ROM contains –1 (word)

20 THE DEVICE MANAGER

ABOUT THE DEVICE MANAGER

While no new routines have been added to the Device Manager, the handling of the existing routines has been significantly improved.

When an Open call is made, installed drivers are searched first (before resources) to avoid replacing a current driver; this search is done by name so be sure that your driver's name is in the driver header. All drivers, exclusive of desk accessories, must have a name that begins with a period; otherwise, the Open call is passed on to the File Manager.

If a driver is already open, Open calls will not be sent to the driver's open routine, preserving its device control entry. A desk accessory will, however, receive another call (certain desk accessories count on this).

If a driver fails to open because of a resource load problem, the Open call terminates with the appropriate error code instead of being passed on to the File Manager (which would usually return the result code fnfErr). If a driver returns a negative result code in register D0 from an Open call, the result code is passed back and the driver is not opened. If a driver returns the result code closeErr in register D0 from a Close call, this result code is passed back and the driver is not closed.

Open, Close, Read, Write, Control, and Status return all results in the ioResult field as well as in register D0. A KillIO call is passed to the driver only if it's open and enabled for Control calls.

The number of device control entries in the 128K ROM has been increased from 32 to 48. The unit table is now a 192-byte nonrelocatable block containing 48 four-byte entries; the standard unit table assignments are as follows:

Unit Number	Device
0	Reserved
1	Hard disk driver: Macintosh XL internal or Hard Disk 20 external
2	.Print driver
3	.Sound driver
4	.Sony driver
5	Modem port asynchronous driver input (.AIn)
6	Modem port asynchronous driver output (.AOut)
7	Printer port asynchronous driver input (.BIn)
8	Printer port asynchronous driver output (.BOut)
9	AppleTalk .MPP driver
10	AppleTalk .ATP driver
11	Reserved
12–26	Desk accessories in System file
27–31	Desk accessories in application files
32–39	SCSI drivers 0–7
40–47	Reserved

THE CHOOSER

The Chooser is a desk accessory that provides a standard interface to help solicit and accept specific choices from the user. It allows new device drivers to prompt the user for choices such as which serial port to use, which AppleTalk zone to communicate with, and which LaserWriter to use.

The Chooser relies heavily on the List Manager for creating, displaying, and manipulating possible user selections. The List Manager is described in chapter 30 of this volume.

Under the Chooser, each device is represented by a **device resource file** in the system folder on the user's system startup disk. (This is an extension of the concept of printer resource files, described in chapter 5 of volume II.) The Chooser accepts three types of device resource files to identify different kinds of devices:

File type	Device type
'PRES'	Serial printer
'PRER'	Non-serial printer
'RDEV'	Other device

The creator of each file is left undefined, allowing each device to have its own icon.

In addition to any actual driver code, each device resource file of type 'PRER' or 'RDEV' contains a set of resources that tell the Chooser how to handle the device. These resources include:

Resource type	Resource ID	Description
'PACK'	–4096	Device package (described below)
'STR '	–4096	Type name for AppleTalk devices
'GNRL'	–4096	NBP timeout and retry information for AppleTalk devices
'STR '	–4093	Left button title
'STR '	–4092	Right button title
'STR '	–4091	String for Chooser to use to label the list when choosing the device
'BNDL'		Icon information
'STR '	–4090	Reserved for use by the Chooser

Warning: You should give your device type a distinctive icon, since this may be the only way that devices are identified in the Chooser's screen display.

Device resource files of type 'PRES' (serial printers) contain only the driver code, without any of the resources listed above. The configuration of such devices is implemented entirely by the Chooser.

The Device Package

The device package is usually written in assembly language, but may be written partially in Pascal. The assembly-language structure of the 'PACK' –4096 resource is as follows:

Offset (hex)	Word
0	BRA.S to offset $10
2	Device ID (word)
4	'PACK' (long word)
8	$F000 (–4096)
A	Version (word)
C	Flags (long word)
10	Start of driver code

The device ID is an integer that identifies the device. The version word differentiates versions of the driver code. The flags field contains the following information:

Bit	Meaning
31	Set if an AppleTalk device
30–29	Reserved (clear to 0)
28	Set if device package can have multiple instances selected at once
27	Set if device package uses left button
26	Set if device package uses right button
25	Set if no saved zone name
24	Set if device package uses actual zone names
23–17	Reserved (clear to 0)
16	Set if device package accepts the newSel message
15	Set if device package accepts the fillList message
14	Set if device package accepts the getSel message
13	Set if device package accepts the select message
12	Set if device package accepts the deselect message
11	Set if device package accepts the terminate message
10–0	Reserved (clear to 0)

Communication with the Chooser

The Chooser communicates with device packages as if they were the following function:

```
FUNCTION Device (message,caller: INTEGER; objName,zoneName:
            StringPtr; p1,p2: LONGINT) : OSErr;
```

The message parameter identifies the operation to be performed. It has one of the following values:

```
CONST newSelMsg     = 12;  {new user selections have been made}
      fillListMsg   = 13;  {fill the list with choices to be made}
      getSelMsg     = 14;  {mark one or more choices as selected}
      selectMsg     = 15;  {a choice has actually been made}
```

```
deselectMsg   = 16;  {a choice has been cancelled}
terminateMsg  = 17;  {lets device package clean up}
buttonMsg     = 19;  {tells driver a button has been selected}
```

The device package should always return noErr, except with select and deselect; with these messages, a result code other than noErr prevents selection or deselection from occurring. The device package must ignore any other messages in the range 0..127 and return noErr. If the message is selectMsg or deselectMsg, it may not call the List Manager.

The caller parameter identifies the caller as the Chooser, with a value of 1. Values in the range 0..127 are reserved; values outside this range may be used by applications.

For AppleTalk devices, the zoneName paramcter is a pointer to a string of up to 32 characters containing the name of the AppleTalk zone in which the devices can be found. If the Chooser is being used with the local zone and bit 24 of the Flags field of the 'PACK' –4096 resource is clear, the string value is '*'; otherwise it's the actual zone name.

The p1 parameter is a handle to a List Manager list of choices for a particular device; this device list must be filled by the device package in response to the fillListMsg message.

Other details of the Chooser messages and their parameters are given below.

The NewSelMsg Parameter

The Chooser sends the newSel message (instead of the select or deselect message) only to device packages that allow multiple selections, when the user changes the selection.

The objName and p2 parameters are not used.

The FillListMsg Parameter

When the Chooser sends the fillList message, the device package should fill a List Manager list filled with choices for a particular device; the p1 parameter is a handle to this list.

The objName and p2 parameters are not used.

The GetSelMsg Parameter

When the Chooser sends the getSel message the device package should mark one or more choices in the given list as currently selected, by a call to LSetSelect.

The objName and p2 parameters are not used.

The SelectMsg Parameter

The Chooser sends the select message whenever a particular choice has become selected, but only to device packages that do not allow multiple selections. The device package may not call the List Manager.

If the device accepts fillList messages, objName is undefined. Otherwise, the objName parameter is a pointer to a string of up to 32 characters containing the name of the device. If the device accepts fillList messages, p2 gives the row number of the list that has become selected; otherwise (if the device is an AppleTalk device) p2 gives the AddrBlock value for the address of the AppleTalk device that has just become selected.

The DeselectMsg Parameter

The Chooser sends the deselect message whenever a particular choice has become deselected, but only to device packages that do not allow multiple selections. The device package may not call the List Manager.

If the device accepts fillList messages, objName is undefined. Otherwise, the objName parameter is a pointer to a string of up to 32 characters containing the name of the device.

If the device accepts fillList messages, p2 gives the row number of the list that has become deselected; otherwise (if the device is an AppleTalk device) p2 gives the AddrBlock value for the address of the AppleTalk device that has just become deselected.

The TerminateMsg Parameter

The Chooser sends the terminate message when the user selects a different device icon, closes the Chooser window, or changes zones. It allows the device package to perform cleanup tasks, if necessary. The device package should not dispose of the device list.

The objName and p2 parameters are not used.

The ButtonMsg Parameter

The Chooser sends the button message when a button in the Chooser display has been clicked.

The low-order byte of the p2 parameter has a value of 1 if the left button has been clicked and 2 if the right button has been clicked.

The objName parameter is not used.

Operation of the Chooser

When the Chooser is first selected from the desk accessory menu, it searches the system folder of the startup disk for device resource files—that is, resource files of type 'PRER', 'PRES', or 'RDEV'. For each one that it finds, it opens the file, fetches the device's icon, fetches the flags long word from the device package, and closes the file. The Chooser then takes the following actions for each device, based on the information just retrieved:

- It displays the device's icon in the Chooser's window.
- If the device is an AppleTalk device and AppleTalk is not connected, the Chooser grays the device's icon.

When the user selects a device icon that is not grayed, the Chooser reopens the corresponding device resource file. It then does the following:

- If the device is type 'PRER' or 'PRES', it sets the current printer type to that device.
- It labels the device's list box with the string in the resource 'STR ' with an ID of –4091.
- If the device is a local printer, the Chooser fills its list box with the two icons for the printer port and modem port serial drivers. Later it will record the user's choice in low memory and parameter RAM.
- If the device accepts fillList messages, the Chooser calls the device package, which should fill column 0 of the list pointed to by p1 with the names (without length bytes) of all available devices in the zone.
- If the device is an AppleTalk device that does not accept fillList messages, the Chooser initiates an asynchronous routine that interrogates the current AppleTalk zone for all devices of the type specified in the device's resource 'STR ' –4096. The NBP retry interval and count are taken from the 'GNRL' resource –4096; the format of this resource consists one byte for the interval followed by another byte for the count. As responses arrive, the Chooser updates the list box.
- To determine which list choices should be currently selected, the Chooser calls the device with the getSel message. The device code should respond by inspecting the list and setting the selected/unselected state of each entry. The Chooser may make this call frequently; for example, each time a new response to the AppleTalk zone interrogation arrives. Hence the device should alter only those entries that need changing. This procedure is not used with serial printers; for them, the Chooser just accesses low memory.
- The Chooser checks the flag in the 'PACK' –4096 resource that indicates whether multiple devices can be active at once, and sets List Manager bits accordingly. Whenever the user selects or deselects a device, the Chooser will call the device package with the appropriate message (if it's accepted). For packages that do not accept multiple active devices, this is the select or deselect message; otherwise it's the newSel message. The device code should implement both mounting and unmounting the device, if appropriate, and recording the user's selections on disk, preferably in the device resource file (which is the current resource file).

When the Chooser is deactivated, it calls the UpdateResFile procedure on the device resource file and flushes the system startup volume.

When the user chooses a different device type icon or closes the Chooser, the Chooser will call the device with the terminate message (if it's accepted). This allows device packages to clean up, if necessary. After this check, the Chooser closes the device resource file (if the device is not the current printer) and flushes the system startup volume.

Writing a Device Driver to Run Under Chooser

The code section of a driver running under chooser is contained in the 'PACK' –4096 resource, as explained earlier. The driver structure remains as described in chapter 6 of Volume II.

Device packages initially have no data space allocated. There are two ways to acquire data space for a device package:

- Use the List Manager
- Create a resource

These options are discussed below.

The best method is to call the List Manager. The Chooser uses column 0 of the device list to store the names displayed in the list box. If the device package currently in use does not accept fillList messages, column 1 stores the four-byte AppleTalk internet addresses of the entities in the list. Therefore, the device package can use column 1 and higher (if it accepts fillList) or column 2 and higher to store data private to itself. The standard List Manager calls can be used to add these columns, place data in them, and retrieve data stored there.

There are several restrictions on data storage in List Manager cells. The list is disposed whenever :

- the user changes device types.
- the user changes the current zone.
- the device package does not accept fillList messages, and a new response to the AppleTalk zone interrogation arrives. The device package will be called with the getSel message immediately afterwards.

When either of the first two situations occurs, the device package is called with the terminate message before the list is disposed.

Another way to get storage space is to create a resource in the device's file. This file is always the current resource file when the package is called; therefore it can issue GetResource calls to get a handle to its storage.

It is important for most device packages to record which devices have been chosen. To do this, the recommended method is to create a resource in the resource file. This resource can be of any type; it fact, it's advantageous to provide your own resource type so that no other program will try to access it. If you choose to use a standard resource type, you should use only resource IDs in the range –4080 to –4065.

SUMMARY OF THE DEVICE MANAGER

Constants

```
CONST   {Chooser message values}

        newSelMsg     = 12; {new user selections have been made}
        fillListMsg   = 13; {fill the list with choices to be made}
        getSelMsg     = 14; {mark one or more choices as selected}
        selectMsg     = 15; {a choice has actually been made}
        deselectMsg   = 16; {a choice has been cancelled}
        terminateMsg  = 17; {lets device package clean up}
        buttonMsg     = 19; {tells driver a button has been selected}

        {caller values}

        chooserID = 1;    {caller value for the Chooser}
```

Routines

```
FUNCTION Device (message,caller: INTEGER; objName,zoneName:
            StringPtr; p1,p2: LONGINT) : OSErr;
```

Assembly-Language Information

Constants

```
; Chooser message values

newSel        .EQU    12    ;new user selections have been made
fillList      .EQU    13    ;fill the list with choices to be made
getSel        .EQU    14    ;mark one or more choices as selected
select        .EQU    15    ;a choice has actually been made
deselect      .EQU    16    ;a choice has been cancelled
terminate     .EQU    17    ;lets device package clean up
button        .EQU    19    ;tells driver a button has been selected

; Caller values

chooserID     .EQU    1     ;caller value for the Chooser
```

Device Package Data Structure

Byte	Value
0	BRA.S to offset $10
2	Device ID (word)
4	'PACK' (long word)
8	$F000 (–4096)
A	Version (word)
C	Flags (long word)
10	Start of driver code

21 THE DISK DRIVER

The Disk Driver has been extended to support the double-sided 3 1/2-inch drive and the Apple Hard Disk 20™ drive; support for the single-sided 3 1/2-inch drive is of course maintained. A second Hard Disk 20 drive, an external double-sided drive, or an external single-sided drive can also be connected through the pass-through connector of a Hard Disk 20.

The Disk Driver's name remains '.Sony' and the reference number for 3 1/2-inch drives (both single-sided and double-sided) is still –5. The drive numbers for the 3 1/2-inch drives—1 for the internal drive and 2 for the external drive—are also unchanged.

The Hard Disk 20 has a reference number of –2 and drive numbers of 3 and 4. The Hard Disk 20 returns 20 tag bytes per sector instead of the 12 bytes returned by the 3 1/2-inch drives.

The new Disk Driver ignores KillIO calls; as before, you cannot make immediate calls to this driver. Read-verify mode is still supported for 3 1/2-inch drives, but has no effect on hard disk drives. A new track cache feature speeds the disk access on 3 1/2-inch drives; an advance control call (described below) let you control this feature.

The DiskEject function, if used with a hard disk drive, returns the Device Manager result code controlErr; at the next Disk Driver vertical retrace task, a disk-in-place event is reposted for that drive.

21 Disk Driver

Assembly-language note: The additional eight bytes of tag data for the Hard Disk 20 are stored in the global variable TFSTagData.

ADVANCED CONTROL CALLS

This section describes several advanced control calls used by the Operating System; you will probably have no need to use them.

csCode = 5

This call verifies that the disk in the drive specified by ioRefNum in the parameter block data structure (including hard disks) is correctly formatted.

csCode = 6 csParam = integer

This call formats the disk in the drive specified by ioRefNum in the parameter block data structure. With the Hard Disk 20, it zeros all blocks. A csParam value of 1 causes it to format a single-sided 3 1/2-inch disk in a double-sided drive; otherwise, the value of csParam should be 0.

> **Warning:** Use this call with care. It's normally used only by the Disk Initialization Package.

csCode = 9 csParam = integer

This call controls the track cache feature. The high-order byte of csParam is nonzero to enable the cache feature and 0 to disable it. The low-order byte of csParam is 1 to install the cache, –1 to remove it, and 0 to do neither. The cache is located in the system heap; the driver will relinquish cache space, if necessary, when the GrowZone function is called for the system heap.

csCode = 21 csParam = ptr (long)

This call works only with the Hard Disk 20; it returns a pointer to an icon data structure whose format is identical to that of an 'ICN#' resource. The drive number must be in ioRefNum in the parameter block data structure.

SUMMARY OF THE DISK DRIVER

Advanced Control Calls

csCode	csParam	Effect
5		Verifies disk formatting
6	integer	Formats a disk
9	integer	Controls track cache feature
21	ptr (long)	Fetches hard disk icon

Assembly-Language Information

Variables

TFSTagData	Additional 8 bytes of Hard Disk 20 tag data

22 THE SERIAL DRIVER

In the 128K ROM, a single new Serial Driver replaces the RAM and ROM Serial Drivers.

> **Note:** The new Serial Driver has a version number of 2. The old ROM driver had a version number of 0, and the old RAM driver a version number of 1.

For best results, include the RAM Serial Drivers as resources of type 'SERD' in the resource fork of your application and continue to use RAMSDOpen and RAMSDClose. If the 128K ROM is present, the new driver is automatically substituted.

The new Serial Driver verifies that the serial port is correctly configured and free; if not, the result code portNotCf or portInUse is returned. When opened, the Serial Driver defaults to hardware handshake *on* (as did the old ROM driver).

The Data Terminal Ready (DTR) line in the RS232 interface is now automatically asserted when the Serial Driver is opened; DTR is negated when it is closed. Control calls let you explicitly set the state of this line, as well as use it to automatically control the input data flow from an external device.

New advanced control calls let you control the DTR line, set certain control options, and modify the translation of parity error default characters; they're described below.

All control and status calls may be immediate. (For information about immediate calls, see chapter 6 of Volume II.)

The following bugs have been fixed:

- The procedure RAMSDClose preserves mouse interrupts during its execution.
- The execution of break and close routines is now synchronized to the current transmission.
- Incoming clock pulses on the CTS line are now detected; if they're present, CTS interrupts are disabled.
- If you open only the input channel of a driver, the Open routine checks to see if the necessary variables have been initialized and exits if they have not.

ADVANCED CONTROL CALLS

This section describes several new advanced control calls. Control calls to the Serial Driver should be made to the output character channel driver.

csCode = 14 csParam through csParam+7 = serShk

This call is identical to a control call with csCode=10 (the SerHShake function, described in the chapter 9 of Volume II) with the additional specification of the DTR handshake option in the eighth byte of its flags parameter (the null field of the SerShk record). You can enable DTR input flow control by setting this byte to a nonzero value. This works symmetrically to hardware handshake output control.

csCode = 16 csParam = byte

This call sets miscellaneous control options. Bits 0–6 should be set to 0 for future options. Bit 7, if set to 1, will cause DTR to be left unchanged when the driver is closed (rather than the normal procedure of negating DTR). This may be used for modem control to prevent the modem from hanging up just because the driver is being closed (such as when the user temporarily exits the terminal program).

csCode = 17

This call asserts DTR.

csCode = 18

This call negates DTR.

csCode = 20 csParam = char csParam+1 = alt char

This call is an extension of call 19, which would simply clear bit 7 of an incoming character when it matched the replacement character. After this call is made, all incoming characters with parity errors will be replaced by the character specified by the ASCII code in csParam. If csParam is 0, no character replacement will be done. If an incoming character is the same as the replacement character specified in csParam, it will be replaced instead by the second character specified in csParam+1.

Note: With this call, the null character (ASCII $00) can be used as the alternate character but not as the first replacement.

SUMMARY OF THE SERIAL DRIVER

Constants

```
CONST  { Indication that DTR is negated }

       dtrNegated = $40;

       { Result codes }

       portInUse   =  -97    {driver Open error, port already in use}
       portNotCf   =  -98    {driver Open error, port not configured for }
                             { this connection}
       memFullErr  =  -108;  {not enough room in heap zone}
```

Data Types

```
     SerShk = PACKED RECORD
                 fXOn:  Byte;  {XOn/XOff output flow control flag}
                 fCTS:  Byte;  {CTS hardware handshake flag}
                 xOn:   CHAR;  {XOn character}
                 xOff:  CHAR;  {XOff character}
                 errs:  Byte;  {errors that cause abort}
                 evts:  Byte;  {status changes that cause events}
                 fInX:  Byte;  {XOn/XOff input flow control flag}
                 fDTR:  Byte   {DTR input flow control flag}
              END;
```

Advanced Control Calls

csCode	csParam	Effect
14	serShk	Set handshake parameters
16	byte	Set miscellaneous control options
17		Asserts DTR
18		Negates DTR
20	2 chars	Replace parity errors, with alternate replacement character

Assembly-Language Information

Constants

```
; Result codes

portInUse    .EQU   -97   ;driver Open error, port already in use
portNotCf    .EQU   -98   ;driver Open error, port not configured for
                          ; this connection
memFullErr   .EQU   -108  ;not enough room in heap zone
```

Structure of Control Information for SerHShake

shFXOn	XOn/XOff output flow control flag (byte)
shFCTS	CTS hardware handshake flag (byte)
shXOn	XOn character (byte)
shXOff	XOff character (byte)
shErrs	Errors that cause abort (byte)
shEvts	Status changes that cause events (byte)
shFInX	XOn/XOff input flow control flag (byte)
shDTR	DTR control flag (byte)

23 THE APPLETALK MANAGER

The two AppleTalk device drivers, named .MPP and .ATP, are included in the 128K ROM. The AppleTalk Manager, however (the interface to the drivers), is not in ROM; your application must link to the appropriate object files.

On the Macintosh Plus, you need only open the .MPP driver; this will also load the .ATP driver and NBP code automatically. Since, in the 128K ROM, device drivers return errors, it's no longer necessary to check whether port B is free and configured for AppleTalk. If port B isn't available, the .MPP driver won't open and the result code portInUse or portNotCf will be returned.

Assembly-language note: When called from assembly language, the Datagram Delivery Protocol (DDP) allows 14 (instead of 12) open sockets.

---

24 THE SYSTEM ERROR HANDLER

A new system error, user alert ID 84, has been added. This error results when the Menu Manager tries to access a menu that's been purged.

25 THE OPERATING SYSTEM UTILITIES

Because in the 128K ROM there can be both an Operating System trap and a Toolbox trap for any given trap number (for details, see the Using Assembly Language chapter), two variants of GetTrapAddress and SetTrapAddress have been added. These new routines, NGetTrapAddress and NSetTrapAddress, require you to specify whether the given trap number refers to an Operating System trap or a Toolbox trap; the following data type is defined for this purpose:

```
TYPE TrapType = (OSTrap,ToolTrap);
```

The RelString function fills the need for a full-magnitude, language-independent string comparison, particularly in the hierarchical file system, where entries are sorted in alphabetical order. Whereas the EqualString function compares two strings only for equality, RelString compares two strings and returns a value indicating whether the the first string is less than, equal to, or greater than the second string.

You can use the existing routine Environs to determine whether the 128K ROM is in use; a description of this procedure is provided below.

OPERATING SYSTEM UTILITY ROUTINES

Assembly language note: To use GetTrapAddress and SetTrapAddress with 128K ROM routines, set bit 9 of the trap word to indicate the new trap numbering. The state of bit 10 then determines whether the intended trap is a Toolbox or Operating System trap. You can set these two bits with the arguments NEWOS and NEWTOOL.

Of course, the 64K ROM versions of GetTrapAddress and SetTrapAddress will fail if applied to traps that exist only in the 128K ROM.

The NGetTrapAddress and NSetTrapAddress routines list the possible permutations of arguments. (The syntax shown applies to the Lisa Workshop Assembler; programmers using another development system should consult its documentation for the proper syntax.)

```
FUNCTION NGetTrapAddress (trapNum: INTEGER; tType: TrapType) :
     LONGINT;  [Not in ROM]
```

NGetTrapAddress is identical to GetTrapAddress except that it requires you to specify in tType whether the given routine is an Operating System or a Toolbox trap.

Trap macro	_GetTrapAddress ,NEWOS _GetTrapAddress ,NEWTOOL	(bit 9 set, bit 10 clear) (bit 9 set, bit 10 set)
On entry	D0: trapNum (word)	
On exit	A0: address of routine	

```
PROCEDURE NSetTrapAddress (trapAddr: LongInt; trapNum: INTEGER;
     tType: TrapType);  [Not in ROM]
```

NSetTrapAddress is identical to SetTrapAddress except that it requires you to specify in tType whether the given routine is an Operating System or a Toolbox trap.

Trap macro	_SetTrapAddress ,NEWOS _SetTrapAddress ,NEWTOOL	(bit 9 set, bit 10 clear) (bit 9 set, bit 10 set)
On entry	A0: trapAddr (address) D0: trapNum (word)	

```
FUNCTION RelString (aStr,bStr: Str255; caseSens,diacSens: BOOLEAN)
          : INTEGER;
```

RelString is similar to EqualString except that it indicates whether the first string is less than, equal to, or greater than the second string by returning either –1, 0, or 1 respectively.

Trap macro	_RelString _RelString ,MARKS _RelString ,CASE _RelString ,MARKS,CASE	 (sets bit 9, for diacSens=FALSE) (sets bit 10, for caseSens=TRUE) (sets bits 9 and 10)
On entry	A0: pointer to first character of first string A1: pointer to first character of second string D0: high-order word: length of first string low-order word: length of second string	
On exit	D0: –1 if first string less than second, 0 if equal, 1 if first string greater than second (long word)	

RelString follows the sort order described in chapter 19 of Volume I except for the reordering of the following ligatures:

Æ falls between Å and a
æ falls between å and B
Œ falls between Ø and o
œ falls between ø and P
ß falls between s and T

If diacSens is FALSE, diacritical marks are ignored; RelString strips diacriticals according to the following table:

A <— Ä, Å, À, Ã
C <— Ç
E <— É
N <— Ñ
O <— Ö, Õ, Ø
U <— Ü
a <— á, à, â, ä, ã, å, ª
c <— ç
e <— é, è, ê, ë
i <— í, ì, î, ï
n <— ñ
o <— ó, ò, ô, ö, õ, ø, º
u <— ú, ù, û, ü
y <— ÿ

Note: This stripping is identical to that performed by the UprString procedure when the diacSens parameter is FALSE.

If caseSens is FALSE, the comparison is not case-sensitive; RelString performs a conversion from lower-case to upper-case characters according to the following table:

A <— a
. . . <— . . .
Z <— z
À <— à
Ã <— ã
Ä <— ä
Å <— å
Æ <— æ
Ç <— ç
É <— é
Ñ <— ñ
Ö <— ö
Õ <— õ
Ø <— ø
Œ <— œ
Ü <— ü

Note: This conversion is identical to that performed by the UprString procedure.

```
PROCEDURE Environs (VAR rom,machine: INTEGER)
```
[Not in ROM]

In the rom parameter, Environs returns the current ROM version number (for a Macintosh XL, the version number of the ROM image installed by MacWorks). To use the 128K ROM information described in this volume, the version number should be greater than or equal to 117 ($75). In the machine parameter, Environs returns an indication of which machine is in use, as follows:

```
CONST macXLMachine  = 0;    {Macintosh XL}
      macMachine    = 1;    {Macintosh 128K, 512K, 512K upgraded, }
                            { 512K enhanced, or Macintosh Plus}
```

Note: The machine parameter does not distinguish between the Macintosh 128K, 512K, 512K upgraded, 512K enhanced, and Macintosh Plus.

Assembly-language note: From assembly language, you can get this information from the word that's at an offset of 8 from the beginning of ROM (which is stored in the global variable ROMBase). The format of this word is $00xx for the Macintosh 128K, 512K, 512K enhanced, or Macintosh Plus, and $xxFF for the Macintosh XL, where xx is the ROM version number. (The ROM version number will always be between $01 and $FE.)

SUMMARY OF THE OPERATING SYSTEM UTILITIES

Constants

```
CONST {Values returned by the Environs procedure}

      macXLMachine  = 0;    {Macintosh XL}
      macMachine    = 1;    {Macintosh 128K, 512K, 512K upgraded, }
                            { 512K enhanced, or Macintosh Plus}
```

Data Types

```
TYPE TrapType = (OSTrap,ToolTrap);
```

Routines

```
FUNCTION   NGetTrapAddress   (trapNum: INTEGER; tType: TrapType) :
                              LongInt;   [Not in ROM]
PROCEDURE  NSetTrapAddress   (trapAddr: LongInt; trapNum: INTEGER; tType:
                              TrapType);   [Not in ROM]
FUNCTION   RelString         (aStr,bStr: Str255; caseSens,diacSens:
                              BOOLEAN) : INTEGER;
PROCEDURE  Environs          (VAR rom,machine: INTEGER)   [Not in ROM]
```

Assembly-Language Information

Routines

Trap macro	On entry	On exit
_GetTrapAddress	_GetTrapAddress ,NEWOS (bit 9 set, bit 10 clear) _GetTrapAddress ,NEWTOOL (bit 9 set, bit 10 set) D0: trapNum (word)	A0: address of routine
_SetTrapAddress	_SetTrapAddress ,NEWOS (bit 9 set, bit 10 clear) _SetTrapAddress ,NEWTOOL (bit 9 set, bit 10 set) A0: trapAddr (address) D0: trapNum (word)	
_RelString	_RelString ,MARKS (sets bit 9, for diacSens=FALSE) _RelString ,CASE (sets bit 10, for caseSens=TRUE) _RelString ,MARKS,CASE (sets bits 9 and 10) A0: ptr to first string A1: ptr to second string D0: high word: length of first string low word: length of second string	D0: –1 if first less than second, 0 if equal, 1 if first greater than second (long)

Variables

ROMBase	Base address of ROM

26 THE DISK INITIALIZATION PACKAGE

This chapter describes the Disk Initialization Package found in the system resource file. The package and its resources together occupy about 5.3K bytes.

The Disk Initialization Package initializes disks, formatting the disk medium and placing the appropriate file directory structure on the disk. Earlier versions of the Disk Initialization Package format a 3 1/2–inch disk on a single side only, creating a 400K-byte volume and placing a flat file directory on the disk. The new version of the Disk Initialization Package can format the 3 1/2–inch disks on either one or both sides, creating 400K or 800K volumes respectively. It will format other devices (such as hard disks) as well; the size of volumes is determined by the driver for the particular device.

When the 128K ROM version of the File Manager is present, all volumes except the 400K, single-sided disks are automatically given hierarchical file directories. (Even the 400K disks can be given a hierarchical directory by holding down the option key.) If the 128K version of the File Manager is not present, all volumes are given flat file directories.

The DIFormat function formats disks in single-sided disk drives as 400K volumes and disks in double-sided drives as 800K volumes; the size of all other volumes is determined by the driver for the particular device.

The DIZero function places a flat file directory on disks in single-sided disk drives and a hierarchical file directory on disks in double-sided drives as 800K volumes. With all other devices, the type of directory placed on a volume is determined by the driver for the particular device.

The DIBadMount function is called with the result code returned by MountVol as a parameter. Based on the value of this result code, on the type of drive containing the disk, and on the disk itself, DIBadMount decides what messages and buttons to display in its dialog box.

The dialog displayed by DIBadMount gets its messages and buttons from a dialog item list ('DITL' resource –6047). The new dialog item list contains messages and buttons for responding to all situations, but it's possible that a new Disk Initialization Package might run into an old dialog item list. The new Disk Initialization Package determines which item list it's using, and makes certain choices as to the best buttons and messages to display.

If the user places a double-sided disk into a single-sided drive, MountVol returns ioErr. If there's a new item list, the message "This is a two-sided disk!" is displayed; if there's an old item list, the message "This disk is unreadable:" is used instead.

If the user tries to erase or format a disk that's write-protected, and there's a new item list, the messages "Initialization failed!" and "This disk is write-protected!" will be displayed. If there's an old item list, the second message is omitted.

If the user tries to erase or format a disk that's not ejectable, and there's a new item list, the Eject button that's normally displayed is replaced by a Cancel button.

If the user tries to erase or format a disk in a double-sided drive, and there's a new item list, three buttons are displayed: Eject, One-sided, and Two-sided. If an old version of the item list is present, only two buttons are displayed: Eject and Initialize. If the user chooses the Initialize button, the disk is formatted as an 800K volume (and if the hierarchical version of the File Manager is present, a hierarchical file directory is written).

If the user tries to erase or format a disk in a single-sided drive, only two buttons are displayed (regardless of which version of the Disk Initialization Package or item list is present): Eject and Initialize. If the user chooses the Initialize button, the disk is formatted as a 400K, flat volume. With other types of devices, the user can choose to eject the volume or format it with a size determined by the driver.

When the result code noErr is passed, DIBadMount can be used to reformat a valid, mounted volume without changing its name. This can be used, for instance, to change the format of a disk in a double-sided drive from single-sided to double-sided. If there's a new item list, your application can specify its own message using the Dialog Manager procedure ParamText; the message can be up to three lines long. The message is stored as the string "^0". (Because the TextEdit procedure TextBox is used to display statText items, word wraparound is done automatically.) If there's an old item list, the message "Initialize this disk?" is displayed instead.

> **Warning:** If your application uses this call, it must call DILoad before ejecting the system disk. This will prevent accidental formatting of the system disk.

> **Note:** The volume to be reformatted must be mounted when DIBadMount is called.

Formatting Hierarchical Volumes

The Disk Initialization Package must set certain volume characteristics when placing a hierarchical file directory on a volume. Default values for these volume characteristics are stored in the 128K ROM; this section is for advanced programmers who want to substitute their own values. The record containing the default values, if defined in Pascal, would look like this:

```
TYPE HFSDefaults =
  PACKED RECORD
    sigWord:    ARRAY[1..2] OF CHAR; {signature word}
    abSize:     LONGINT;    {allocation block size in bytes}
    clpSize:    LONGINT;    {clump size in bytes}
    nxFreeFN:   LONGINT;    {next free file number}
    btClpSize:  LONGINT;    {B*-Tree clump size in bytes}
    rsrv1:      INTEGER;    {reserved}
    rsrv2:      INTEGER;    {reserved}
    rsrv3:      INTEGER;    {reserved}
  END;
```

The default values for these fields are as follows:

Field	**Default value**
sigWord	'BD'
abSize	0
clpSize	4 * abSize
nxFreeFN	16
btClpSize	0

To supply your own values for these fields, create a similar, nonrelocatable record containing the desired values and place a pointer to it in the global variable FmtDefaults. To restore the system defaults, simply clear FmtDefaults.

The sigWord must equal 'BD' (meaning “big disk”) for the volume to be recognized as a hierarchical volume. If the specified allocation block size is 0, the allocation block size is calculated according to the size of the volume:

abSize = (1 + (volSize in blocks / 64K)) * 512 bytes

If the specified B*-tree clump size is 0, the clump size for both the catalog and extent trees is calculated according to the size of the volume:

btClpSize = (volSize in blocks)/128 * 512bytes

SUMMARY OF THE DISK INITIALIZATION PACKAGE

Variables

FmtDefaults   Pointer to substitute values for hierarchical volume characteristics

27 THE FINDER INTERFACE

The Finder has been modified to work with the hierarchical file system. In the 64K ROM, the user's perceived desktop hierarchy of folders and files is essentially an illusion maintained (at great expense) by the Finder. In the 128K ROM version of the File Manager, this hierarchy is recorded in the file directory itself, relieving the Finder of the task of maintaining this information.

THE DESKTOP FILE

Most of the information used by the Finder is kept in a resource file named Desktop. (The Finder doesn't display this file on the Macintosh desktop, to ensure that the user won't tamper with it.) On flat volumes, file and folder information is kept in resources known as file objects (resources of type 'FOBJ'). On hierarchical volumes, the only dynamic file object data remaining in the Desktop file are the Get Info comments. The other information about files and folders is maintained by the File Manager; for more details, see the section "Information Used by the Finder" in chapter 19 of this volume.

With flat volumes, the Finder enumerates the entire volume; this means that it can always locate a particular application by scanning through all the file objects in memory. With hierarchical volumes, however, the Finder searches only open folders, so there's no guarantee that it will see the application. A new data structure, called the **application list**, is kept in the Desktop file for launching applications from their documents in the hierarchical file system. For each application in the list, an entry is maintained that includes the name and signature of the application, as well as the directory ID of the folder containing it.

Whenever an application is moved or renamed, its old entry in the list is removed, and a new entry is added to the top of the list. The list is rebuilt when the desktop is rebuilt; this makes the rebuilding process much slower since the entire volume must be scanned.

> **Note:** The user has control over the search order in the sense that the most recently moved or added applications will be at the top of the list and will be matched first.

28 THE MACINTOSH PLUS HARDWARE

This chapter describes the hardware features of the Macintosh Plus. Two of these features—the 800K internal disk drive and the 128K ROM—are also found in the Macintosh 512K enhanced. This chapter covers only the new features and does not repeat information already covered in chapter 2 of Volume III.

> **Note:** A partially upgraded Macintosh 512K is identical to the Macintosh 512K enhanced, while a completely upgraded Macintosh 512K includes all the features of the Macintosh Plus.

This chapter is oriented toward assembly-language programmers and assumes you're familiar with the basic operation of microprocessor-based devices. Knowledge of the Macintosh Operating System will also be helpful. To learn how your program can determine the hardware environment in which it's operating, see the description of the Environs procedure in chapter 25 of this volume.

> **Warning:** Memory sizes, addresses and other data specific to the Macintosh Plus are presented in this chapter. To maintain software compatibility across the Macintosh line, and to allow for future changes to the hardware, you're *strongly advised* to use the Toolbox and Operating System routines wherever provided. In particular, use the low-memory global variables to reference hardware; *never* use absolute addresses.

OVERVIEW OF THE HARDWARE

Features of the Macintosh 512K enhanced (not found in the Macintosh 128K and 512K) are:

- 800K internal disk drive
- 128K ROM

Features of the Macintosh Plus are:

- 800K internal disk drive
- 128K ROM
- SCSI high-speed peripheral port
- 1Mb RAM, expandable to 2Mb, 2.5Mb, or 4Mb.
- 2 Mini-8 connectors for serial ports, replacing the 2 DB-9 connectors found on the Macintosh 128K, 512K, and 512K enhanced.
- keyboard with built-in cursor keys and numeric keypad

The Macintosh Plus contains the Motorola MC68000 microprocessor clocked at 7.8336 megahertz, random access memory (RAM), read-only memory (ROM), and several chips that enable it to communicate with external devices. In addition to the five I/O devices found in the Macintosh 128K, 512K, and 512K enhanced (the video display, sound generator, VIA, SCC and IWM), the Macintosh Plus contains a NCR 5380 Small Computer Standard Interface (SCSI) chip for high-speed parallel communication with devices such as hard disks.

In the Macintosh Plus, the 16 Mb of addressable space is divided into four equal sections. The first four megabytes are for RAM, the second four megabytes are for ROM and SCSI, the third are for the SCC, and the last four are for the IWM and the VIA. Since the devices within each block may have far fewer than four megabytes of individually addressable locations or registers, the addressing for a device may "wrap around" (a particular register appears at several different addresses) within its block.

RAM

The Macintosh Plus RAM is provided in four packages known as Single In-line Memory Modules (SIMMs). Each SIMM contains eight surface-mounted Dynamic RAM (DRAM) chips on a small printed circuit board with electrical "finger" contacts along one edge. Various RAM configurations are possible depending on whether two or four SIMMs are used and on the density of the DRAM chips that are plugged into the SIMMs:

- If the SIMMs contain 256K-bit DRAM chips, two SIMMs will provide 512K bytes of RAM, or four SIMMs will provide 1Mb of RAM (this is the standard configuration).

- If the SIMMs contain 1M-bit DRAM chips, two SIMMs will provide 2Mb of RAM, or four SIMMs will provide 4Mb of RAM.

- If two of the SIMMs contain 1M-bit DRAM chips, and two of the SIMMs contain 256K-bit DRAM chips, then these four SIMMs will provide 2.5Mb of RAM. For this configuration, the 1M-bit SIMMs must be placed in the sockets closest to the 68000 CPU.

Warning: Other configurations, such as a single SIMM or a pair of SIMMs containing DRAMs of different density, are not allowed. If only two SIMMs are installed, they must be placed in the sockets closest to the MC68000.

The SIMMs can be changed by simply releasing one and snapping in another. However, there are also two resistors on the Macintosh Plus logic board (in the area labelled "RAM SIZE") which tell the electronics how much RAM is installed. If two SIMMs are plugged in, resistor R9 (labeled "ONE ROW") must be installed; if four SIMMs are plugged in, this resistor must be removed. Resistor R8 (labelled "256K BIT") must be installed if all of the SIMMs contain 256K-bit DRAM chips. If either two or four of the SIMMs contain 1M-bit chips, resistor R8 must be removed.

Each time you turn on the Macintosh Plus, system software does a memory test and determines how much RAM is present in the machine. This information is stored in the global variable MemTop, which contains the address (plus one) of the last byte in RAM.

ROM

The Macintosh Plus contains two 512K-bit (64K x 8) ROM chips, providing 128K bytes of ROM. This is the largest size of ROM that can be installed in a Macintosh 128K, 512K, or 512K enhanced. The Macintosh Plus ROM sockets, however, can accept ROM chips of up to 1M-bit (128K x 8) in size. A configuration of two 1M-bit ROM chips would provide 256K bytes of ROM.

THE VIDEO INTERFACE

28 Hardware

The starting addresses of the screen buffers depend on the amount of memory present in the machine. The following table shows the starting address of the main and the alternate screen buffer for various memory configurations of the Macintosh Plus:

System	Main Screen	Alternate
Macintosh Plus, 1Mb	$FA700	$F2700
Macintosh Plus, 2Mb	$1FA700	$1F2700
Macintosh Plus, 2.5Mb	$27A700	$272700
Macintosh Plus, 4Mb	$3FA700	$3F2700

Warning: To ensure that software will run on Macintoshes of different memory size, as well as on future Macintoshes, use the address stored in the global variable ScrnBase. Also, the alternate screen buffer may not be available in future versions of the Macintosh and may not be found in some software configurations of current Macintoshes.

THE SOUND GENERATOR

The starting addresses of the sound buffers depend on the amount of memory present in the machine. The following table shows the starting address of the main and the alternate sound buffer for various memory configurations of the Macintosh Plus:

System	Main Sound	Alternate
Macintosh Plus, 1Mb	$FFD00	$FA100
Macintosh Plus, 2Mb	$1FFD00	$1FA100
Macintosh Plus, 2.5Mb	$27FD00	$27A100
Macintosh Plus, 4Mb	$3FFD00	$3FA100

> **Warning:** To ensure that software will run on Macintoshes of different memory size, as well as future Macintoshes, use the address stored in the global variable SoundBase. Also, the alternate sound buffer may not be available in future versions of the Macintosh and may not be found in some software configurations of current Macintoshes.

THE SCC

The Macintosh Plus uses two Mini-8 connectors for the two serial ports, replacing the two DB-9 connectors used for the serial ports on the Macintosh 128K, 512K, and 512K enhanced.

The Mini-8 connectors provide an output handshake signal, but do not provide the +5 volts and +12 volts found on the Macintosh 128K, 512K, and 512K enhanced serial ports.

The output handshake signal for each Macintosh Plus serial port originates at the SCC's Data Terminal Ready (DTR) output for that port, and is driven by an RS423 line driver. Other signals provided include input handshake/external clock, Transmit Data + and –, and Receive Data + and –.

Figure 1 shows the Mini-8 pinout for the SCC serial connectors.

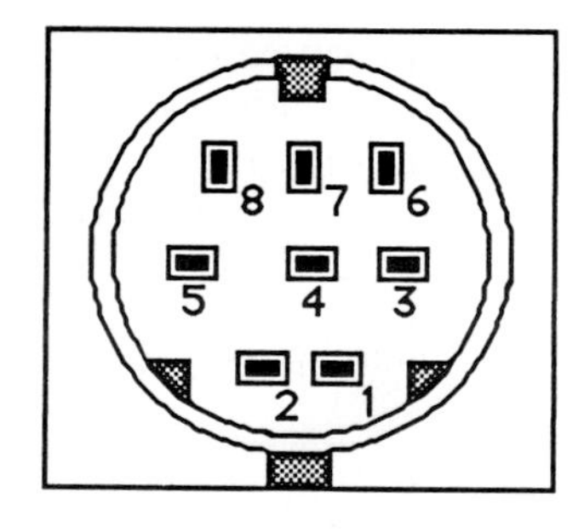

1	Output handshake
2	Input handshake / external clock
3	Transmit data –
4	Ground
5	Receive data –
6	Transmit data +
7	(not connected)
8	Receive data +

Figure 1. Pinout for SCC Serial Connectors

Diagram

Figure 2 shows a circuit diagram for the Macintosh Plus serial ports.

Extron
Yellow = ground = 4
green = 3 = Xdata
3 = Receive Data
5 = Ground

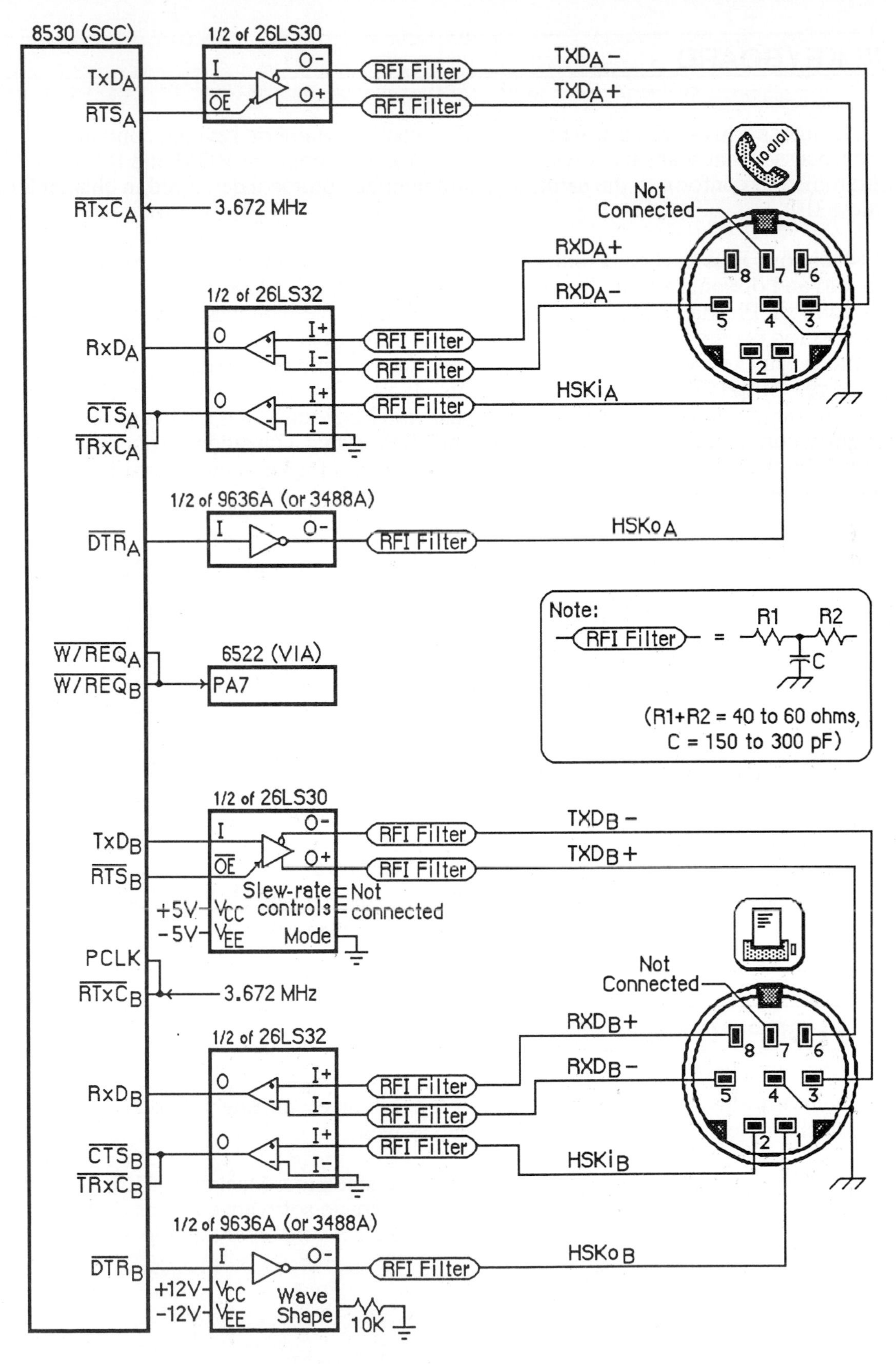

Figure 2. Circuit Diagram for the Macintosh Plus Serial Ports

28 Hardware

THE KEYBOARD

The Macintosh Plus keyboard, which includes a built-in numeric keypad, contains a microprocessor that scans the keys. The microprocessor contains ROM and RAM, and is programmed to conform to the same keyboard interface protocol described in chapter 2 of Volume III.

The Macintosh Plus keyboard reproduces all of the key-down transitions produced by the keyboard and optional keypad used by the Macintosh 128K, 512K, and 512K enhanced; the Macintosh Plus keyboard is also completely compatible with these other machines. If a key transition occurs for a key that used to be on the optional keypad in *lowercase*, the Macintosh Plus keyboard still responds to an Inquiry command by sending back the Keypad response ($79) to the Macintosh Plus. If a key transition occurs for an key that used to be on the optional keypad in *uppercase*, the Macintosh Plus keyboard responds to an Inquiry command by sending back the Shift Key–down Transition response ($71), followed by the Keypad response ($79). The responses for key-down transitions on the Macintosh Plus are shown (in hexadecimal) in Figure 3.

`	1	2	3	4	5	6	7	8	9	0	-	=	Backspace
65	25	27	29	2B	2F	2D	35	39	33	3B	37	31	67

Tab	Q	W	E	R	T	Y	U	I	O	P	[	]
61	19	1B	1D	1F	23	21	41	45	3F	47	43	3D

Caps Lock	A	S	D	F	G	H	J	K	L	;	'	Return
73	01	03	05	07	0B	09	4D	51	4B	53	4F	49

Shift	Z	X	C	V	B	N	M	,	.	/	Shift	↑
71	0D	0F	11	13	17	5B	5D	57	5F	59	71	1B

Option	⌘	space	\	←	→	↓
75	6F	63	55	0D	05	11

Clear	=	/	*
0F	11	1B	05
7	8	9	–
33	37	39	1D
4	5	6	+
2D	2F	31	0D
1	2	3	Enter
27	29	2B	19
0		.	
25		03	

U.S. and International Keyboard

Figure 3. Key-Down Transitions

THE FLOPPY DISK INTERFACE

The Macintosh Plus has an internal double-sided disk drive; an external double-sided drive or the older single-sided drive, can be attached as well.

> **Note:** The external double-sided drive can be attached to a Macintosh 512K through the back of a Hard Disk 20. The Hard Disk 20 start-up software contains a device driver for this drive and the hierarchical (128K ROM) version of the File Manager.

The double-sided drive can format, read, and write both 800K double-sided disks and 400K single-sided disks. The operation of the drive with double-sided disks differs from that on single-sided disks. With double-sided disks, a single mechanism positions two read/write heads—one above the disk and one below—so that the drive can access two tracks simultaneously—one on the top side, and a second, directly beneath the first, on the bottom side. This lets the drive read or write two complete tracks of information before it has to move the heads, significantly reducing access time. For 400K disks, the double-sided drive restricts itself to one side of the disk.

Warning: Applications (for instance, copy protection schemes) should never interfere with, or depend on, disk speed control. The double-sided drive controls its own motor speed, ignoring the speed signal (PWM) from the Analog Signal Generator (ASG).

THE REAL-TIME CLOCK

The Macintosh Plus real-time clock is a new custom chip. The commands described in chapter 2 of Volume III for accessing the Macintosh 512K clock chip are also used to access the new chip. The new chip includes additional parameter RAM that's reserved by Apple. The parameter RAM information provided in chapter 13 of Volume II, as well as the descriptions of the routines used for accessing that information, apply for the new clock chip as well.

THE SCSI INTERFACE

The NCR 5380 **Small Computer Standard Interface** (SCSI) chip controls a high-speed parallel port for communicating with up to seven SCSI peripherals (such as hard disks, streaming tapes, and high speed printers). The Macintosh Plus SCSI port can be used to implement all of the protocols, arbitration, interconnections, etc. of the SCSI interface as defined by the ANSI X3T9.2 committee.

The Macintosh Plus SCSI port differs from the ANSI X3T9.2 standard in two ways. First, it uses a DB-25 connector instead of the standard 50-pin ribbon connector. An Apple adapter cable, however, can be used to convert the DB-25 connector to the standard 50-pin connector. Second, power for termination resistors is not provided at the SCSI connector nor is a termination resistor provided in the Macintosh Plus SCSI circuitry.

Warning: Do *not* connect an RS232 device to the SCSI port. The SCSI interface is designed to use standard TTL logic levels of 0 and +5 volts; RS232 devices may impose levels of –25 and +25 volts on some lines, thereby causing damage to the logic board.

The NCR 5380 interrupt signal is not connected to the processor, but the progress of a SCSI operation may be determined at any time by examining the contents of various status registers in the NCR 5380. SCSI data transfers are performed by the MC68000; pseudo-DMA mode operations can assert the NCR 5380 DMA Acknowledge (DACK) signal by reading or writing to the appropriate address (see table below). Approximate transfer rates are 142K bytes per second for nonblind transfers and 312K bytes per second for blind transfers. (With nonblind transfers, each byte transferred is polled, or checked.)

Figure 4 shows the DB-25 pinout for the SCSI connector at the back of the Macintosh Plus.

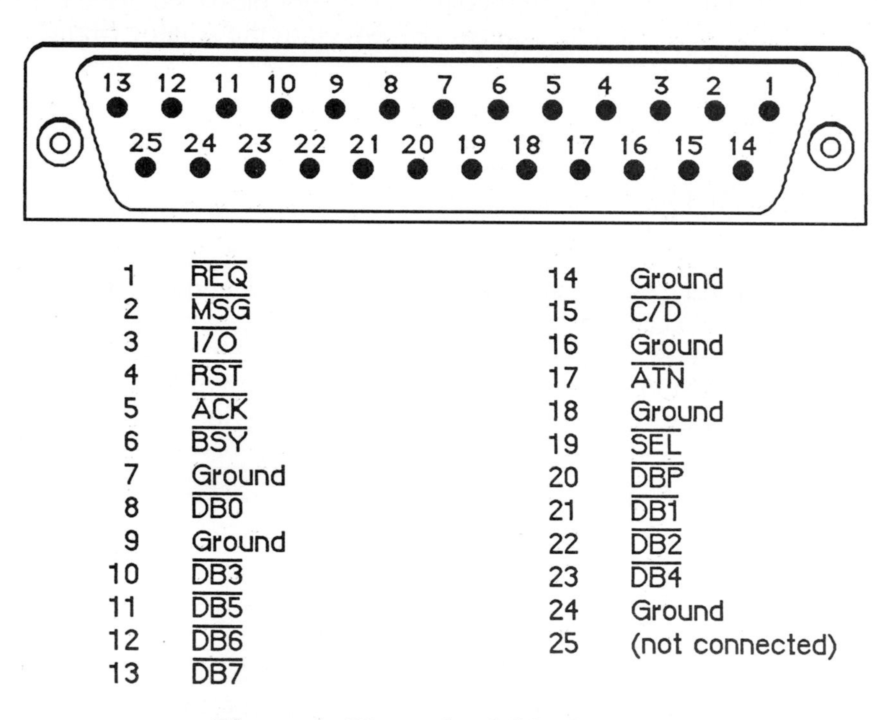

Figure 4. Pinout for SCSI Connector

The locations of the NCR 5380 control and data registers are given in the following table as offsets from the constant scsiWr for write operations, or scsiRd for read operations. These base addresses are not available in global variables; instead of using absolute addresses, you should use the routines provided by the SCSI Manager (covered in chapter 31 of this volume).

Read and write operations must be made in bytes. Read operations must be to even addresses and write operations must be to odd addresses; otherwise an undefined operation will result.

The address of each register is computed as follows:

$580drn

where **r** represents the register number (from 0 through 7),
n determines whether it a read or write operation
(0 for reads, or 1 for writes), and
d determines whether the DACK signal to the NCR 5380 is asserted.
(0 for not asserted, 1 is for asserted)

Here's an example of the address expressed in binary:

0101 1000 0000 00d0 0rrr 000n

Note: Asserting the DACK signal applies only to write operations to the output data register and read operations from the input data register.

Symbolic Location	Memory Location	NCR 5380 Internal Register
scsiWr+sODR+dackWr	$580201	Output Data Register with DACK
scsiRd+sIDR+dackRd	$580260	Current SCSI Data with DACK
scsiWr+sODR	$580001	Output Data Register
scsiWr+sICR	$580011	Initiator Command Register
scsiWr+sMR	$580021	Mode Register
scsiWr+sTCR	$580031	Target Command Register
scsiWr+sSER	$580041	Select Enable Register
scsiWr+sDMAtx	$580051	Start DMA Send
scsiWr+sTDMArx	$580061	Start DMA Target Receive
scsiWr+sIDMArx	$580071	Start DMA Initiator Receive
scsiRd+sCDR	$580000	Current SCSI Data
scsiRd+sICR	$580010	Initiator Command Register
scsiRd+sMR	$580020	Mode Registor
scsiRd+sTCR	$580030	Target Command Register
scsiRd+sCSR	$580040	Current SCSI Bus Status
scsiRd+sBSR	$580050	Bus and Status Register
scsiRd+sIDR	$580060	Input Data Register
scsiRd+sRESET	$580070	Reset Parity/Interrupt

Note: For more information on the registers and control structure of the SCSI, consult the technical specifications for the NCR 5380 chip.

SUMMARY

Constants

```
; SCSI base addresses

scsiRd      .EQU    $580000    ;base address for read operations
scsiWr      .EQU    $580001    ;base address for write operations


; SCSI offsets for DACK

dackRd      .EQU    $200       ;for use with sOCR and sIDR
dackWr      .EQU    $200       ;for use with sOCR and sIDR

; SCSI offsets to NCR 5380 register

sCDR        .EQU    $00        ;Current SCSI Read Data (read)
sOCR        .EQU    $00        ;Output Data Register (write)
sICR        .EQU    $10        ;Initiator Command Register (read/write)
sMR         .EQU    $20        ;Mode Register (read/write)
sTCR        .EQU    $30        ;Target Command Register (read/write)
sCSR        .EQU    $40        ;Current SCSI Bus Status (read)
sSER        .EQU    $40        ;Select Enable Register (write)
sBSR        .EQU    $50        ;Bus & Status Register (read)
sDMAtx      .EQU    $50        ;DMA Transmit Start (write)
sIDR        .EQU    $60        ;Data input register (read)
sTDMArx     .EQU    $60        ;Start Target DMA receive (write)
sRESET      .EQU    $70        ;Reset Parity/Interrupt (read)
sIDMArx     .EQU    $70        ;Start Initiator DMA receive (write)
```

29 THE SYSTEM RESOURCE FILE

This chapter describes the contents of the System file version 3.2 whose creation date is June 4, 1986.

The System file, also known as the system resource file, contains standard resources that are shared by all applications, and are used by the Macintosh Toolbox and Operating System as well. This file can be modified by the user with the Installer and Font/DA Mover programs.

Warning: You should not add resources to, or delete resources from, the system resource file directly.

Note: Some of the resources in the system resource file are also contained in the 128K ROM; they're duplicated in the system resource file for compatibility with machines not equipped with the 128K ROM. Other resources are put in the system resource file because they are too large to be put in ROM.

The system resource file contains the standard Macintosh packages and the resources they use (or own):

- the List Manager Package ('PACK' resource 0), and the standard list definition procedure ('LDEF' resource 0)
- the Disk Initialization Package ('PACK' resource 2), and code (resource type 'FMTR') used in formatting disks
- the Standard File Package ('PACK' resource 3), and resources used to create its alerts and dialogs (resource types 'ALRT', 'DITL', and 'DLOG')
- the Floating-Point Arithmetic Package ('PACK' resource 4)
- the Transcendental Functions Package ('PACK' resource 5)
- the International Utilities Package ('PACK' resource 6)
- the Binary-Decimal Conversion Package ('PACK' resource 7)

Certain device drivers (including desk accessories) and the resources they use (or own) are also found in the system resource file; these resources include:

- the .PRINT driver ('DRVR' resource 2) that communicates between the Printing Manager and the printer
- the .MPP and .ATP drivers ('DRVR' resources 9 and 10 respectively) used by AppleTalk
- the Control Panel desk accessory ('DRVR' resource 15) and the bit maps (resource type 'bmap') and windows (resource type 'WIND') used in displaying its various options

- the Chooser desk accessory ('DRVR' resource 16), and the dialogs, icons, list definition procedures, and strings (resource types 'DITL', 'DLOG', 'ICON', and 'LDEF') that it uses (or owns)

Other general resources contained in the system resource file include:

- standard definition procedures for creating windows, menus, controls, lists, and so on
- system fonts and font families (resource types 'FONT' and 'FOND')
- system icons
- code for patching bugs in ROM routines (resource type 'PTCH')
- initialization resources (described below) used during system startup

INITIALIZATION RESOURCES

The system resource file contains initialization resources (resource type 'INIT') used during system startup. A mechanism has been provided so that applications can supply code to be executed during system startup *without* adding resources of type 'INIT' to the system resource file. Instead of putting your code in the system resource file, you should create a separate file with a file type of 'INIT' (or for Chooser devices, file type 'RDEV').

A special initialization resource in the system resource file, 'INIT' resource 31, searches the System Folder of the system startup volume for files of type 'INIT' or 'RDEV'. When it finds one, it opens the file (with ResLoad set to FALSE) and uses GetIndResource (with ResLoad set to TRUE) to find all resources in that file of type 'INIT'. It calls each resource it finds. After calling the last resource, it closes the file, and continues searching for other files of type 'INIT' or 'RDEV'.

Warning: If you do not want your 'INIT' resources to be released, be sure to call the Resource Manager procedure DetachResource.

Note: The order in which your 'INIT' resources are called depends on the order in which your 'INIT' and 'RDEV' files are opened, and on the order of the 'INIT' resources within these files; these orders are not predictable.

Assembly-language note: The 'INIT' resource 31 saves all registers and places the handle to your 'INIT' resource in register A0.

The System Startup Environment

This section discusses the organization of the Macintosh Plus RAM at the time your 'INIT' files are loaded (see Figure 1); most the information presented here is useful only to assembly-language programmers.

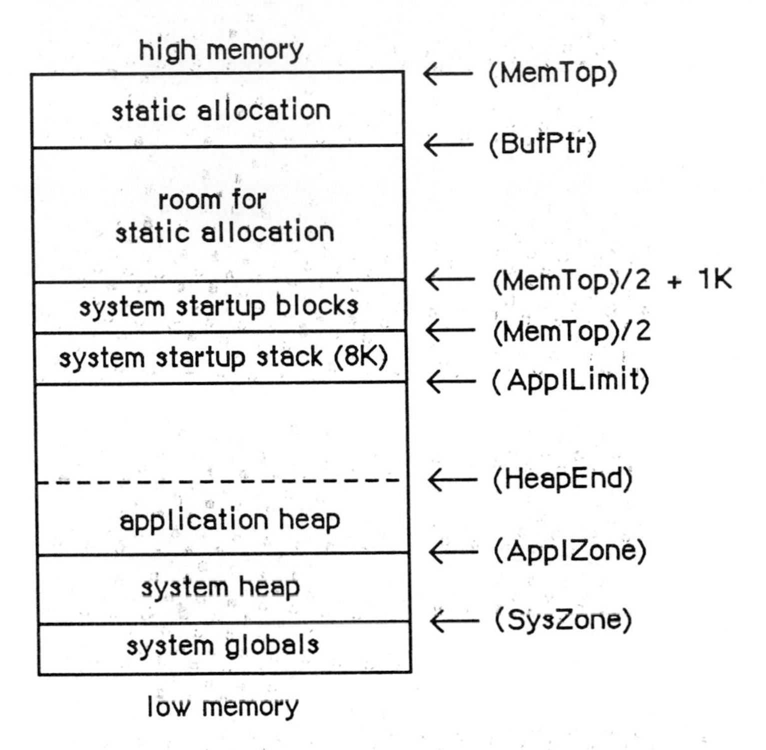

Figure 1. Macintosh Plus RAM at System Startup

The global variables, shown in parentheses, contain the addresses of the indicated areas.

The application heap limit (stored in the global variable ApplLimit) is set to 8K below the beginning of the boot stack to protect the stack.

Static allocation off the address contained in the global variable BufPtr is useful when a large amount of space is needed which will never be deallocated (once space is allocated, it may not be deallocated unless no one has allocated space below). An 'INIT' resource may obtain permanent space by moving BufPtr down, but no further than the location of the boot blocks (MemTop/2 + 1K). (If it's necessary to allocate space below MemTop/2 + 1K, contact Developer Technical Support for details.) It may also use the application zone for temporary heap memory.

> **Warning:** An 'INIT' resource that wants to grow the system heap should be aware that its associated resource map is open in the application heap at the time.

To avoid their being deallocated when the application heap is initialized, vertical retrace tasks, AppleTalk listeners, and RAM-based drivers (and their storage) should be placed in the system heap or in statically allocated space.

30 THE LIST MANAGER PACKAGE

ABOUT THIS CHAPTER

This chapter describes the List Manager Package, which lets you create, display, and manipulate lists.

You should already be familiar with:

- resources, as discussed in the Resource Manager chapter
- the basic concepts and structures behind QuickDraw, particularly points, rectangles, and grafPorts
- the Toolbox Event Manager and the Window Manager
- packages in general, as described in the Package Manager chapter

Warning: Early versions of the system resource file may not contain the List Manager Package.

ABOUT THE LIST MANAGER PACKAGE

The List Manager Package is a tool for storing and updating elements of data within a list and for displaying the list in a rectangle within a window. It handles all hit-testing, selection, and scrolling of **list elements** within that list. In its simplest form, the List Manager Package can be used to display a "text-only" list of names; with some additional effort, it can be used to display an array of images and text.

A list element is simply a group of consecutive bytes of data, so it can be used to store anything—a name, the bits of an icon, or the resource ID of an icon. There's no specific restriction on the size of a list element, but the total size of a list cannot exceed 32K bytes.

Appearance of Lists

A list is drawn in a window. When you create a list, you need to supply a pointer to the window to be used; the grafPort of this window becomes the port in which drawing is done.

You must also supply a rectangle in which to display the list. You specify whether the list should use scroll bars and a size box. If you request scroll bars, they're drawn outside the rectangle (but within the window). If you request a size box, the List Manager leaves room for one but does not draw it; to draw the size box, see the Window Manager procedure DrawGrowIcon. The rectangle can take up the entire area of the content region (except for the space needed by scroll bars, if any), or it can occupy only a small portion of the content region.

List elements are displayed in **cells**; an element can be seen as the contents of a cell. Cells provide the basic structure of a list, and may or may not contain list elements. While list elements (the actual data) may vary in length, the cells in which they're displayed must be the same size for any given list. You can specify the horizontal and vertical size of a cell when you create a list; if either dimension is unspecified, the List Manager calculates a default dimension.

The dimensions of a list are always specified as a number of rows and columns of cells. When you create a list, you can specify the number of cells it is to contain initially; if you don't, it's created with no cells. To add cells to an empty list, you call routines that add entire rows or columns of cells at a time. For instance, to add a single column of 15 cells to an empty list, you would first call a routine to add one column, followed by a routine adding 15 rows.

All cells are initially empty. Once you've added the rows and columns of a list, you can set the values of the cells. At some later point, you can also add empty rows and columns to a list that already contains data.

Drawing Lists

The List Manager provides a drawing mode that you can set either on or off. When the drawing mode is on, all routines that affect the contents of cells, the number of rows or columns, the size of the window, or which cells are visible within the rectangle will cause drawing to happen.

In certain cases, such as the insertion or setting of many cells (typically when the list is created), drawing is either unsightly or slow. In these cases, you'll want to set the drawing mode to off; when the action is completed, you can set the drawing mode back to on.

The appearance and behavior of a list is determined by a routine called its **list definition procedure**, which is stored as a resource in a resource file. The List Manager calls the definition procedure to perform any additional list initialization (such as the allocation of storage space for the application), to draw a cell, to invert the highlight state of a cell, and to dispose of any data it may have allocated.

The system resource file includes a list definition procedure for a standard text-only list. If you'd like another type of list, you'll have to write a list definition procedure, as described later in the section "Defining Your Own Lists".

LIST RECORDS

The List Manager maintains all the information it requires for its operations on a particular list in a **list record**. A list record includes:

- A pointer to the grafPort used by the list; it's set to the port of the window specified when the list is created.
- The rectangle, given in the window's local coordinates, in which the list is to be displayed.

- A rectangle that specifies, by row and column, the dimensions of the list.
- A rectangle that determines, by row and column, which cells are currently visible.
- A handle to the list definition procedure, which actually performs the drawing of the cells.
- The size of a cell.
- A field containing flags that control the selection process.

The list record also contains a handle to the cell data. The data is stored as a contiguous block of data in list order (cells 0..n of row 0, cells 0..n of row 1, and so on). The cell data is locked down only while it's being searched.

The last field of the list record is an array of integers containing the offset of each cell's data within the contiguous block of cell data. The high-order bit of an array element is set if the corresponding cell is selected; the remaining 15 bits contain the offset. This provides the maximum total data size of 32K, and an overhead of one word per cell.

Warning: Since a variety of routines are provided for accessing cell data, you should never need to directly access the array of offsets or the data itself.

The List Record Data Structure

The exact data structure of a list record is as follows:

```
TYPE Cell = Point;

     DataArray  = PACKED ARRAY [0..32000] OF CHAR;
     DataPtr    = ^DataArray;
     DataHandle = ^DataPtr;

     ListRec =
        RECORD
          rView:        Rect;          {list's display rectangle}
          port:         GrafPtr;       {list's grafPort}
          indent:       Point;         {indent distance}
          cellSize:     Point;         {cell size}
          visible:      Rect;          {boundary of visible cells}
          vScroll:      ControlHandle;  {vertical scroll bar}
          hScroll:      ControlHandle;  {horizontal scroll bar}
          selFlags:     SignedByte;    {selection flags}
          lActive:      BOOLEAN;       {TRUE if active}
          lReserved:    SignedByte;    {reserved}
          listFlags:    SignedByte;    {automatic scrolling flags}
          clikTime:     LONGINT;       {time of last click}
          clikLoc:      Point;         {position of last click}
          mouseLoc:     Point;         {current mouse location}
          lClikLoop:    Ptr;           {routine for LClick}
          lastClick:    Cell;          {last cell clicked}
          refCon:       LONGINT;       {list's reference value}
          listDefProc:  Handle;        {list definition procedure}
```

```
        userHandle:   Handle;       {additional storage}
        dataBounds:   Rect;         {boundary of cells allocated}
        cells:        DataHandle;   {cell data}
        maxIndex:     INTEGER;      {used internally}
        cellArray:    ARRAY [1..1] OF INTEGER  {offsets to data}
      END;

    ListPtr     = ^ListRec;
    ListHandle = ^ListPtr;
```

RView is the rectangle, given in the local coordinates of the grafPort, in which the list is displayed. Room for scroll bars is *not* included in this rectangle. If the list has scroll bars and is to fill the entire window, rView should be 15 points smaller in each dimension than the grafPort.

Port is the grafPort used by the list; it's set to the port of the window specified when the list is created. Indent is the distance in pixels that the list definition procedure should indent from the topLeft of the cell when drawing the contents. The default value for indent is 0, but it can be set by the list definition procedure.

CellSize is the size of a cell in pixels. If it's not specified when the list is created, a default cell size is set. CellSize.v is set to the ascent plus descent plus leading of the port's font, and cellSize.h is set to

(rView.right – rView.left) DIV (dataBounds.right – dataBounds.left)

A cell is a box in which a list element is displayed. Cells are identified by their column and row numbers. In Figure 1, for instance, the highlighted cell is in column 1, row 2.

Cells are declared as points, using the Point data type simply as a way of specifying the column and row number of a cell. Similarly, visible and dataBounds use the Rect data type to specify a rectangular set of cells as two diagonally opposite cell coordinates (rather than two diagonally opposite points in the local coordinates of a grafPort).

DataBounds is the boundary of the cells currently allocated, specified by row and column. The list in Figure 1 (assuming the entire list is visible) has seventeen rows and five columns of cells. DataBounds for this list can be represented, using the QuickDraw rectangle notation (left,top)(right,bottom), as (0,0)(5,17). Notice that the column and row specified for the bottom right of dataBounds are 1 greater in each dimension than the column and row number of the bottom right cell. Thus, you can test to see if a cell is a valid cell within the boundary of a list using the statement:

```
IF PtInRect(c,myList^^.dataBounds) THEN...
```

The visible rectangle reflects which cells are currently within the visible part of the list; it's calculated by the List Manager according to the values you specify for rView, dataBounds, and cellSize when you create the list. (Visible.topLeft is the row and column of the top left visible cell; visible.botRight is 1 greater in both dimensions than the row and column of the bottom right visible cell.) For example, if only four cells—row 2, column 0; row 2, column 1; row 3, column 0; and row 3, column 1—are visible, the visible rectangle is (0,2)(2,4). You can test to see if a cell is visible using the statement:

```
IF PtInRect(c,myList^^.visible) THEN...
```

A Sample

Cell 0,0	Cell 1,0	Cell 2,0	Cell 3,0	Cell 4,0
Cell 0,1	Cell 1,1	Cell 2,1	Cell 3,1	Cell 4,1
Cell 0,2	Cell 1,2	Cell 2,2	Cell 3,2	Cell 4,2
Cell 0,3	Cell 1,3	Cell 2,3	Cell 3,3	Cell 4,3
Cell 0,4	Cell 1,4	Cell 2,4	Cell 3,4	Cell 4,4
Cell 0,5	Cell 1,5	Cell 2,5	Cell 3,5	Cell 4,5
Cell 0,6	Cell 1,6	Cell 2,6	Cell 3,6	Cell 4,6
Cell 0,7	Cell 1,7	Cell 2,7	Cell 3,7	Cell 4,7
Cell 0,8	Cell 1,8	Cell 2,8	Cell 3,8	Cell 4,8
Cell 0,9	Cell 1,9	Cell 2,9	Cell 3,9	Cell 4,9
Cell 0,10	Cell 1,10	Cell 2,10	Cell 3,10	Cell 4,10
Cell 0,11	Cell 1,11	Cell 2,11	Cell 3,11	Cell 4,11
Cell 0,12	Cell 1,12	Cell 2,12	Cell 3,12	Cell 4,12
Cell 0,13	Cell 1,13	Cell 2,13	Cell 3,13	Cell 4,13
Cell 0,14	Cell 1,14	Cell 2,14	Cell 3,14	Cell 4,14
Cell 0,15	Cell 1,15	Cell 2,15	Cell 3,15	Cell 4,15
Cell 0,16	Cell 1,16	Cell 2,16	Cell 3,16	Cell 4,16

Figure 1. A Sample List

SelFlags contains selection flags for the List Manager. It's initialized to 0; with this setting, the List Manager selects cells according to the Macintosh User Interface Guidelines. The meaning of these flags is explained below in the section "Cell Selection Algorithm". The listFlags field contains automatic scrolling flags; the List Manager sets these flags automatically when you specify scroll bars. There are predefined constants that let you set or test the status of the corresponding bits:

```
CONST lDoVAutoScroll = 2; {set to allow automatic vertical scrolling}
      lDoHAutoScroll = 1; {set to allow automatic horizontal }
                          { scrolling}
```

ClikLoc is the position of the last mouse click in local coordinates; you can use it in the list definition procedure to get the position within the cell. LClikLoop is a pointer to the routine to be called during the LClick function, as described later. LastClick contains the cell coordinates of the last cell clicked in.

RefCon is the list's reference value field, which the application may store into and access for any purpose. In addition, the application may use the field userHandle to store a handle to an additional storage area.

CellArray contains offsets to the cell data. For each list element, this includes the bit indicating whether the cell is selected or not.

The LClikLoop Field

The lClikLoop field of a list record lets you specify a routine that will be called repeatedly (by the LClick function, described below) as long as the mouse button is held down within the rView rectangle or its scroll bars.

> **Note:** The LClick function performs automatic scrolling if the mouse is dragged outside the visible rectangle, so there's no need to write a list click loop routine to do automatic scrolling.

The list click loop routine has no parameters and returns a Boolean value. You could declare a list click loop routine named MyClikLoop like this:

```
FUNCTION MyClikLoop : BOOLEAN;
```

The function should return TRUE. You must put a pointer to your list click loop routine in the lClikLoop field of the list record so that the List Manager will call your routine.

> **Warning:** Returning FALSE from your list click loop routine tells the LClick function that the mouse button has been released, which aborts LClick.

Assembly-language note: Your routine should set register D0 to 1; returning 0 in register D0 aborts LClick. For your convenience, register D5 contains the current mouse location.

CELL SELECTION ALGORITHM

The default algorithm used by the List Manager for user selection of cells follows the techniques described in the Macintosh User Interface Guidelines, as summarized below.

1. If neither the Shift nor the Command key is held down, a click causes all current selections to be deselected, and the cell receiving the click to be selected. While the mouse button is held down and the mouse moved around, only the cell under the cursor is selected.

2. If the Shift key is held down, then as long as the mouse button is down, the List Manager expands and shrinks a selected rectangle that's defined by the mouse location and the "anchor". When the mouse is first pressed, the List Manager calculates the smallest rectangle that encloses *all* selected cells. If the click is above or to the left of this rectangle (or on the top left corner), the bottom right corner of the rectangle becomes the anchor; otherwise the top left corner becomes the anchor. (If no cells are selected, the clicked cell is used as the anchor.)

3. If the Command key is held down, then while the mouse button is down, all cells that the mouse passes over are either selected or deselected. Like FatBits in MacPaint, if the initial cell was off, cells are turned on; otherwise they're turned off.

The selFlags byte, initialized to 0 by the List Manager, contains flags that let you change the way selections work. Each flag is specified by a bit, as illustrated in Figure 2.

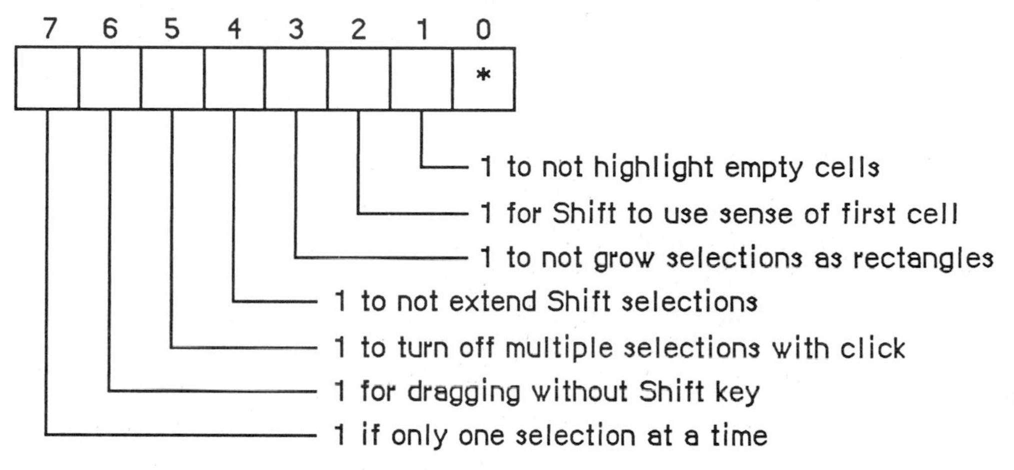

Figure 2. Selection flags

The List Manager provides a predefined constant for each flag, in which the bit corresponding to that flag is set.

```
CONST lOnlyOne     = -128; {set if only one selection at a time}
      lExtendDrag  = 64;   {set for dragging without Shift key}
      lNoDisjoint  = 32;   {set to turn off multiple selections with }
                           { click}
      lNoExtend    = 16;   {set to not extend Shift selections}
      lNoRect      = 8;    {set to not expand selections as }
                           { rectangles}
      lUseSense    = 4;    {set for Shift to use sense of first cell}
      lNoNilHilite = 2;    {set to not highlight empty cells}
```

Setting one or more of bits 5–7 modifies the selection algorithm in the following ways:

- If you set the lOnlyOne bit, only one cell can be selected at a time.
- If you set the lNoDisjoint bit, multiple cells can be selected, but everything is deselected when the mouse button is pressed (even if the Shift or Command keys are held down).
- If you set the lExtendDrag bit, clicking and dragging selects all cells in its path. (It works best if you also set lNoDisjoint, lNoRect, lUseSense, and lNoExtend.)

Bits 2–4 affect Shift selection. If all three are set, Shift selection works exactly like Command selection.

- If you set the lNoRect bit, Shift selections are not dragged out as rectangles, but instead select everything they pass over. They use the anchor point, but do not shrink selections when you back over them.
- If you set the lNoExtend bit, the click is used as the anchor point for Shift selections, and current selections are ignored.
- If you set the lUseSense bit, the cell that's clicked determines whether cells are turned off or on.

Bit 1, the lNoNilHilite bit, determines whether or not empty cells can be selected. If you set this bit, cells not containing data cannot be selected (that is, the list definition procedure isn't called to highlight empty cells).

Note: For the convenience of your application's user, remember to conform to the Macintosh User Interface Guidelines for selection.

USING THE LIST MANAGER PACKAGE

The List Manager Package is automatically read into memory from the system resource file when one of its routines is called; it occupies a total of about 5K bytes.

Before using the List Manager, you must initialize QuickDraw, the Font Manager, the Window Manager, the Menu Manager, and TextEdit, in that order.

Before creating a list, you must create a window in which the drawing will take place. To create a new list, call the LNew function. When you're done using a list, you should dispose of its data with LDispose. Before you dispose of the list, make sure you dispose of any data that you may have stored in the userHandle or refCon fields of the list record.

To change the size of a list's cells, call LCellSize.

The procedure LDoDraw controls whether operations performed on cells by List Manager routines cause drawing on the screen.

To add rows or columns to the list, call LAddRow and LAddColumn. To delete rows or columns, call LDelRow and LDelColumn. These routines do all necessary updating of the screen if you've set drawing on with LDoDraw.

To assign a value to a cell, call the procedure LSetCell. To append data to a cell, you can call LAddToCell; to clear the contents of a cell, call LClrCell. To get a cell's data, call LGetCell. The new value of a cell is displayed if you've set drawing on.

Warning: If you add or delete rows or columns, change the data in a cell, or call a routine that may move or purge memory, pointers (to a cell's data) obtained by earlier calls to the List Manager may no longer be valid.

To select or deselect a cell, call LSetSelect. To determine whether or not a cell is selected, call LGetSelect. LGetSelect can also be used to find the next selected cell in the list.

The Window Manager NewWindow or GetNewWindow call generates an update event for the entire window. Call LUpdate in response to the update event, and all visible cells in the update region will be drawn (or redrawn). When you change the value or selection of a cell from your program, it's redisplayed only if drawing is on. If drawing is off, you can call the procedure LDraw to display the contents of the cell.

If a mouse-down event occurs within the list's window, call LClick. This routine tracks the mouse, selecting cells and scrolling the display as necessary. The result of LClick is a Boolean value that is TRUE if a double-click occurred. You can discover which cell received the double-click by calling LLastClick.

If an activate or deactivate event occurs for the window containing the list, you should call the procedure LActivate. This routine highlights the selected cells and scroll bars as necessary.

If the window containing the list has a size box (and you want the list to grow along with the window), call the Window Manager routines GrowWindow and SizeWindow as usual, then call LSize with the new size of the list. The list is automatically expanded to fill the new area and the scroll bars are updated accordingly. The drawing mode does *not* affect the updating of scroll bars in LSize.

You can find a cell with specified contents by calling LSearch. The default search routine is the International Utilities Package function IUMagIDString, but you can pass LSearch another search routine if you wish. Given a cell, you can call LNextCell to find the next cell in the list.

You can find the local coordinates of a given cell by calling LRect. To scroll the list, call LScroll. You can call LAutoScroll to make sure that the first selected cell is visible. It automatically places the first selected cell in the top left corner of the visible rectangle.

All the data in a list is stored as a single block. You can find the offset of a particular cell's data using LFind.

LIST MANAGER PACKAGE ROUTINES

Assembly-language note: You can invoke each of the List Manager routines with a macro that has the same name as the routine preceded by an underscore. These macros expand to invoke to trap macro _Pack 0. The package determines which routine to execute from a **routine selector**, an integer that's passed to it in a word on the stack. The routine selectors are as follows:

```
lActivate   .EQU  0          lAutoScroll .EQU   16
lAddColumn  .EQU  4          lCellSize   .EQU   20
lAddRow     .EQU  8          lClick      .EQU   24
lAddToCell  .EQU  12         lClrCell    .EQU   28
```

```
lDelColumn  .EQU    32          lNew         .EQU    68
lDelRow     .EQU    36          lNextCell    .EQU    72
lDispose    .EQU    40          lRect        .EQU    76
lDoDraw     .EQU    44          lScroll      .EQU    80
lDraw       .EQU    48          lSearch      .EQU    84
lFind       .EQU    52          lSetCell     .EQU    88
lGetCell    .EQU    56          lSetSelect   .EQU    92
lGetSelect  .EQU    60          lSize        .EQU    96
lLastClick  .EQU    64          lUpdate      .EQU    100
```

Creating and Disposing of Lists

```
FUNCTION LNew (rView,dataBounds: Rect; cSize: Point; theProc:
            INTEGER; theWindow: WindowPtr; drawIt,hasGrow,
            scrollHoriz,scrollVert: BOOLEAN) : ListHandle;
```

Call LNew to create a new list. It returns a handle to the new list. The list's grafPort is set to theWindow's port. If drawIt is FALSE, the list is not displayed.

RView specifies, in the local coordinates of theWindow, the rectangle in which the list will be displayed. (Remember that this doesn't include space for scroll bars. If the list, including scroll bars, is to fill the entire window, rView should be 15 points smaller in each dimension than theWindow's portRect.)

DataBounds is the rectangle for specifying the initial array dimensions of the list. For example to preallocate space for a list that's 5 cells across by 10 cells down, you should set dataBounds to (0,0)(5,10). If you want to allocate the space for a one-column list, set dataBounds to (0,0)(1,0) and use LAddRow.

CSize.h and cSize.v are the desired height and width of each cell in pixels; if they're not specified, a default cell size is calculated (as described above).

TheProc is the resource ID of your list definition procedure; for a text-only list, pass 0 and the default list definition procedure (about 150 bytes in size) will be used. The list definition procedure is called to initialize itself after all other list record fields have been initialized; thus, it can use any of the values in the list record (or set particular fields, such as the indent distance).

If hasGrow is TRUE, the scroll bars are sized so that there's room for a size box in the standard position. It's up to the program to display the size box (using the Window Manager procedure DrawGrowIcon). If scrollHoriz is TRUE, a horizontal scroll bar is placed immediately below rView and all horizontal scrolling functions are implemented. If scrollVert is TRUE, a vertical scroll bar is placed immediately to the right of rView and all vertical scrolling functions are implemented.

The visible rectangle is set to contain as many cells of cSize (or the default) as will fit into rView. If the cells do not fit exactly into rView, the visible rectangle is rounded up to the nearest cell. Scrolling will always allow all cells to be fully displayed. The selection flags are set to 0, and the active flag is set to TRUE.

Note: Scrolling looks best if rView is a multiple of cSize.v in height.

```
PROCEDURE LDispose (lHandle: ListHandle);
```

Call LDispose when you are through using a list. It issues a close call to the list definition procedure, and calls the Memory Manager procedure DisposHandle for the data handle, the Control Manager procedure DisposeControl for both scroll bars (if they're there), and DisposHandle for the list record.

> **Note:** Calling LDispose is *much* faster than deleting one row at a time.

Adding and Deleting Rows and Columns

```
FUNCTION LAddColumn (count,colNum: INTEGER; lHandle: ListHandle) :
            INTEGER;
```

LAddColumn inserts into the given list the number of columns specified by the count parameter, starting at the column specified by colNum. Column numbers that are greater than or equal to colNum are increased by count. If colNum is not within dataBounds, new last columns are added. The number of the first added column is returned and dataBounds.right is increased by count. All cells added are empty. If there are no cells (because dataBounds.top = dataBounds.bottom), no cells are added, but dataBounds is still extended. If drawing is on and the added columns (which are empty) are visible, the list and its scroll bars are updated.

```
FUNCTION LAddRow (count,rowNum: INTEGER; lHandle: ListHandle) :
            INTEGER;
```

LAddRow inserts the number of rows specified by the count parameter, starting at the row specified by rowNum. Row numbers that are greater than or equal to rowNum are increased by count. If rowNum is not within dataBounds, new last rows are added. The number of the first added row is returned, and dataBounds.bottom is increased by count. All cells added are empty. If there are no cells (because dataBounds.left = dataBounds.right), no cells are added, but dataBounds is still extended. If drawing is on and the added rows (which are empty) are visible, the list and its scroll bars are updated.

```
PROCEDURE LDelColumn (count,colNum: INTEGER; lHandle: ListHandle);
```

LDelColumn deletes the number of columns specified by the count parameter, starting with the column specified by colNum. Column numbers that are greater than colNum are decreased by count. If colNum is not within dataBounds, nothing is done. DataBounds.right is decreased by count. If drawing is on and the deleted columns were visible, the list and its scroll bars are updated.

If count is 0, or

colNum = dataBounds.left AND count >= dataBounds.right – dataBounds.left

all the data in the list is quickly deleted, dataBounds.right is set to dataBounds.left, and the number of rows is left unchanged.

```
PROCEDURE LDelRow (count,rowNum: INTEGER; lHandle: ListHandle);
```

LDelRow deletes the number of rows specified by the count parameter, starting with the row specified by rowNum. Row numbers that are greater than rowNum are decreased by count. If rowNum is not within dataBounds, nothing is done. DataBounds.bottom is decreased by count. If drawing is on and the deleted rows were visible, the list and its scroll bars are updated.

If count is 0, or

rowNum = dataBounds.top AND count > = dataBounds.bottom – dataBounds.top

all the data in the list is quickly deleted, dataBounds.bottom is set to dataBounds.top, and the number of columns is left unchanged.

Operations on Cells

```
PROCEDURE LAddToCell (dataPtr: Ptr; dataLen: INTEGER; theCell:
            Cell; lHandle: ListHandle);
```

LAddToCell appends the data pointed to by dataPtr and of length dataLen to the cell specified by theCell in lHandle. If drawing is off, you must turn drawing on and call LDraw (or LUpdate) to display the cell's new value.

```
PROCEDURE LClrCell (theCell: Cell; lHandle: ListHandle);
```

LClrCell clears the contents of the specified cell (by setting the length to 0). If theCell is not a valid cell, nothing is done. If drawing is off, you must turn drawing on and call LDraw to display the cell's new value (or simply call the Window Manager procedure InvalRect).

```
PROCEDURE LGetCell (dataPtr: Ptr; VAR dataLen: INTEGER; theCell:
            Cell; lHandle: ListHandle);
```

Given a cell in theCell, LGetCell copies the cell's data to the location specified by dataPtr; dataLen is the maximum number of bytes allowed. If the data is longer than dataLen, only dataLen bytes are copied into the location specified by dataPtr. If the data is shorter than dataLen, dataLen is set to the true length of the cell's data.

```
PROCEDURE LSetCell (dataPtr: Ptr; dataLen: INTEGER; theCell: Cell;
            lHandle: ListHandle);
```

LSetCell places the data pointed to by dataPtr and of length dataLen into the specified cell. It replaces any data that was already in the cell. If dataLen is 0, this is equivalent to LClrCell. If theCell is not a valid cell, nothing is done. If drawing is off, you must turn drawing on and call LDraw (or LUpdate) to display the cell's new value.

```
PROCEDURE LCellSize (cSize: Point; lHandle: ListHandle);
```

LCellSize sets the cellSize field in the list record to cSize and updates the visible rectangle to contain cells of this size. This command should be used only before any cells have been drawn.

```
FUNCTION LGetSelect (next: BOOLEAN; VAR theCell: Cell; lHandle:
            ListHandle) : BOOLEAN;
```

If next is FALSE, LGetSelect returns TRUE if the specified cell is selected, or FALSE if not. If next is TRUE, LGetSelect returns in c the cell coordinates of the next selected cell in the row that is *greater than or equal to theCell*. If there are no more cells in the row, it returns in theCell the cell coordinates of the next selected cell in the next row. If there are no more rows, FALSE is returned.

```
PROCEDURE LSetSelect (setIt: BOOLEAN; theCell: Cell; lHandle:
            ListHandle);
```

If setIt is TRUE, LSetSelect selects the cell and redraws if it is visible and was previously unselected. If setIt is FALSE, it deselects the cell and redraws if necessary.

Mouse Location

```
FUNCTION LClick (pt: Point; modifiers: INTEGER; lHandle: ListHandle)
            : BOOLEAN;
```

Call LClick when there is a mouse-down event in the destination rectangle or its scroll bars. Pt is the mouse location in local coordinates. Modifiers is the modifiers word from the event record. LHandle is the list to be tracked. The result is TRUE if a double-click occurred (and the two clicks took place within the same cell).

LClick keeps control until the mouse is released; each time through its inner loop, it calls the routine whose pointer is in the lClikLoop field of the list record.

If the mouse is in the visible rectangle, cells are selected according to the state of the modifiers and the selection flags. If the mouse was in the cells but is dragged outside the list's rectangle, the list is auto-scrolled. If the mouse was in a control, the control's definition procedure is called to track the mouse. To discover which cell was clicked in, use the LLastClick function.

```
FUNCTION LLastClick (lHandle: ListHandle) : Cell;
```

LLastClick returns the cell coordinates of the last cell clicked in. If no cell has been clicked in since LNew, the value returned (for both integers) is negative.

> **Note:** The value returned by this call is not the last cell double-clicked in, or the last cell selected, but merely the last cell clicked in.

Accessing Cells

```
PROCEDURE LFind (VAR offset,len: INTEGER; theCell: Cell; lHandle:
          ListHandle);
```

Given a cell in theCell, LFind returns the offset and the length in bytes of the cell's data. If an invalid cell is specified, offset and len are set to –1. A similar procedure, LGetCell, is more convenient to use from Pascal.

```
FUNCTION LNextCell (hNext,vNext: BOOLEAN; VAR theCell: Cell;
          lHandle: ListHandle) : BOOLEAN;
```

Given a cell in theCell, LNextCell returns in theCell the next cell in the list. If both hNext and vNext are TRUE, theCell is first advanced to the next cell in the row. If there are no more cells in the row, theCell is set to the first cell in the next row. If there are no more rows, FALSE is returned. If only hNext is TRUE, theCell is advanced within the current row. If only vNext is TRUE, theCell is advanced within the current column. FALSE is returned if there are no remaining cells in the row or column.

```
PROCEDURE LRect (VAR cellRect: Rect; theCell: Cell; lHandle:
          ListHandle);
```

LRect returns in cellRect the local (QuickDraw) coordinates of the cell specified by theCell. If an invalid cell is specified, (0,0)(0,0) is returned in cellRect.

```
FUNCTION LSearch (dataPtr: Ptr; dataLen: INTEGER; searchProc: Ptr;
          VAR theCell: Cell; lHandle: ListHandle) : BOOLEAN;
```

LSearch searches for the first cell greater than or equal to theCell that contains the specified data. If a cell containing matching data is found, the function result TRUE is returned, and the cell coordinates are returned in theCell. If searchProc is NIL, the International Utilities Package function IUMagIDString is called to compare the specified data with the contents of each cell. If searchProc is not NIL, the routine pointed to by searchProc is called.

> **Note:** Your searchProc should have the same parameters as the IUMagIDString function.

```
PROCEDURE LSize (listWidth,listHeight: INTEGER; lHandle:
          ListHandle);
```

You'll usually call LSize immediately after the Window Manager procedure SizeWindow. It causes the bottom right of the list to be adjusted so that the list is the width and height indicated by listWidth and listHeight. The contents of the list and the scroll bars are adjusted and redrawn as necessary. The values of listWidth and listHeight do not include the scroll bars; for a list that entirely fills the window, listWidth and listHeight should be 15 fewer pixels than the portRect if both scroll bars are present.

List Display

```
PROCEDURE LDraw (theCell: Cell; lHandle: ListHandle);
```

Call LDraw after updating a cell's data or selection status. (You can achieve the same result by invalidating the cell's rectangle and calling LUpdate in response to the update event.) The List Manager makes its grafPort the current port, sets the clipping region to the cell's rectangle, and calls the list definition procedure to draw the cell. It restores the clipping region and port before exiting.

```
PROCEDURE LDoDraw (drawIt: BOOLEAN; lHandle: ListHandle);
```

LDoDraw sets the List Manager's drawing mode to the state specified by drawIt. If drawIt is TRUE, changes made by most List Manager calls will cause some sort of drawing to take place. If drawIt is FALSE, all cell drawing is disabled. (Two exceptions: The scroll bars are still updated after LSize, and the scroll arrows are still highlighted if the user clicks them.)

The recommended use of LDoDraw is to disable drawing while you're building a list (that is, adding rows or columns, setting or changing cell values, or setting default selections). Once you've finished building the list, you should then re-enable drawing. In general, drawing should be on while you're in your event loop and dispatching events to the List Manager.

```
PROCEDURE LScroll (dCols,dRows: INTEGER; lHandle: ListHandle);
```

LScroll scrolls the given list by the number of columns and rows specified in dCols and dRows, either positively (down and to the right) or negatively (up and to the left). Scrolling is pinned to the list's dataBounds. If drawing is on, LScroll does all necessary updating of the screen.

```
PROCEDURE LAutoScroll (lHandle: ListHandle);
```

For the given list, LAutoScroll scrolls the list until the first selected cell is visible. It automatically places the first selected cell in the top left corner of the visible rectangle.

```
PROCEDURE LUpdate (theRgn: RgnHandle; lHandle: ListHandle);
```

LUpdate should be called in response to an update event. TheRgn should be set to the visRgn of the list's port (for more details, see the BeginUpdate procedure in the Window Manager chapter). It redraws any visible cells in lHandle that intersect theRgn. It also redraws the controls, if necessary.

```
PROCEDURE LActivate (act: BOOLEAN; lHandle: ListHandle);
```

Call LActivate to activate or deactivate the list specified by lHandle (in response to an activate event in the window containing the list). The act parameter should be set to TRUE to activate the list, or FALSE to deactivate the list. LActivate highlights or unhighlights the selections, and shows or hides the scroll bars (but not the size box, if any).

DEFINING YOUR OWN LISTS

The List Manager calls a list definition procedure to perform any additional list initialization (such as the allocation of storage space for the application), to draw a cell, to invert the highlight state of a cell, and to dispose of any data it may have allocated. The system resource file includes a default list definition procedure for a standard text-only list; you may, however, wish to define your own type of list with special features.

To define your own type of list, you write a list definition procedure and store it in a resource file as a resource of type 'LDEF'. The standard list definition procedure has a resource ID of 0; your definition procedure should have a different ID.

When you create a list, you provide the resource ID of the list definition procedure to be used. The List Manager calls the Resource Manager to access the list definition procedure with the given resource ID. The Resource Manager reads the list definition procedure into memory and returns a handle to it. The List Manager then stores this handle in the listDefProc field of the list record.

The List Definition Procedure

The list definition procedure is usually written in assembly language, but may be written in Pascal.

Assembly-language note: The procedure's entry point must be at the beginning.

You may choose any name you wish for your list definition procedure. Here's how you would declare one named MyList:

```
PROCEDURE MyList (lMessage: INTEGER; lSelect: BOOLEAN; lRect: Rect;
            lCell: Cell; lDataOffset,lDataLen: INTEGER; lHandle:
            ListHandle);
```

The lMessage parameter identifies the operation to be performed. It has one of the following values:

```
CONST lInitMsg    = 0;   {do any additional list initialization}
      lDrawMsg    = 1;   {draw the cell }
      lHiliteMsg  = 2;   {invert cell's highlight state}
      lCloseMsg   = 3;   {take any additional disposal action}
```

LSelect is used for both the drawing and highlighting operations; it's TRUE if the cell should be selected.

LRect indicates the rectangle in which a cell should be drawn. LDataOffset is the offset into the cell data of the cell to be drawn or highlighted; lDataLen is the length in bytes of that cell's data. LHandle is the handle to the list record.

The routines that perform these operations are described below.

> **Note:** "Routine" here doesn't necessarily mean a procedure or function. While it's a good idea to set these up as subfunctions within the list definition procedure, you're not required to do so.

The Initialize Routine

The list definition procedure is called by the LNew function with an initMsg message after all list initialization has been completed. Since all default settings have been stored in the list record, this routine is a good place to change any of these settings. This routine can also be used to allocate any private storage needed by the list definition procedure.

The Draw Routine

The list definition procedure receives a lDrawMsg message when a cell needs to be drawn. The lSelect parameter is TRUE if the given cell should be selected.

LRect is the rectangle in which the cell should be drawn. The draw routine sets the clipping region of the list's window to this rectangle.

LDataOffset is the offset into the cell data of the cell to be drawn; lDataLen is the length of that cell's data in bytes.

The Highlight Routine

The definition procedure receives a lHiliteMsg message when a cell's data is visible and its highlight state needs to be inverted (from selected to deselected or vice versa). This routine is provided for the extra speed usually gained by using an invert operation instead of a combination of the draw and highlight operations.

The parameters for this routine are identical to those for the lDrawMsg routine. If you want (for instance, if highlighting is more complicated than mere inversion), you can simply call your lDrawMsg routine when you get a lHiliteMsg message.

The Close Routine

The definition procedure receives a lCloseMsg message in response to a LDispose call. If any private storage was allocated by the definition procedure, this routine should dispose of it.

SUMMARY OF THE LIST MANAGER PACKAGE

Constants

```
CONST { Masks for automatic scrolling }

      lDoVAutoscroll = 2  {set to allow automatic vertical scrolling}
      lDoHAutoscroll = 1  {set to allow automatic horizontal scrolling}

      { Masks for selection flags }

      lOnlyOne     = -128; {set if only one selection at a time}
      lExtendDrag  = 64;   {set for dragging without Shift key}
      lNoDisjoint  = 32;   {set to turn off multiple selections with }
                           { click}
      lNoExtend    = 16;   {set to not extend Shift selections}
      lNoRect      = 8;    {set to not grow selections as rectangles}
      lUseSense    = 4;    {set for Shift to use sense of first cell}
      lNoNilHilite = 2;    {set to not highlight empty cells}

      { Messages to list definition procedure }

      lInitMsg   = 0;  {initialize list, set defaults, allocate space}
      lDrawMsg   = 1;  {draw the indicated cell data}
      lHiliteMsg = 2;  {invert (select/deselect) the state of a cell}
      lCloseMsg  = 3;  {dispose of list and any associated data}
```

Data Types

```
TYPE Cell = Point;

     DataArray  = PACKED ARRAY [0..32000] OF CHAR;
     DataPtr    = ^DataArray;
     DataHandle = ^DataPtr;

     ListRec =
        RECORD
          rView:       Rect;          {list's display rectangle}
          port:        GrafPtr;       {list's grafPort}
          indent:      Point;         {indent distance}
          cellSize:    Point;         {cell size}
          visible:     Rect;          {boundary of visible cells}
          vScroll:     ControlHandle; {vertical scroll bar}
          hScroll:     ControlHandle; {horizontal scroll bar}
          selFlags:    SignedByte;    {selection flags}
          lActive:     BOOLEAN;       {TRUE if active}
          lReserved:   SignedByte;    {reserved}
          listFlags:   SignedByte;    {automatic scrolling flags}
          clikTime:    LONGINT;       {time of last click}
          clikLoc:     Point;         {position of last click}
          mouseLoc:    Point;         {current mouse location}
          lClikLoop:   Ptr;           {routine for LClick}
```

```
        lastClick:    Cell;         {last cell clicked}
        refCon:       LONGINT;      {list's reference value}
        listDefProc:  Handle;       {list definition procedure}
        userHandle:   Handle;       {additional storage}
        dataBounds:   Rect;         {boundary of cells allocated}
        cells:        DataHandle;   {cell data}
        maxIndex:     INTEGER;      {used internally}
        cellArray:    ARRAY [1..1] OF INTEGER  {offsets to data}
      END;

   ListPtr    = ^ListRec;
   ListHandle = ^ListPtr;
```

Routines

Creating and Disposing of Lists

```
FUNCTION   LNew      (rView,dataBounds: Rect; cSize: Point; theProc:
                      INTEGER; theWindow: WindowPtr; drawIt,
                      hasGrow,scrollHoriz,scrollVert: BOOLEAN) :
                      ListHandle;
PROCEDURE LDispose   (lHandle: ListHandle);
```

Adding and Deleting Rows and Columns

```
FUNCTION   LAddColumn  (count,colNum: INTEGER; lHandle: ListHandle) :
                        INTEGER;
FUNCTION   LAddRow     (count,rowNum: INTEGER; lHandle: ListHandle) :
                        INTEGER;
PROCEDURE LDelColumn   (count,colNum: INTEGER; lHandle: ListHandle);
PROCEDURE LDelRow      (count,rowNum: INTEGER; lHandle: ListHandle);
```

Operations on Cells

```
PROCEDURE LAddToCell  (dataPtr: Ptr; dataLen: INTEGER; theCell: Cell;
                       lHandle: ListHandle);
PROCEDURE LClrCell    (theCell: Cell; lHandle: ListHandle);
PROCEDURE LGetCell    (dataPtr: Ptr; VAR dataLen: INTEGER; theCell:
                       Cell; lHandle: ListHandle);
PROCEDURE LSetCell    (dataPtr: Ptr; dataLen: INTEGER; theCell: Cell;
                       lHandle: ListHandle);
PROCEDURE LCellSize   (cSize: Point; lHandle: ListHandle );
FUNCTION   LGetSelect  (next: BOOLEAN; VAR theCell: Cell; lHandle:
                       ListHandle) : BOOLEAN;
PROCEDURE LSetSelect  (setIt: BOOLEAN; theCell: Cell; lHandle:
                       ListHandle);
```

Mouse Location

```
FUNCTION LClick       (pt: Point; modifiers: INTEGER; lHandle:
                       ListHandle) : BOOLEAN;
FUNCTION LLastClick   (lHandle: ListHandle) : Cell;
```

Accessing Cells

```
PROCEDURE LFind      (VAR offset,len: INTEGER; theCell: Cell; lHandle:
                      ListHandle);
FUNCTION  LNextCell  (hNext,vNext: BOOLEAN; VAR theCell: Cell; lHandle:
                      ListHandle) : BOOLEAN
PROCEDURE LRect      (VAR cellRect: Rect; theCell: Cell; lHandle:
                      ListHandle);
FUNCTION  LSearch    (dataPtr: Ptr; dataLen: INTEGER; searchProc: Ptr;
                      VAR theCell: Cell; lHandle: ListHandle) : BOOLEAN;
PROCEDURE LSize      (listWidth,listHeight: INTEGER; lHandle:
                      ListHandle);
```

List Display

```
PROCEDURE LDraw        (theCell: Cell; lHandle: ListHandle);
PROCEDURE LDoDraw      (drawIt: BOOLEAN; lHandle: ListHandle);
PROCEDURE LScroll      (dCols,dRows: INTEGER; lHandle: ListHandle);
PROCEDURE LAutoScroll  (lHandle: ListHandle);
PROCEDURE LUpdate      (theRgn: RgnHandle; lHandle: ListHandle);
PROCEDURE LActivate    (act: BOOLEAN; lHandle: ListHandle);
```

List Definition Procedure

```
PROCEDURE MyListDef (lMessage: INTEGER; lSelect: BOOLEAN; lRect: Rect;
                     lCell: Cell; lDataOffset,lDataLen: INTEGER;
                     lHandle: ListHandle);
```

Assembly-Language Information

Constants

```
; Automatic scrolling flags

lDoVAutoscroll  .EQU  1    ;set to allow automatic vertical scrolling
lDoHAutoscroll  .EQU  0    ;set to allow automatic horizontal scrolling

; Selection flags

lOnlyOne      .EQU  7    ;set if only one selection at a time
lExtendDrag   .EQU  6    ;set for dragging without Shift key
lNoDisjoint   .EQU  5    ;set to turn off multiple selections with
                         ; click
lNoExtend     .EQU  4    ;set to not extend Shift selections
lNoRect       .EQU  3    ;set to not grow selections as rectangles
lUseSense     .EQU  2    ;set for Shift to use sense of first cell
lNoNilHilite  .EQU  1    ;set to not highlight empty cells
```

```
; Messages to list definition procedure

lInitMsg      .EQU  0    ;initialize list, set defaults, allocate space
lDrawMsg      .EQU  1    ;draw the indicated cell data
lHiliteMsg    .EQU  2    ;invert (select/deselect) the state of a cell
lCloseMsg     .EQU  3    ;dispose of list and any associated data

; Routine selectors
; (Note:  You can invoke each of the List Manager routines with a macro
;  that has the same name as the routine preceded by an underscore.)

lActivate     .EQU  0
lAddColumn    .EQU  4
lAddRow       .EQU  8
lAddToCell    .EQU  12
lAutoScroll   .EQU  16
lCellSize     .EQU  20
lClick        .EQU  24
lClrCell      .EQU  28
lDelColumn    .EQU  32
lDelRow       .EQU  36
lDispose      .EQU  40
lDoDraw       .EQU  44
lDraw         .EQU  48
lFind         .EQU  52
lGetCell      .EQU  56
lGetSelect    .EQU  60
lLastClick    .EQU  64
lNew          .EQU  68
lNextCell     .EQU  72
lRect         .EQU  76
lScroll       .EQU  80
lSearch       .EQU  84
lSetCell      .EQU  88
lSetSelect    .EQU  92
lSize         .EQU  96
lUpdate       .EQU  100
```

List Record Data Structure

rView	List's display rectangle (rectangle; 8 bytes)
port	List's grafPort (portRec bytes)
indent	Indent distance (point; long)
cellSize	Cell size (point; long)
visible	Boundary of visible cells (rectangle; 8 bytes)
vScroll	Handle to vertical scroll bar
hScroll	Handle to horizontal scroll bar
selFlags	Selection flags (byte)
lActive	Nonzero if active (byte)
clikTime	Time of last click (long)
clikLoc	Position of last click (point; long)
mouseLoc	Current mouse location (point; long)
lClikLoop	Pointer to routine to be called during LClick

lastClick	Last cell clicked (point; long)
refCon	Reference value (long)
listDefHandle	Handle to list definition procedure
userHandle	Handle to user storage
dataBounds	Boundary of cells allocated (rectangle; 8 bytes)
cells	Handle to cell data
maxIndex	Used internally (word)
cellArray	Offsets to cells

Trap Macro Name

_Pack0

(Note: You can invoke each of the List Manager routines with a macro that has the same name as the routine preceded by an underscore.)

31 THE SCSI MANAGER

ABOUT THIS CHAPTER

This chapter describes the SCSI Manager, the part of the Operating System that controls the exchange of information between a Macintosh and peripheral devices connected through the Small Computer Standard Interface (SCSI).

The SCSI Manager is the Macintosh implementation of an SCSI bus and its attached devices. This chapter describes the routines and data structures you'll use to communicate between a Macintosh and peripherals over an SCSI bus. It also explains how to write an SCSI device driver that's capable of performing the Macintosh system startup.

This chapter provides information needed to connect a device to the Macintosh via an SCSI bus; it is *not* intended as a guide to designing an SCSI device. A familiarity with the American National Standard Committee (ANSC) documentation for SCSI, specifically the ANSC X3T9.2/82-2 draft proposal, is assumed; the information provided in the draft proposal will not be repeated in this chapter.

You should also already be familiar with:

- the use of devices and device drivers, as described in the Device Manager chapter
- sectors and file tags, as described in the Disk Driver chapter
- any documentation provided with the particular SCSI device you want to connect to the Macintosh

ABOUT THE SCSI MANAGER

The **Small Computer Standard Interface** (SCSI) is a specification of mechanical, electrical, and functional standards for connecting small computers with intelligent peripherals such as hard disks, printers, and optical disks. The SCSI Manager is the part of the Operating System that provides routines and data structures for communicating between a Macintosh and peripheral devices according to this industry-standard interface.

Up to eight devices can be connected, in a daisy-chain configuration, to an SCSI bus. When two SCSI devices communicate with each other, one acts as the **initiator** and the other as the **target**. The initiator asks the target to perform a certain operation, such as reading a block of data. An SCSI device typically has a fixed role as an initiator or target; for instance, the Macintosh acts as initiator to a variety of peripherals acting as targets. There may also be intelligent peripherals capable of acting as initiators. Multiple initiators (as well as multiple targets) are allowed on an SCSI bus, but only one Macintosh can be connected to an SCSI bus at a time.

Each device on the bus has a unique ID, an integer from 0 to 7. The Macintosh always has an ID of 7; peripheral devices should choose another number.

At any given time, the Apple SCSI bus is in one of eight phases. When no SCSI device is actively using the bus, the bus is in the **bus free phase**.

Since multiple initiators are possible, an initiator must first gain control of the bus; this process is called the **arbitration phase**.

> **Note:** If more than one initiator arbitrates for use of the bus at the same time, the initiator with the higher ID gains control first. Once an initiator (regardless of ID) gains control of the bus, no other device can interrupt that session.

Once the initiator has gained control of the bus, it selects the target device that will be asked to perform a certain operation; this phase, known as the **selection phase**, includes an acknowledgement from the target that it has been selected. In the event that the target suspends (or disconnects) the communication, an optional phase, known as the **reselection phase**, lets the target reconnect to the initiator.

In the **command phase**, the initiator tells the target what operation to perform. The **data phase** follows; this is when the actual transfer of data between initiator and target takes place. When the operation is completed, the target sends two completion bytes. The first byte contains status information and the second contains a message; they constitute the **status phase** and **message phase** respectively.

A typical communication might involve a Macintosh requesting a block of data to be read from a hard disk connected via an SCSI bus. The Macintosh waits for a bus free phase to occur and then arbitrates for use of the bus. It selects the hard disk as target and sends the command for the read operation. The hard disk transfers the requested data back to the Macintosh, completing the session by sending the status and message bytes.

USING THE SCSI MANAGER

The SCSI Manager is automatically initialized when the system starts up. To gain control of the SCSI bus, call SCSIGet. To select a target device to perform an operation (such as reading or writing data), call SCSISelect. The SCSICmd function tells the target device what operation to perform.

To transfer data from the target device to the Macintosh, you can call SCSIRead; SCSIWrite transfers data from the Macintosh to the target device. The read and write operations can be performed without polling and waiting for the /REQ line on each data byte by calling SCSIRBlind and SCSIWBlind, respectively. All four read/write functions require a transfer instruction block telling the SCSI Manager what to do with the data bytes transferred during the data phase.

The SCSIComplete function gives the current command a specified number of ticks to complete and then returns the status and message bytes.

You can obtain a bit map of the SCSI control and status bits by calling SCSIStat. To reset the SCSI bus (typically when a device has left it in a suspended phase), call SCSIReset.

Describing the Operation to be Performed

You tell the SCSI Manager what operation to perform by passing a pointer to a command descriptor block; the SCSI command structure is outlined in the ANSC document X3T9.2/82-2.

When the command to be performed involves a transfer of data (such as a read or write operation), you also need to pass a pointer to a **transfer instruction block**, which tells the SCSI Manager what to do with the data bytes transferred during the data phase. A transfer instruction block contains a pseudo-program consisting of a variable number of instructions; it's similar to a subroutine except that the instructions are provided and interpreted by the SCSI Manager itself. The instructions are of a fixed size and have the following structure:

```
TYPE SCSIInstr = RECORD
                    scOpcode: INTEGER; {operation code}
                    scParam1: LONGINT; {first parameter}
                    scParam2: LONGINT  {second parameter}
                 END;
```

Eight instructions are available; their operation codes are specified with the following predefined constants:

```
CONST scInc    = 1;  {SCINC instruction}
      scNoInc  = 2;  {SCNOINC instruction}
      scAdd    = 3;  {SCADD instruction}
      scMove   = 4;  {SCMOVE instruction}
      scLoop   = 5;  {SCLOOP instruction}
      scNOp    = 6;  {SCNOP instruction}
      scStop   = 7;  {SCSTOP instruction}
      scComp   = 8;  {SCCOMP instruction}
```

A description of the instructions is given below.

opcode = scInc param1 = buffer param2 = count

The SCINC instruction moves count data bytes to or from buffer, incrementing buffer by count when done.

opcode = scNoInc param1 = buffer param2 = count

The SCNOINC instruction moves count data bytes to or from buffer, leaving buffer unmodified.

opcode = scAdd param1 = addr param2 = value

The SCADD instruction adds the given value to the address in addr. (The addition is performed as an MC68000 long operation.)

opcode = scMove param1 = addr1 param2 = addr2

The SCMOVE instruction moves the value pointed at by addr1 to the location pointed to by addr2. (The move is an MC68000 long operation.)

opcode = scLoop   param1 = relAddr   param2 = count

The SCLOOP instruction decrements count by 1. If the result is greater than 0, pseudo-program execution resumes at the current address+relAddr. If the result is 0, pseudo-program execution resumes at the next instruction. RelAddr should be a signed multiple of the instruction size (10 bytes). For example, to loop to the immediately preceding instruction, the relAddr field would contain –10. To loop forward by three instructions, it would contain 30.

opcode = scNOp   param1 = NIL   param2 = NIL

The SCNOP instruction does nothing.

opcode = scStop   param1 = NIL   param2 = NIL

The SCSTOP instruction terminates the pseudo-program execution, returning to the calling SCSI Manager routine.

opcode = scComp   param1 = addr   param2 = count

The SCCOMP instruction is used only with a read command. Beginning at addr, it compares incoming data bytes with memory, incrementing addr by count when done. If the bytes do not compare equally, an error is returned to the read command.

Example

This example gives a transfer instruction block for a transfer of six 512-byte blocks of data from or to address $67B50.

```
SCINC    $67B50   512
SCLOOP   -10      6
SCSTOP
```

SCSI MANAGER ROUTINES

Assembly-language note: Unlike most other Operating System routines, the SCSI Manager routines are stack-based. You can invoke each of the SCSI routines with a macro that has the same name as the routine preceded by an underscore. These macros, however, aren't trap macros themselves; instead they expand to invoke the trap macro _SCSIDispatch. The SCSI Manager determines which routine to execute from the **routine selector**, an integer that's passed to it in a word on the stack. The routine selectors are as follows:

```
scsiReset     .EQU   0
scsiGet       .EQU   1
scsiSelect    .EQU   2
scsiCmd       .EQU   3
scsiComplete  .EQU   4
scsiRead      .EQU   5
scsiWrite     .EQU   6
scsiRBlind    .EQU   8
scsiWBlind    .EQU   9
scsiStat      .EQU   10
```

Most of the SCSI Manager routines return an integer result code of type OSErr. Each routine lists all of the applicable result codes, along with a short description of what the result code means. Lengthier explanations of all the result codes can be found in the summary at the end of this chapter.

Warning: The error codes returned by SCSI Manager routines typically indicate only that a given operation failed. To determine the actual cause of the failure, you need to send another SCSI command asking the device what went wrong.

```
FUNCTION SCSIReset : OSErr;
```

SCSIReset resets the SCSI bus.

Result codes	noErr	No error
	commErr	Breakdown in SCSI protocols

```
FUNCTION SCSIGet : OSErr;
```

SCSIGet arbitrates for use of the SCSI bus.

Result codes	noErr	No error
	commErr	Breakdown in SCSI protocols

```
FUNCTION SCSISelect (targetID: INTEGER) : OSErr;
```

SCSISelect selects the device whose ID is in targetID.

Result codes	noErr	No error
	commErr	Breakdown in SCSI protocols

```
FUNCTION SCSICmd (buffer: Ptr; count: INTEGER) : OSErr;
```

SCSICmd sends the command pointed to by buffer to the selected target device. The size of the command in bytes is specified in count.

Result codes	noErr	No error
	commErr	Breakdown in SCSI protocols
	phaseErr	Phase error

```
FUNCTION SCSIRead (tibPtr: Ptr) : OSErr;
```

SCSIRead transfers data from the target to the initiator, as specified in the transfer instruction block pointed to by tibPtr.

Result codes	noErr	No error
	badParmsErr	Unrecognized instruction in transfer instruction block
	commErr	Breakdown in SCSI protocols
	compareErr	Data comparison error (with scComp command in transfer instruction block)
	phaseErr	Phase error

```
FUNCTION SCSIRBlind (tibPtr: Ptr) : OSErr;
```

SCSIRBlind is functionally identical to SCSIRead, but does not poll and wait for the /REQ line on each data byte. Rather, the /REQ line is polled only for the first byte transferred by each SCINC, SCNOINC, or SCCOMP instruction. For instance, given the following transfer instruction block

```
SCINC     $67B50   512
SCLOOP    -10      6
SCSTOP
```

SCSIRBlind polls and waits only for the first byte of each 512-byte block transferred.

Result codes	noErr	No error
	badParmsErr	Unrecognized instruction
	commErr	Breakdown in SCSI protocols
	compareErr	Data comparison error
	phaseErr	Phase error

```
FUNCTION SCSIWrite (tibPtr: Ptr) : OSErr;
```

SCSIWrite transfers data from the initiator to the target, as specified in the command descriptor block pointed to by tibPtr.

Result codes	noErr	No error
	badParmsErr	Unrecognized instruction
	commErr	Breakdown in SCSI protocols
	phaseErr	Phase error

```
FUNCTION SCSIWBlind (tibPtr: Ptr) : OSErr;
```

SCSIWBlind is functionally identical to SCSIWrite, but does not poll and wait for the /REQ line on each data byte. As with SCSIRBlind, SCSIWBlind polls the /REQ line only for the first byte transferred by each SCINC, SCNOINC, or SCCOMP instruction.

Result codes	noErr	No error
	badParmsErr	Unrecognized instruction
	commErr	Breakdown in SCSI protocols
	phaseErr	Phase error

```
FUNCTION SCSIComplete (VAR stat,message: INTEGER; wait: LONGINT) :
     OSErr;
```

SCSIComplete gives the current command wait number of ticks to complete; the two completion bytes are returned in stat and message.

Result codes	noErr	No error
	commErr	Breakdown in SCSI protocols
	phaseErr	Phase error

```
FUNCTION SCSIStat : INTEGER;
```

This function returns a bit map of SCSI control and status bits; these bits are shown in Figure 1. See the NCR 5380 SCSI chip documentation for a description of these signals. (Bits 0–9 are complements of the SCSI bus standard signals.)

15							8	7							0
END DMA	DMA REQ	PTY ERR	INT REQ	PHS MAT	BSY ERR	ATN	ACK	RST	BSY	REQ	MSG	C/D	I/O	SEL	DBP

Figure 1. SCSI Control and Status Bits

Result codes	noErr	No error
	commErr	Breakdown in SCSI protocols
	phaseErr	Phase error

WRITING A DRIVER FOR AN SCSI BLOCK DEVICE

Device drivers are usually written in assembly language. The structure of a device driver is described in the Device Manager chapter. This section presents additional information to enable SCSI block devices to perform the Macintosh system startup.

For each attached SCSI device, the ROM attempts to read in its driver prior to system startup. In order to be loaded, the device must place two data structures in the first two physical blocks. A **driver descriptor map** must be put at the start of physical block 0; it identifies the various device drivers available for loading (see Figure 2). The drivers can then be located anywhere else on the device and can be as large as necessary.

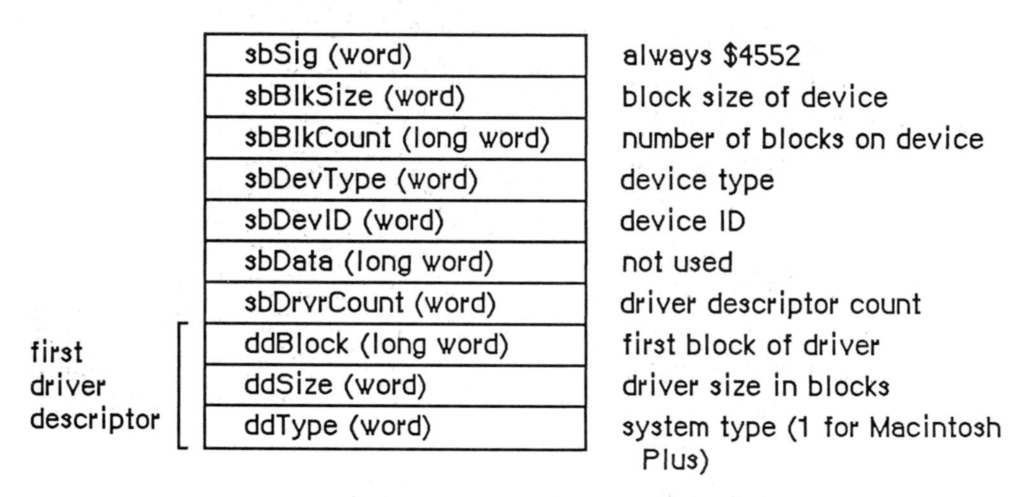

Figure 2. Driver Descriptor Map

A second data structure, the **device partition map**, must be put at the start of physical block 1; it describes the allocation of blocks on the device for different partitions and/or operating systems (see Figure 3).

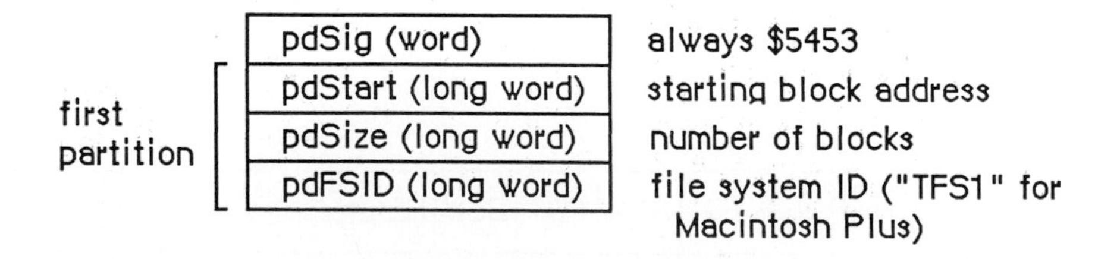

Figure 3. Device Partition Map

Since there's no field in the device partition map for specifying the number of partitions, you need to signal the end of the map with a partition whose pdStart, pdSize, and pdFSID fields are set to 0.

The system startup procedure takes the following steps:

1. It attempts to select the first target device on the bus by its ID, beginning with the device, if any, having an ID of 6.

2. It reads the first 256 bytes of physical block 0, checking for the signature indicating a valid driver descriptor map ($4552). It then reads the device partition map from physical block 1 and checks for the proper signature ($5453).

3. It searches the driver descriptor map for a driver for the Macintosh.

4. It reads the driver from the indicated physical blocks into the system heap, using standard SCSI read commands. It checks for a proper driver signature.

5. It calls the driver to install itself, and passes a pointer to the device partition map for examination by the driver.

6. It performs steps 1 through 5 for all other SCSI devices on the bus.

Note: During system startup, the SCSI Manager may call SCSIReset after your driver has been loaded.

Since the driver is called to install itself, it must contain code to set up its own entry in the unit table and to call its own Open routine. An example of how to do this can be obtained from

Developer Technical Support.
Mail Stop 3-T
Apple Computer, Inc.
20525 Mariani Avenue
Cupertino, CA 95014

SUMMARY OF THE SCSI MANAGER

Constants

```
CONST { Transfer instruction operation codes }

      scInc      = 1;   {SCINC instruction}
      scNoInc    = 2;   {SCNOINC instruction}
      scAdd      = 3;   {SCADD instruction}
      scMove     = 4;   {SCMOVE instruction}
      scLoop     = 5;   {SCLOOP instruction}
      scNop      = 6;   {SCNOP instruction}
      scStop     = 7;   {SCSTOP instruction}
      scComp     = 8;   {SCCOMP instruction}

      { SCSI Manager result codes }

      scBadParmsErr = 4;  {unrecognized instruction in transfer }
                          { instruction block}
      scCommErr     = 2;  {breakdown in SCSI protocols:  usually no }
                          { device connected or bus not terminated}
      scCompareErr  = 6;  {data comparison error during read (with }
                          { SCCOMP instruction in transfer }
                          { instruction block)}
      scPhaseErr    = 5;  {phase error:  target and initiator not in }
                          { agreement as to type of information to }
                          { transfer}
```

Data Types

```
TYPE SCSIInstr = RECORD
                   scOpcode: INTEGER;  {operation code}
                   scParam1: LONGINT;  {first parameter}
                   scParam2: LONGINT   {second parameter}
                 END;
```

Routines

```
FUNCTION SCSIReset :    OSErr;
FUNCTION SCSIGet :      OSErr;
FUNCTION SCSISelect    (targetID: INTEGER) : OSErr;
FUNCTION SCSICmd       (buffer: Ptr; count: INTEGER) : OSErr;
FUNCTION SCSIRead      (tibPtr: Ptr) : OSErr;
FUNCTION SCSIRBlind    (tibPtr: Ptr) : OSErr;
FUNCTION SCSIWrite     (tibPtr: Ptr ) : OSErr;
FUNCTION SCSIWBlind    (tibPtr: Ptr) : OSErr;
FUNCTION SCSIComplete  (VAR stat,message: INTEGER; wait: LONGINT) :
                        OSErr;
FUNCTION SCSIStat :     INTEGER;
```

Assembly-Language Information

Constants

```
; Transfer instruction operation codes

scInc    .EQU    1    ;SCINC instruction
scNoInc  .EQU    2    ;SCNOINC instruction
scAdd    .EQU    3    ;SCADD instruction
scMove   .EQU    4    ;SCMOVE instruction
scLoop   .EQU    5    ;SCLOOP instruction
scNOp    .EQU    6    ;SCNOP instruction
scStop   .EQU    7    ;SCSTOP instruction
scComp   .EQU    8    ;SCCOMP instruction

; Routine selectors
; (Note:  You can invoke each of the SCSI Manager routines with a macro
;  that has the same name as the routine preceded by an underscore.)

scsiReset     .EQU    0
scsiGet       .EQU    1
scsiSelect    .EQU    2
scsiCmd       .EQU    3
scsiComplete  .EQU    4
scsiRead      .EQU    5
scsiWrite     .EQU    6
scsiRBlind    .EQU    8
scsiWBlind    .EQU    9
scsiStat      .EQU    10

; SCSI Manager result codes

scBadParmsErr  .EQU    4    ;unrecognized instruction in transfer
                            ; instruction block
scCommErr      .EQU    2    ;breakdown in SCSI protocols:  usually no
                            ; device connected or bus not terminated
scCompareErr   .EQU    6    ;data comparison error during read (with
                            ; scComp command in transfer instruction
                            ; block)
scPhaseErr     .EQU    5    ;phase error:  target and initiator not in
                            ; agreement as to type of information to
                            ; transfer
```

Trap Macro Name

_SCSIDispatch

(Note: You can invoke each of the SCSI Manager routines with a macro that has the same name as the routine preceded by an underscore.)

32 THE TIME MANAGER

ABOUT THIS CHAPTER

This chapter describes the Time Manager, the part of the Operating System that lets you schedule a routine to be executed after a given number of milliseconds have elapsed.

ABOUT THE TIME MANAGER

The Time Manager provides the user with an asynchronous "wakeup" service with 1-millisecond accuracy; it can have any number of outstanding wakeup requests. The Time Manager is independent of clock speed or interrupts, and should be used in place of cycle-counting timing loops.

An application can add any number of tasks for the Time Manager to schedule. These tasks can perform any desired action so long as they don't make any calls to the Memory Manager, directly or indirectly, and don't depend on handles to unlocked blocks being valid. They must preserve all registers other than A0–A3 and D0–D3. If they use application globals, they must also ensure that register A5 contains the address of the boundary between the application globals and the application parameters; for details, see SetUpA5 and RestoreA5 in chapter 13.

> **Note:** To perform periodic actions that do allocate and release memory, you can use the Desk Manager procedure SystemTask.

Information describing each Time Manager task is contained in the Time Manager queue; you need only supply a pointer to the routine to be executed. The Time Manager queue is a standard Macintosh queue, as described in the Operating System Utilities chapter. Each entry in the Time Manager queue has the following structure:

```
TYPE TMTask = RECORD
                qLink:    QElemPtr;   {next queue entry}
                qType:    INTEGER;    {queue type}
                tmAddr:   ProcPtr;    {pointer to routine}
                tmCount:  INTEGER     {reserved}
              END;
```

USING THE TIME MANAGER

The Time Manager is automatically initialized when the system starts up. Since the "sleep" time for a given task can be as small as 1 millisecond, you need to install a queue element in the Time Manager queue before actually making the wakeup request; to do this, call InsTime. To make the actual wakeup request, call PrimeTime. When you're done, call RmvTime to remove the element from the queue.

TIME MANAGER ROUTINES

```
PROCEDURE InsTime (tmTaskPtr: QElemPtr);
```

Trap macro	_InsTime
On entry	A0: tmTaskPtr (pointer)
On exit	D0: result code (word)

InsTime adds the task specified by tmTaskPtr to the Time Manager queue. InsTime returns one of the result codes listed below.

Result codes	noErr	No error

```
PROCEDURE PrimeTime (tmTaskPtr,count: LONGINT);
```

Trap macro	_PrimeTime
On entry	A0: tmTaskPtr (pointer) D0: count (long word)
On exit	D0: result code (word)

PrimeTime schedules the routine specified by tmTaskPtr to be executed after count milliseconds have elapsed. The queue element must already be inserted into the queue by a call to InsTime before making the PrimeTime call. The PrimeTime routine returns immediately, and the specified routine will be executed after count milliseconds have elapsed.

Result codes	noErr	No error

```
PROCEDURE RmvTime (tmTaskPtr: QElemPtr);
```

Trap macro	_RmvTime
On entry	A0: tmTaskPtr (pointer)
On exit	D0: result code (word)

RmvTime removes the task specified by tmTaskPtr from the Time Manager queue. RmvTime returns one of the result codes listed below.

Result codes	noErr	No error

SUMMARY OF THE TIME MANAGER

Data Types

```
TYPE TMTask = RECORD
                qLink:      QElemPtr; {next queue entry}
                qType:      INTEGER;  {queue type}
                tmAddr:     ProcPtr;  {pointer to task}
                tmCount:    INTEGER   {reserved}
              END;
```

Routines

```
PROCEDURE InsTime     (tmTaskPtr: QElemPtr);
PROCEDURE RmvTime     (tmTaskPtr: QElemPtr);
PROCEDURE PrimeTime   (tmTaskPtr,count: LONGINT);
```

Assembly-Language Information

Routines

Trap macro	On entry	On exit
_InsTime	A0: tmTaskPtr (ptr)	D0: result code (word)
_RmvTime	A0: tmTaskPtr (ptr)	D0: result code (word)
_PrimeTime	A0: tmTaskPtr (ptr) D0: count (long)	D0: result code (word)

Structure of Time Manager Queue Entry

qLink	Pointer to next queue entry
qType	Queue type (word)
tmAddr	Pointer to task
tmCount	Reserved (word)

APPENDIX A: ROUTINES THAT MAY MOVE OR PURGE MEMORY

This appendix lists all the new routines that may move or purge blocks in the heap. As described in chapter 1 of Volume II, calling these routines may cause problems if a handle has been dereferenced. None of these routines may be called from within an interrupt, such as in a completion routine or a VBL task.

DelMenuItem
Draw1Control
FindDItem
FontMetrics
Get1IndResource
Get1IndType
Get1NamedResource
Get1Resource
HideDItem
InsMenuItem
MeasureText
MoveHHi
NewEmptyHandle
OpenRFPerm
PStr2Dec
Dec2Str
CStr2Dec
ShowDItem
TEAutoView
TEPinScroll
TESelView
TrackBox
UpdtControl
UpdtDialog
ZoomWindow

APPENDIX B: SYSTEM TRAPS

This appendix lists the trap macros for the new Toolbox and Operating System routines and their corresponding trap word values in hexadecimal. The "Name" column gives the trap macro name (without its initial underscore character). In those cases where the name of the equivalent Pascal call is different, the Pascal name appears indented under the main entry. The routines in Macintosh packages are listed under the macros they invoke after pushing a routine selector onto the stack; the routine selector follows the Pascal routine name in parentheses.

There are two tables: The first is ordered alphabetically by name; the second is ordered numerically by trap number, for use when debugging. (The trap number is the last two digits of the trap word unless the trap word begins with A9, in which case the trap number is 1 followed by the last two digits of the trap word.)

Warning: Traps that aren't currently used by the system are reserved for future use.

Name		Trap word
CalcMask		A838
CopyMask		A817
Count1Resources		A80D
Count1Types		A81C
DelMenuItem		A952
Draw1Control		A96D
FindDItem		A984
Fix2Frac		A841
Fix2Long		A840
Fix2X		A843
FixAtan2		A818
FixDiv		A84D
FontMetrics		A835
Frac2Fix		A842
Frac2X		A845
FracCos		A847
FracDiv		A84B
FracMul		A84A
FracSin		A848
FracSqrt		A849
Get1IxResource		A80E
Get1IndResource		
Get1IxType		A80F
Get1IndType		
Get1NamedResource		A820
Get1Resource		A81F
HClrRBit		A068
HFSDispatch		A260
OpenWD	(1)	
CloseWD	(2)	

Name		Trap word
CatMove	(5)	
DirCreate	(6)	
GetWDInfo	(7)	
GetFCBInfo	(8)	
GetCatInfo	(9)	
SetCatInfo	(10)	
SetVolInfo	(11)	
LockRng	(16)	
UnlockRng	(17)	
HGetState		A069
HideDItem		A827
HSetRBit		A067
HSetState		A06A
InsMenuItem		A826
Long2Fix		A83F
MaxApplZone		A063
MaxBlock		A061
MaxSizeRsrc		A821
MeasureText		A837
MoveHHi		A064
NewEmptyHandle		A066
OpenRFPerm		A9C4
Pack0		A9E7
LActivate	(0)	
LAddColumn	(4)	
LAddRow	(8)	
LAddToCell	(12)	
LAutoScroll	(16)	
LCellSize	(20)	
LClick	(24)	

Appendices

Name		Trap word
LClrCell	(28)	
LDelColumn	(32)	
LDelRow	(36)	
LDispose	(40)	
LDoDraw	(44)	
LDraw	(48)	
LFind	(52)	
LGetCell	(56)	
LGetSelect	(60)	
LLastClick	(64)	
LNew	(68)	
LNextCell	(72)	
LRect	(76)	
LScroll	(80)	
LSearch (84)		
LSetCell	(88)	
LSetSelect	(92)	
LSize	(96)	
LUpdate	(100)	
Pack7		A9EE
PStr2Dec	(2)	
Dec2Str	(3)	
CStr2Dec	(4)	
Pack8		A816
Pack9		A82B
Pack10		A82C
Pack11		A82D
Pack12		A82E
Pack13		A82F
Pack14		A830
Pack15		A831
(Pack 8–Pack 15 reserved for future use)		
PPostEvent		A12F
PurgeSpace		A062
RelString		A050
RsrcMapEntry		A9C5
SCSIDispatch		A815
SCSIReset	(0)	
SCSIGet	(1)	
SCSISelect	(2)	
SCSICmd	(3)	
SCSIComplete	(4)	
SCSIRead	(5)	
SCSIWrite	(6)	
SCSIInstall	(7)	
SCSIRBlind	(8)	
SCSIWBlind	(9)	
SCSIStat	(10)	
SeedFill		A839
SetFScaleDisable		A834
ShowDItem		A828
StackSpace		A065
TEAutoView		A813
TEPinScroll		A812
TESelView		A811
TrackBox		A83B
Unique1ID		A810
UpdtControl		A953
UpdtDialog		A978
X2Fix		A844
X2Frac		A846
ZoomWindow		A83A

Trap word	Name	
A050	RelString	
A067	HSetRBit	
A068	HClrRBit	
A069	HGetState	
A06A	HSetState	
A061	MaxBlock	
A062	PurgeSpace	
A063	MaxApplZone	
A064	MoveHHi	
A065	StackSpace	
A066	NewEmptyHandle	
A12F	PPostEvent	
A260	HFSDispatch	
	OpenWD	(1)
	CloseWD	(2)
	CatMove	(5)
	DirCreate	(6)
	GetWDInfo	(7)
	GetFCBInfo	(8)
	GetCatInfo	(9)
	SetCatInfo	(10)
	SetVolInfo	(11)
	LockRng	(16)
	UnlockRng	(17)
A80D	Count1Resources	
A80E	Get1IxResource	
	Get1IndResource	
A80F	Get1IxType	
	Get1IndType	
A810	Unique1ID	
A81C	Count1Types	
A81F	Get1Resource	
A811	TESelView	
A812	TEPinScroll	
A813	TEAutoView	

Trap word	Name	
A815	SCSIDispatch	
	SCSIReset	(0)
	SCSIGet	(1)
	SCSISelect	(2)
	SCSICmd	(3)
	SCSIComplete	(4)
	SCSIRead	(5)
	SCSIWrite	(6)
	SCSIInstall	(7)
	SCSIRBlind	(8)
	SCSIWBlind	(9)
	SCSIStat	(10)
A816	Pack8	
A817	CopyMask	
A818	FixAtan2	
A820	Get1NamedResource	
A821	MaxSizeRsrc	
A82B	Pack9	
A82C	Pack10	
A82D	Pack11	
A82E	Pack12	
A82F	Pack13	
A830	Pack14	
A831	Pack15	
A834	SetFScaleDisable	
A835	FontMetrics	
A826	InsMenuItem	
A827	HideDItem	
A828	ShowDItem	
A836	GetMaskTable	
A837	MeasureText	
A838	CalcMask	
A839	SeedFill	
A83A	ZoomWindow	
A83B	TrackBox	
A83F	Long2Fix	
A840	Fix2Long	
A841	Fix2Frac	
A842	Frac2Fix	
A843	Fix2X	
A844	X2Fix	
A845	Frac2X	
A846	X2Frac	

Trap word	Name	
A847	FracCos	
A848	FracSin	
A849	FracSqrt	
A84A	FracMul	
A84B	FracDiv	
A84D	FixDiv	
A952	DelMenuItem	
A953	UpdtControl	
A96D	Draw1Control	
A978	UpdtDialog	
A984	FindDItem	
A9C4	OpenRFPerm	
A9C5	RsrcMapEntry	
A9E7	Pack0	
	LActivate	(0)
	LAddColumn	(4)
	LAddRow	(8)
	LAddToCell	(12)
	LAutoScroll	(16)
	LCellSize	(20)
	LClick	(24)
	LClrCell	(28)
	LDelColumn	(32)
	LDelRow	(36)
	LDispose	(40)
	LDoDraw	(44)
	LDraw	(48)
	LFind	(52)
	LGetCell	(56)
	LGetSelect	(60)
	LLastClick	(64)
	LNew	(68)
	LNextCell	(72)
	LRect	(76)
	LScroll	(80)
	LSearch	(84)
	LSetCell	(88)
	LSetSelect	(92)
	LSize	(96)
	LUpdate	(100)
A9EE	Pack7	
	PStr2Dec	(2)
	Dec2Str	(3)
	CStr2Dec	(4)

APPENDIX C: GLOBAL VARIABLES

This appendix gives an alphabetical list of all system global variables described in this volume, along with their locations in memory.

Name	Location	Contents
ApFont ID	$984	Font number of application font (word)
BootDrive	$210	Working directory reference number for system startup volume (word)
CurDirStore	$398	Directory ID of directory last opened (long)
DefVCBPtr	$352	Pointer to default volume control block
DrvQHdr	$308	Drive queue header (10 bytes)
FCBSPtr	$34E	Pointer to file-control-block buffer
FractEnable	$BF4	Nonzero to enable fractional widths (byte)
FSFCBLen	$3F6	Size of a file control block; on 64K ROM, it contains –1 (word)
FSQHdr	$360	File I/O queue header (10 bytes)
IntlSpec	$BA0	International software installed if not equal to –1 (long)
LastFOND	$BC2	Handle to last family record used
MemErr	$220	Current value of MemError (word)
ROMBase	$2AE	Base address of ROM
RomMapInsert	$B9E	Flag for whether to insert map to the ROM resources (byte)
SFSaveDisk	$214	Negative of volume reference number, used by Standard File Package (word)
SysFontFam	$BA6	If nonzero, the font number to use for system font (word)
SysFontSize	$BA8	If nonzero, the size of the system font (word)
TmpResLoad	$B9F	Temporary SetResLoad state for calls using ROMMapInsert (byte)
ToExtFS	$3F2	Pointer to external file system
VCBQHdr	$356	Volume-control-block queue header (10 bytes)
WidthListHand	$8E4	Handle to a list of handles to recently-used width tables
WidthPtr	$B10	Pointer to global width table
WidthTabHandle	$B2A	Handle to global width table

GLOSSARY

access path: A description of the route that the File Manager follows to access a file; created when a file is opened.

access path buffer: Memory used by the File Manager to transfer data between an application and a file.

active end: In a selection, the location to which the insertion point moves to complete the selection.

allocation block: Volume space composed of multiples of logical blocks.

anchor point: In a selection, the location of the insertion point when the selection was started.

application list: A data structure, kept in the Desktop file, for launching applications from their documents in the hierarchical file system. For each application in the list, an entry is maintained that includes the name and signature of the application, as well as the directory ID of the folder containing it.

arbitration phase: The phase in which an initiator attempts to gain control of the bus.

asynchronous execution: After calling a routine asynchronously, an application is free to perform other tasks until the routine is completed.

block map: Same as volume allocation block map.

bus free phase: The phase in which no SCSI device is actively using the bus.

catalog tree file: A file that maintains the relationships between the files and directories on a hierarchical directory volume. It corresponds to the file directory on a flat directory volume.

cell: The basic component of a list from a structural point of view; a cell is a box in which a list element is displayed.

Chooser: A desk accessory that provides a standard interface for device drivers to solicit and accept specific choices from the user.

closed file: A file without an access path. Closed files cannot be read from or written to.

clump: A group of contiguous allocation blocks. Space is allocated to a new file in clumps to promote file contiguity and avoid fragmentation.

clump size: The number of allocation blocks to be allocated to a new file.

command phase: The phase in which the SCSI initiator tells the target what operation to perform.

completion routine: Any application-defined code to be executed when an asynchronous call to a routine is completed.

data buffer: Heap space containing information to be written to a file or device driver from an application, or read from a file or device driver to an application.

data fork: The part of a file that contains data accessed via the File Manager.

data phase: The phase in which the actual transfer of data between an SCSI initiator and target takes place.

default directory: A directory that will be used in File Manager routines whenever no other directory is specified. It may be the root directory, in which case the default directory is equivalent to the default volume.

default volume: A volume that will receive I/O during a File Manager routine call, whenever no other volume is specified.

device partition map: A data structure that must be placed at the start of physical block 1 of an SCSI device to enable it to perform Macintosh system startup. It describes the allocation of blocks on the device.

device resource file: An extension of the printer resource file, this file contains all the resources needed by the Chooser for operating a particular device (including the device driver code).

directory: A subdivision of a volume that can contain files as well as other directories; equivalent to a folder.

directory ID: A unique number assigned to a directory, which the File Manager uses to distinguish it from other directories on the volume. (It's functionally equivalent to the file number assigned to a file; in fact, both directory IDs and file numbers are assigned from the same set of numbers.)

drive number: A number used to identify a disk drive. The internal drive is number 1, the external drive is number 2, and any additional drives will have larger numbers.

drive queue: A list of disk drives connected to the Macintosh.

driver descriptor map: A data structure that must be placed at the start of physical block 0 of an SCSI device to enable it to perform Macintosh system startup. It identifies the various device drivers on the device.

end-of-file: See **logical end-of-file** or **physical end-of-file.**

extent: A series of contiguous allocation blocks.

extent descriptor: A description of an extent, consisting of the number of the first allocation block of the extent followed by the length of the extent in blocks.

extent record: A data record, stored in the leaf nodes of the extents tree file, that contains three extent descriptors and a key identifying the record.

extents tree file: A file that contains the locations of the files on a volume.

family record: A data structure, derived from a family resource, that contains all the information describing a font family.

file: A named, ordered sequence of bytes; a principal means by which data is stored and transmitted on the Macintosh.

file catalog: A hierarchical file directory.

file control block: A fixed-length data structure, contained in the file-control-block buffer, where information about an access path is stored.

file-control-block buffer: A nonrelocatable block in the system heap that contains one file control block for each access path.

file directory: The part of a volume that contains descriptions and locations of all the files and directories on the volume. There are two types of file directories: hierarchical file directories and flat file directories.

file I/O queue: A queue containing parameter blocks for all I/O requests to the File Manager.

file number: A unique number assigned to a file, which the File Manager uses to distinguish it from other files on the volume. A file number specifies the file's entry in a file directory.

font: A complete set of characters of one typeface, which may be restricted to a particular size and style, or may comprise multiple sizes, or multiple sizes and styles, as in the context of menus.

font family: A group of fonts of one basic design but with variations like weight and slant.

font record: A data structure, derived from a font resource, that contains all the information describing a font.

fork: One of the two parts of a file; see **data fork** and **resource fork.**

full pathname: A pathname beginning from the root directory.

global width table: A data structure in the system heap used by the Font Manager to communicate fractional character widths to QuickDraw.

initiator device: An SCSI device that initiates a communication by asking another device (known as the target device) to perform a certain operation.

I/O request: A request for input from or output to a file or device driver; caused by calling a File Manager or Device Manager routine asynchronously.

list definition procedure: A procedure called by the List Manager that determines the appearance and behavior of a list.

list element: The basic component of a list from a logical point of view, a list element is simply bytes of data. In a list of names, for instance, the name Melvin might be a list element.

List Manager: The part of the Operating System that provides routines for creating, displaying, and manipulating lists.

list record: The internal representation of a list, where the List Manager stores all the information it requires for its operations on that list.

locked file: A file whose data cannot be changed.

locked volume: A volume whose data cannot be changed. Volumes can be locked by either a software flag or a mechanical setting.

logical block: Volume space composed of 512 consecutive bytes of standard information and an additional number of bytes of information specific to the disk driver.

logical end-of-file: The position of one byte past the last byte in a file; equal to the actual number of bytes in the file.

mark: A marker used by the File Manager to keep track of where it is during a read or write operation.

master directory block: Part of the data structure of a flat directory volume; contains the volume information and the volume allocation block map.

message phase: The phase in which the target sends one byte of message information back to the initiator.

mounted volume: A volume that has been inserted into a disk drive and has had descriptive information read from it by the File Manager.

newline character: Any character, but usually Return (ASCII code $0D), that indicates the end of a sequence of bytes.

newline mode: A mode of reading data where the end of the data is indicated by a newline character (and not by a specific byte count).

off-line volume: A mounted volume with all but the volume control block released.

offspring: For a given directory, the set of files and directories for which it is the parent.

on-line volume: A mounted volume with its volume buffer and descriptive information contained in memory.

open file: A file with an access path. Open files can be read from and written to.

open permission: Information about a file that indicates whether the file can be read from, written to, or both.

parameter block: A data structure used to transfer information between applications and certain Operating System routines.

parent: For a given file or directory, the directory immediately above it in the tree.

parent ID: The directory ID of the directory containing a file or directory.

partial pathname: A pathname beginning from any directory other than the root directory.

pathname: A series of concatenated directory and file names that identifies a given file or directory. See also **partial pathname** and **full pathname**.

path reference number: A number that uniquely identifies an individual access path; assigned when the access path is created.

physical end-of-file: The position of one byte past the last allocation block of a file; equal to 1 more than the maximum number of bytes the file can contain without growing.

reselection phase: An optional phase in which the SCSI initiator allows a target device to reconnect itself to the initiator.

resource fork: The part of a file that contains data used by an application (such as menus, fonts, and icons). The resource fork of an application file also contains the application code itself.

root directory: The directory at the base of a file catalog.

routine selector: For routines that expand to the same macro, an integer that's pushed onto the stack or placed into a register before the macro is invoked, to identify which routine to execute. For instance, all SCSI routines expand to invoke the trap macro _SCSIDispatch; each routine has a selector that's passed to the SCSI Manager in a word on the stack before _SCSIDispatch is invoked.

SCSI: See **Small Computer Standard Interface**.

SCSI Manager: The part of the Operating System that controls the exchange of information between a Macintosh and peripheral devices connected through the Small Computer Standard Interface (SCSI).

selection phase: The phase in which the initiator selects the target device that will be asked to perform a certain operation.

Small Computer Standard Interface (SCSI): A specification of mechanical, electrical, and functional standards for connecting small computers with intelligent peripherals such as hard disks, printers, and optical disks.

status phase: The phase in which the SCSI target sends one byte of status information back to the initiator.

subdirectory: Any directory other than the root directory.

synchronous execution: After calling a routine synchronously, an application cannot continue execution until the routine is completed.

Time Manager: The part of the Operating System that lets you schedule a routine to be executed after a given number of milliseconds have elapsed.

target device: An SCSI device (typically an intelligent peripheral) that receives a request from an initiator device to perform a certain operation.

unmounted volume: A volume that hasn't been inserted into a disk drive and had descriptive information read from it, or a volume that previously was mounted and has since had the memory used by it released.

valence: The number of offspring for a given directory.

volume: A piece of storage medium formatted to contain files; usually a disk or part of a disk. A 3 1/2-inch Macintosh disk is one volume.

volume allocation block map: A list of 12-bit entries, one for each allocation block, that indicate whether the block is currently allocated to a file, whether it's free for use, or which block is next in the file. Block maps exist both on flat directory volumes and in memory.

volume attributes: Information contained on volumes and in memory indicating whether the volume is locked, whether it's busy (in memory only), and whether the volume control block matches the volume information (in memory only).

volume bit map: A data structure containing a sequence of bits, one bit for each allocation block, that indicate whether the block is allocated or free for use. Volume bit maps exist both on hierarchical directory volumes and in memory.

volume buffer: Memory used initially to load the master directory block, and used thereafter for reading from files that are opened without an access path buffer.

volume control block: A nonrelocatable block that contains volume-specific information.

volume-control-block queue: A list of the volume control blocks for all mounted volumes.

volume information: Volume-specific information contained on a volume, including the volume name and the number of files on the volume.

volume information block: Part of the data structure of a hierarchical directory volume; it contains the volume information.

volume reference number: A unique number assigned to a volume as it's mounted, used to refer to the volume.

working directory: An alternative way of referring to a directory. When opened as a working directory, a directory is given a working directory reference number that's used to refer to it in File Manager calls.

working directory control block: A data structure that contains the directory ID of a working directory, as well as the volume reference number of the volume on which the directory is located.

working directory reference number: A temporary reference number used to identify a working directory. It can be used in place of the volume reference number in all File Manager calls; the File Manager uses it to get the directory ID and volume reference number from the working directory control block.

INDEX

E

F

G

H

I, J

K

L

M

N

O

P

Q

R

S

X, Y

Z